Dollars and Deficits

Inflation, Monetary Policy and the Balance of Payments

MILTON FRIEDMAN

Paul Snowden Russell
Distinguished Service Professor of Economics
University of Chicago

PRENTICE-HALL, INC., ENGLEWOOD CLIFFS, NEW JERSEY

PRENTICE-HALL INTERNATIONAL, INC., *London*
PRENTICE-HALL OF AUSTRALIA, PTY. LTD., *Sydney*
PRENTICE-HALL OF CANADA, LTD., *Toronto*
PRENTICE-HALL OF INDIA PRIVATE LTD., *New Delhi*
PRENTICE-HALL OF JAPAN, INC., *Tokyo*

Library of Congress Catalog Card Number: 68-9465

Printed in the United States of America

Current Printing (last digit):
10 9 8 7 6 5 4 3 2 1

This book is also being published in a
cloth edition under the title of
Dollars and Deficits: Living with
America's Economic Problems.

Preface

The essays in this book were written over a period spanning nearly two decades. If I were rewriting them today, I would change many of them in detail, to accommodate what I have learned in that period and to adapt them to changes in economic circumstances. I have refrained from this temptation, however, and published them as they stood, not only because I begrudged the time that it would have taken to rewrite them but even more because I would not have changed the major thesis expressed in any of the items and that point—so important to the reader in judging how well foresight has been supported by hindsight—would have been concealed by extensive revision.

The criteria used in selecting the essays were first, that they be intelligible to the public at large, second, that they deal with inflation, monetary policy, and the balance of payments, and third, that they avoid undue duplication. No papers were omitted because they contained predictions that were contradicted by the actual later course of events. The introductory essay was written especially for this book. Others of my essays, directed to professional economists, are published in *Essays in Positive Economics* (University of Chicago Press, 1956) and *The Optimum Quantity of Money and Other Essays* (Aldine Publishing Co., 1968). Many of them cover the same issues dealt with in this book on a more technical level.

In the course of writing these essays, I have benefited greatly from the criticisms of numerous colleagues, students, and other friends. Some are acknowledged in notes attached to particular essays, but more, I fear, go unacknowledged. My major indebtedness is to my teachers and colleagues at the University of Chicago who kept alive a tradition and a body of thought that nearly expired in the rest of the academic world.

I am indebted to *Harvard University Press, Journal of Law and Economics, The University of Chicago Press, Newsweek, Foundation of Economic Education*, and *Nationalekonomiska Foreningens Forhandlingar* for permission to reprint.

My wife, Rose Director Friedman, selected the essays to be included in this volume and has done most of the work of seeing the book through the press—a labor of true love for which I am deeply grateful.

Milton Friedman
Capitaf
Ely, Vermont
June 25, 1968

Contents

Inflation

PART ONE

v

Monetary
Policy

PART TWO

Why Economists
Disagree

INTRODUCTION   Let three economists gather and
there are bound to be at least four opinions about desirable economic policy—so runs the standard cliché,
naturally followed by: if doctors disagree, how can
patients prescribe?

Like most cliches, these are half-truths. The
appearance of disagreement among economists is
grossly exaggerated. In talking with one another,
economists naturally spend little time repeating what
all accept. They discuss their disagreements. When
they present their views in public, the same pressures that impel a businessman to differentiate his
product from his competitors' impel an economist to
present his views in a form that makes them appear
distinctive and individual. Parrots are not much imi-
tated—at least deliberately.

Even more important, economists who present
their views to the public temper their strictly economic judgements with considerations of political ac-

1

ceptability and feasibility, and do so to very different degrees. A classical example was John Maynard Keynes' advocacy of a tariff for Britain in 1931. Qua economist, he favored devaluation of the pound as the best remedy for Britain's economic ills. But he concluded that devaluation was not politically feasible. Hence he came out for a tariff as a way, albeit an unsatisfactory way, to achieve the equivalent of a concealed devaluation. Within six months of Keynes' advocacy of a tariff, Britain devalued. Keynes, of course, with his unusual flexibility, immediately reversed himself and no longer supported a tariff—but, as he notes in a footnote added subsequently when one of his pieces urging a tariff was reprinted, not all of those whom he had converted were equally adaptable.[1]

A current example—in an area not dealt with in this book—is the minimum wage rate. It would be hard to find a reputable economist—of whatever political persuasion—who does not agree that legal minimum wage rates increase unemployment among the unskilled. It would be almost as hard to find one who regards other consequences of legal minimum wage rates as sufficiently favorable to outweigh the adverse effects on employment. Yet most economists are deterred from advocating elimination of legal minimum wage rates because they recognize that this would be widely regarded as "reactionary" and "hard-hearted." They choose instead to remain silent on the issue.

Another example, directly relevant to the third part of this book, concerns the price of gold and of the dollar. Probably the great majority of economists who specialize in money and international trade favors abandoning any fixed price for gold and permitting greater flexibility in the price of the dollar (i.e. in exchange rates). Yet many an economist has hesitated to recommend such policies because he knew that officials in Washington were strongly opposed to them and even more to public discussion of them. Instead, he has proffered second-best solutions for our balance of payments problem.

This example illustrates also a different relation between economic and political considerations. The present arrangements

[1] John Maynard Keynes, *Essays in Persuasion* (New York: Harcourt Brace & Co., 1932), p. 286.

for gold and exchange rates involve agreements among countries implemented partly by an international agency, the International Monetary Fund. The adoption of different arrangements would have implications for the political relations among countries. Some economists, who might favor a free price for gold and floating exchange rates if they considered only the economic effects of such a policy, believe that the political consequences would be adverse, and so adverse as to more than counterbalance the economic gains. As concerned citizens, they properly feel impelled in their public pronouncements to take into account all the effects of proposed changes in policy and not only the economic effects.

As some of these examples suggest, economists have not turned out to be good forecasters about what is politically feasible. That is one reason why I have been inclined myself to give little weight to political feasibility—in the sense of the prospect that any proposal will be quickly or readily enacted. (Of course, weight must be given to political feasibility in a very different sense, namely, how any measure would work once enacted— given the political system within which it operates.) I am a professional economist, an amateur political scientist. Is it reasonable—and in the public interest—for me to let my amateur political judgement override my professional economic judgement?

In any event, the tendency to mix economic with political judgements is a major reason why public expressions of opinion give an exaggerated impression of the disagreements among economists on economic matters proper.

By contrast with this appearance of disagreement, experience over many years has impressed me with a very different phenomenon. Time and again, I have attended discussion sessions among economists and non-economists. Regardless of the topic, and regardless of how widely separated the reputed political positions of the professional economists present, the economists soon coalesce into a single group vis-à-vis the remaining participants. Their training gives them a common approach in attacking problems; the widely accepted common core of economic theory leads them rapidly to reach the same conclusions from common premises. It is the old story of the quarrelsome family ganging up on the outsiders.

3

But a half-truth is half true. Though much exaggerated, disagreement there is among economists on the causes and cures for our economic ills—as any knowledgeable reader of this book will quickly recognize. No doubt I have not been immune to the temptation to differentiate my product. But even if full allowance is made for my sins in this respect, my views on desirable policy have not coincided and do not now coincide with the views of many other economists, though, in fairness both to myself and my professional colleagues, I must add that I have far more company now than I did when many of the items in this book were first written—much less because of my persuasiveness than because of the persuasiveness of economic events.

How can there be such disagreements? How can it be that, after nearly two centuries of the scientific study of economics (which began seriously with Adam Smith's *Wealth of Nations* published in 1776), after numerous and elaborate studies of empirical evidence, after prolonged internal professional discussion, economists can disagree on such apparently simple matters as whether a tax increase will reduce inflationary pressure and, if so, by how much, whether a given monetary policy action will raise or lower interest rates, whether a higher or a lower price of gold would improve the balance of payments—let alone whether one or another of these measures should be adopted. And if economists do disagree on such questions, how can the citizen prescribe? Why should you give any special credence to my views in preference to the views of other reputable economists?

These are hard questions that admit of no easy answer—or at least none that I know of—and about which I have myself very mixed feelings. On one level, the task of the professional economist is surely first to persuade his fellow economists—and only when something of a professional consensus has been established, to tender advice to the public at large. If I cannot persuade my fellow economists, how can I have enough confidence in my nostrums to peddle them to the public? And how can I expect the public to accept mine rather than the other fellows'?

On another level, it is unwise to refrain from appealing to the public until a professional consensus emerges. A profession no less than a person develops accepted patterns of thought that are highly resistant to change.[2] This has its merits, but let there be no appeal outside the profession, and resistance to change will be carried too far. The history of science and of invention shows that, time and again, it is the maverick, the outsider, the person attacking vested intellectual or economic interests, who produces the new insight, the new invention, the fresh direction, the correction of long accepted error.

This argument is buttressed by the strictly practical consideration that the public must often choose—the sick patient cannot wait until full agreement has been reached among medical researchers about the nature, the cause, and the cure of his malady. Where there is a professional consensus, fine, but where there is not, better that the public know how wide is the range of considered opinions than that it be lulled by contrived unanimity among experts.

The dilemma is real and admits of no simple solution. We shall have to muddle along, choosing our physicians and our economists as best we can, by relying on whatever indirect clues and leads establish our confidence in one opinion rather than another or whatever evidence of past success we can get to guide us for the future.

While I cannot therefore offer the reader any easy way to choose his economists, it may help him in making his choice if I indicate what seem to me the main sources of disagreement—real disagreement not expressed disagreement dominated by political considerations—among economists about the three areas of economic policy discussed in this book: inflation, monetary policy, and the balance of payments.

Disagreement about policy ultimately arises from a difference of opinion about either the *consequences* of the policy proposed—a difference in scientific judgement—or the *desirability* of those consequences—a difference in value judgement.

---

[2] For a fascinating example in another field, see Robert Ardrey, *African Genesis* (New York, Atheneum, 1961), which describes the conditioned reflex of the anthropology profession to the findings and theories of anthropologists, mostly from South Africa, that contradicted what were regarded as settled conclusions in the profession about the origin of man. I was particularly fascinated by the story because it so closely paralleled the fight in economics by some of us against entrenched Keynesianism.

I have long argued that policy differences among economists in the United States derive primarily from differences in scientific rather than in value judgements. This is particularly true for the issues discussed in this book. There is widespread agreement among economists on the desirability of relatively stable prices, high and stable levels of employment, and maximum freedom of international trade. This agreement is widely shared by the public at large for prices and employment but not for international trade. (This is one topic on which the technical body of economic analysis has produced a wide consensus among economists that differs from the naive bias toward "protection" in the body politic.) The agreement on these broad goals is greater than on the harder question of how much of each one to sacrifice if they prove incompatible—yet even here the main disagreement is on the scientific question of how much one goal can in fact be promoted by sacrificing another.

Differences in value judgements doubtless play a larger role for other economic policies—in particular, those connected more directly with the distribution of income. But even for such policies, much of the difference is scientific. I oppose, for example, our present highly graduated personal income tax not because I prefer inequality of income to equality but because I believe that our present tax is a fraud and a delusion which treats people in the same economic position differently, widens rather than narrows differences in income, and produces a great waste of human talent and ingenuity. And many economists who place equality of realized income far higher in their scale of values than I do agree with this evaluation.

Though I remain persuaded that differences in scientific judgement are far more important than differences in value judgement, a number of qualifications to this general proposition have increasingly impressed themselves on me—qualifications that arise mostly from the interaction between scientific and value judgements. Any scientific judgement necessarily involves elements of uncertainty. Economics deals with phenomena that are complex, varied, and interdependent. An economic change may affect hundreds of millions of people and numerous economic, political, and social phenomena. What happens in one place on the globe or in one segment of the economy may have its main effects not in that place or in that segment, but in very different ones. To take a clear and striking example: the perfecting of the cyanide process for extracting gold from low grade ore around 1890 had major effects on the gold industry in South Africa and on the whole development of South Africa—but it also produced twenty years of world-wide price inflation, and, among other far-reaching effects, destroyed William Jennings Bryan as a serious contender for the presidency of the United States.[3]

A scholar's basic values undoubtedly affect the way he resolves the inevitable uncertainties in his scientific judgements when he comes to recommend policies—and it is proper that they should. A person like myself who regards freedom as the major objective in relations among individuals and who believes (itself a scientific not a value judgement) that the preservation of freedom requires limiting narrowly the role of government and placing primary reliance on private property, free markets, and voluntary arrangements—such a person will resolve his doubts about the precise effects of any measure in favor of policies relying on the market. By contrast, a person who regards welfare or security as the major objective in social relations and who believes (again a scientific not a value judgement) that this objective can best be attained by governmental measures controlling and regulating private activity—such a person will resolve his doubts in favor of policies relying on government. Each will place the burden of proof differently—one on the proponent of governmental intervention, the other, on the proponent of laissez-faire.[4]

A second way that basic values enter into policy choices is through differences in time perspective. Given the same scientific judgements, the choice among policies will often depend on the importance attached to the short-term vs. the long-term consequences of the policies.

Interestingly, there tends to be a close connection between beliefs about the role of government and time perspective. The

[3] See Milton Friedman and Anna J. Schwartz, *Monetary History of the United States, 1867-1960* (Princeton University Press for the National Bureau of Economic Research, 1963), p. 8.

[4] See my *Capitalism and Freedom* (University of Chicago Press, 1962), esp. chapter 1, for my own value position.

7

liberal in the original sense—the person who gives primacy to freedom and believes in limited government—tends to take the long view, to put major emphasis on the ultimate and permanent consequences of policies rather than on the immediate and possible transitory consequences. The modern liberal—the person who gives primacy to welfare and believes in greater governmental control—tends to take the short view, to put primary emphasis on the immediate effects of policy measures.

This connection is one of reciprocal cause and effect. The man who has a short time perspective will be impatient with the slow workings of voluntary arrangements in producing changes in institutions. He will want to achieve changes at once, which requires centralized authority that can override objections. Hence he will be disposed to favor a greater role for government. But conversely, the man who favors a greater role for government will thereby be disposed to have a shorter time perspective. Partly, he will be so disposed because centralized government can achieve changes of some kinds rapidly; hence he will feel that if the longer term consequences are adverse, he—through the government—can introduce new measures that will counter them, that he can have his cake and eat it. Partly, he will have a short time perspective because the political process demands it. In the market, an entrepreneur can experiment with a new innovation without first persuading the public. He need only have confidence that after he has made his innovation enough of the public will buy his product to make it pay. He can afford to wait until they do. Hence, he can have a long time perspective. In the political process, an entrepreneur must first get elected in order to be in a position to innovate. To get elected, he must persuade the public in advance. Hence he must look at immediate results that he can offer the public. He may not be able to take a very long time perspective and still hope to be in power.[5]

My own policy position has undoubtedly been affected by these interconnections between value judgements and scientific judgements. Certainly, the monetary policy I have come to favor

[5] I am indebted for this point to a perceptive paper by W. Allen Wallis written for a "rational debate" under the auspices of the American Enterprise Institute for Public Policy Research. The paper will be published in a book containing the transcript of the debate.

—a steady rate of growth in the quantity of money—is highly congenial to my preference for limited government and, where government is essential, for limiting government so far as possible by clearly specified rules rather than granting wide discretion to government officials. Certainly the policy I have long favored for adjusting international financial transactions—a system of freely floating exchange rates determined in private markets without governmental intervention—fits in with my preference for the maximum use of the market and for the avoidance of government interference. And both of these, providing for institutional change and the avoidance of day-to-day government tinkering, reflect my tendency to take a long view rather than a short.

These connections are spelled out explicitly in several of the items in this book (especially chapters six and twelve). Yet they explain only in part—and perhaps in minor part—the specific policy positions I have adopted. Many economists with whom I agree most fully about basic values—men like Ludwig von Mises, Jacques Rueff, Friedrich Hayek, Henry Simons, Lionel Robbins— do not agree with my policy positions in this area. They favor achieving automaticity and limitations on government by using a gold or other commodity standard and fixed exchange rates, or by an "independent" central bank, or by some alternative monetary rule, rather than by a steady growth in the quantity of money plus floating exchange rates. On the other side, many economists who would classify themselves as modern liberals—men like Harry Johnson, James Meade, and James Tobin—share my views about balance of payment policy though not about monetary policy.

To look at the matter from a different angle, no value judgements can explain why I have been led to the conclusion that is the central theme of the first part of this book—that inflation is primarily a monetary phenomenon. There is nothing about that conclusion that is more congenial to my values than, for example, the view—held by many businessmen—that inflation is a result of strong labor unions and monopolistic producers, or the view— also widely held—that inflation is a result of government deficits. Indeed, in some ways these latter two explanations would be more congenial to my political and social values.

9

Again, no value judgement can explain why I regard the quantity of money rather than the rate of interest or "money market conditions" as the crucial variable for monetary policy—the central theme of the second part of this book. Or why I have been unable to find—so far—any more sensitive and satisfactory rule for monetary policy than a steady rate of growth. Or why I regard monetary policy as playing a more critical role than fiscal policy in promoting economic stability or producing economic instability.

And certainly, as already implied, my rejection of a gold standard as an appropriate mechanism under present conditions for imposing "discipline" on monetary and fiscal policy, and my advocacy of a free market price for both gold and the dollar—the central theme of the third part of this book—cannot be explained by my value position.

So I am led to return to the proposition with which I started: the major reasons for differences of opinion among economists on inflation, monetary policy, and the balance of payments are not differences in values but differences in scientific judgements about both economic and non-economic effects.

For these topics, differences in scientific judgements about economic effects center primarily on the role of money in economic affairs.[6] This is an issue on which professional opinion has fluctuated widely. Before the Great Contraction of 1929-33, the dominant opinion attributed great importance to the quantity of money in determining the level of prices and the course of the business cycle. The Great Contraction produced a drastic change in this attitude. It was widely—though as I shall point out, erroneously—believed that monetary forces could explain neither the duration nor the intensity of that traumatic episode. Equally important—because you cannot beat a theory without a theory—Keynes, in his great work *The General Theory of Employment,*

[6] The next few pages draw on "The Role of Monetary Policy," *American Economic Review*, March 1968, esp. pp. 1-3. Compare also "Post-War Trends in Monetary Theory and Policy," *National Banking Review* (September 1964), pp. 1-9 and "The Monetary Theory and Policy of Henry Simons," *Journal of Law and Economics* (October, 1967), pp. 1-13. All three essays are reprinted in my *The Optimum Quantity of Money and other Essays* (Aldine Publishing Company, 1968).

Interest, and Money (1936), offered an appealing alternative interpretation.

Said Keynes, the relation between nominal income and the quantity of money—what economists call the velocity of circulation of money—is highly unstable and undependable, particularly under conditions of unemployment. Under such conditions, he said, people are willing to vary the amount of money they hold within wide limits in response to small changes in rates of interest. Hence changes in the quantity of money would have little economic effect beyond producing small changes in interest rates. Alvin Hansen, and many of Keynes' other American followers, went farther. Even if changes in the quantity of money did alter interest rates substantially, they said, the changes in the rate of interest in turn would have little effect on spending. Interest rates, they claimed, are a minor factor in determining how much businessmen want to invest in additional capital, and a negligible factor in determining what fraction of their income consumers want to spend.

What matters, said Keynes and his disciples, is not velocity —that is a will-of-the-wisp—but the relation between investment and government spending, on the one hand, and income, on the other. People have a highly stable "propensity to consume," they contended, so that the amount they spend on consumption and the amount they save depends directly and dependably on the size of their incomes. If the amount that the public wants to save out of an income corresponding to full employment is less than the amount that businessmen want to invest plus the amount that government is willing to spend in excess of its tax receipts, there will be a conflict that can only be resolved by a lower level of income in order to reduce saving to the amount that can be "absorbed" by "offsets to saving" (investment and government spending in excess of taxes, to speak loosely). This lower income will put downward pressure on prices but, in the modern world, this will show up mostly in output and employment. In any event, they argued, price declines would do little good, because they lower both costs and income.

On this view, the Great Contraction—and similar if milder episodes—reflected a collapse of investment spending, or a shortage of investment opportunities, or an excess of thriftiness on the part of the public. Monetary policy could do nothing to counter such a decline. Expanding the quantity of money would simply lead people to substitute money for other securities in their portfolios without any significant effect on spending. However, there was available an alternative—fiscal policy. Government spending could make up for insufficient private investment. Tax reduction could undermine stubborn thriftiness.

These views came to be widely accepted in the economics profession. For some decades, monetary policy was believed by all but a few reactionary souls to have been rendered obsolete. Money did not matter. What mattered was fiscal policy—government spending and taxing. That was the key instrument for controlling economic fluctuations, for achieving full employment, stable prices, and balance of payments equilibrium.

There is always a long lag before a change of opinion among the leaders of any profession is transmitted to the bulk of the profession. And there is an even longer lag before it is transmitted to public opinion in general. Only now is the Keynesian emphasis on fiscal policy becoming "conventional wisdom," to the intelligent layman; until only a few years ago, the elementary economics textbooks taught essentially the doctrine that I have just outlined, in about as stark and unqualified a form.

Yet the vanguard of professional opinion started to shift away from this unvarnished Keynesian position nearly two decades ago, and by now has swung very far indeed. Already by 1953, in a lecture I gave in Sweden, reprinted as Chapter 2 below, I was able to record the beginnings of a revival of belief in monetary policy.

Early postwar experience provided the immediate stimulus for a reaction away from the view that money doesn't matter. Many countries adopted "cheap money" policies under the influence of Keynesian ideas. Every country that did so was forced sooner or later to give up the pretense that it could indefinitely keep "the" rate of interest at a low level. In this country, the public denouement came with the Federal Reserve-Treasury Accord in 1951. Inflation, stimulated by cheap money policies, not the widely heralded postwar depression, turned out to be the order of the day.

The revival of belief in the role of money and in monetary policy was strongly fostered also by developments in economic theory that pointed out a channel—namely, changes in wealth—whereby changes in the quantity of money can affect aggregate demand even if they do not alter interest rates. These developments undermined Keynes' key theoretical proposition, namely, that even in a world of flexible prices, a position of full employment might not exist. Henceforth, unemployment had again to be explained by rigidities or imperfections, not as the natural outcome of a fully operative process.

More important than any of these developments for my own personal views—perhaps also for the profession—was a re-examination of the evidence for the Great Contraction of 1929-33. Keynes and most other economists of the time believed that the Great Contraction in the U.S. from 1929 to 1933 occurred despite aggressive expansionary policies by the monetary authorities. Naturally, the monetary authorities proclaimed at the time that they were doing everything possible to stem the depression, that they were doing their best but that forces beyond their control meant that their best was not good enough. And many economists, Henry Simons and J. M. Keynes among them, accepted this apologia, at least in large part. It was this evidence, more than anything else, I believe, that led them to conclude that the Depression could not be explained in monetary terms. After all, Keynes himself had not only shared but helped develop and spread the earlier views that the quantity of money plays a critical role in inflation and economic fluctuations.[7] And it was the apparent impossibility of explaining the Great Contraction in monetary terms that, more than anything else, made the economics profession so receptive to Keynes' message.

As is pointed out in Chapter 4 below, recent studies have demonstrated that the facts were very different from what they appeared to be to so many at the time.[8] The U.S. monetary authorities followed highly deflationary policies, not expansionary ones. The quantity of money in the U.S. fell by one-third in the course of the contraction. And it fell not because there were no

[7] Particularly in *Monetary Reform* (New York: Harcourt, Brace and Co., 1924).

[8] See Friedman and Schwartz, *A Monetary History of the United States*, ch. 7.

willing borrowers. It fell because the Federal Reserve System forced or permitted a sharp reduction in the monetary base, because it failed to exercise the responsibilities assigned to it in the Federal Reserve Act to provide liquidity to the banking system. The Great Contraction is tragic testimony to the power of money —not as Keynes and so many of his contemporaries believed, evidence of its unimportance.

Facts are stubborn things. Sooner or later, they must be accommodated to. Had the facts for 1929-33—and for other episodes—been as Keynes apparently assumed them to have been, I could not hold the views I do about the role of money. Had Keynes recognized that the facts were what they were, he would have had to modify his views.

But theories are stubborn things too. Nothing is harder than for men to face facts that threaten to undermine strongly held beliefs, to change views arrived at over a long period. And there are no such things as unambiguous facts. They are always subject to more than one interpretation. So it has been a slow process for the re-evaluation of the monetary experience to alter received opinion.

This process has been hastened by another body of facts— the lack of success of the Keynesian approach in predicting the short-term course of the economy. The ratio of investment-type spending to income has proved far less stable and predictable than Keynes and his disciples thought that it would be. Some years ago, David Meiselman and I made extensive tests of the relative stability of the ratio (or its reciprocal, the Keynesian multiplier) and the velocity of circulation of money.[9] We concluded that velocity was considerably stabler than the Keynesian multiplier—indeed, that most of the evidence was consistent with the view that the multiplier is useless for predictive purposes except as a disguised reflection of monetary change. This paper produced a barrage of criticisms from other economists followed by rejoinders by us, and re-rejoinders by them. The upshot, however, was a far cry from the original Keynesian, "money does not mat-

[9] "The Relative Stability of Monetary Velocity and the Investment Multiplier in the United States, 1897-1958," in *Stabilization Policies*, Committee on Money and Credit (Englewood Cliffs, N.J.: Prentice-Hall, 1963).

ter," position. Our critics all granted that the quantity of money played an important role in determining short-term fluctuations in income. But they interpreted the evidence as showing that the multiplier process also played an important role and berated us for overstating our case.

It was this experience that led me to tell a reporter for *Time* Magazine that "in one sense, we are all Keynesians now; in another, no one is a Keynesian any longer." We all use the Keynesian language and apparatus; none of us any longer accepts the initial Keynesian conclusions. (Unfortunately, *Time* only quoted the phrase "We are all Keynesians now" and thus gave a highly misleading impression of my opinion.)

Recent experience has produced another striking bit of evidence on the relative importance of monetary and fiscal forces that has had its impact on opinion. In 1966, there was a sharp reduction in the rate of monetary growth. At the same time, fiscal policy became decidedly more expansionary; the high employment budget showed a deficit—a rapidly growing deficit. The monetary change was deflationary, the fiscal change inflationary. The result—some six to nine months after the monetary change— was a slowdown in the economy in the first six months of 1967— succeeded by an upturn some 6 months after a shift to an expansionary monetary policy. Monetary effects clearly dominated fiscal effects. (See Chapter 5 below.)

The cumulative effect of this evidence has produced such a change in professional opinion that I felt impelled in my 1967 presidential address to the American Economic Association, to warn that "the pendulum may well have swung too far, that . . . we are in danger of assigning to monetary policy a larger role than it can perform, in danger of asking it to accomplish tasks that it cannot achieve, and, as a result, in danger of preventing it from making the contribution that it is capable of making." [10]

The true test of a scientific theory—of a set of propositions about a class of observable phenomena—is whether it works, whether it correctly predicts the consequences of changes in conditions. But this is not an easy test to apply in any field and certainly not in economics. Controlled experiments permitting the

[10] "The Role of Monetary Policy," *op. cit.*, p. 5.

near-isolation of one or a few forces are virtually impossible. We must test our propositions by observing uncontrolled experience that involves a large number of people, numerous economic variables, frequent changes in other circumstances, and, at that, is imperfectly recorded. The interpretation of the experience is further complicated because the experience affects directly many of the observers, often giving them reasons, irrelevant from a scientific point of view, to prefer one rather than another interpretation of the complex and ever-changing course of events.

Under these circumstances, little wonder that economists often disagree. The remarkable thing is rather the wide area of agreement, the common body of knowledge about how the economic system works.

Inflation

PART ONE   There is widespread concern in the U.S. today about the dangers of price inflation. Prices, which doubled during World War II, have continued to creep up in the postwar period, and recently have been doing so at an accelerated pace. The current rate of inflation, around 3 to 4 per cent per year, is high by U.S. standards. But it is moderate or low compared to the rates of inflation that other countries are experiencing now or have experienced in earlier periods. Hence, we have much to learn about the causes and consequences of inflation by observing experience over a wide span of space and time.

   The first of the three items in this section is an attempt to present and interpret this experience for a lay audience. It consists of two lectures delivered in Bombay, India, in 1963 and a transcript of the question and answer periods that followed. Because of the audience addressed, the illustrations are largely

Indian, but the reader will have little trouble in translating them into American terms, since the basic phenomena are identical. Indeed, in one important respect, the Indian situation of 1963 was a foretaste of what was to come in the U.S.—namely, with respect to international trade and payments. At that time, India had an extensive system of exchange controls; the U.S. did not. But the same pressures which produced Indian exchange controls—the attempt to peg exchange rates despite domestic inflation—have produced exchange controls in the U.S. Our controls are still mild compared to the sweeping controls in India. However, if inflation continues to accelerate and we continue to try to peg exchange rates, exchange control is bound to become more pervasive and more severe. Hence, India's experience can well serve as a cautionary tale for us.

The key propositions stressed in these lectures are (1) that inflation is always and everywhere a monetary phenomenon, produced in the first instance by an unduly rapid growth in the quantity of money, (2) that the reasons for the rapid growth in the quantity of money are very diverse, varying from occasion to occasion, (3) that inflation has very different effects when it is anticipated than when it is unanticipated, and (4) that attempts to suppress price rises without removing their basic source do far more harm than good. If inflation cannot be avoided, then let it be open, not suppressed.

The second item in this section, a talk given in Sweden in 1954, was an attempt to interpret the special features of the U.S. situation to a group of sophisticated European observers. In contrast to the Indian lectures, it stressed those features that are special to the U.S. rather than those that are common to all inflations.

It is hard for readers today to recapture the attitudes that prevailed in the decade after World War II. Those attitudes were dominated by the Great Depression and the Keynesian revolution in economic thought that followed. It was widely held that the great danger in the postwar era was an economic collapse involving falling prices and massive unemployment. When a mild recession occurred in 1948 to 1949, many observers feared the beginning of a major collapse. Though these fears proved unfounded, apprehension was by no means removed, partly because the occurrence of the Korean War enabled the subsequent recovery to be interpreted as another wartime inflationary episode.

The Swedish talk was written and delivered partway through the next recession, which began in mid-1953 and ended in 1954. That downturn revived all the earlier fears. Some prominent business forecasters issued alarming predictions that, unless massive action was taken, another major contraction, like that from 1929-33, was in store for the U.S., and these predictions were taken seriously both in the U.S. and abroad.

In the talk, I tried to explain why, in my opinion, these fears were unfounded, why the changes that had occurred in the U.S. fiscal, monetary, and banking structure rendered a serious depression highly unlikely—at least until the U.S. had first experienced a major inflation. As I reread the talk nearly 15 years later, I find only one major respect in which I would alter the predictions I made about the likely future course of the U.S. economy. That has to do with timing. I thought developments would occur faster than they have in fact occurred. Had I been asked to specify where we would be in 1968 on the generally inflationary path I then foresaw, I would have put us farther on that course than the point at which we now are. The forces of inertia are stronger than I then anticipated.

The final item in this section is an examination of a specific U.S. example of a general policy discussed in the Indian lectures —namely, a policy of trying to attack inflation by holding down specific prices. This policy is for the moment dormant. The failures of the guideposts policy in 1966 and 1967 were so blatant that today it is hardly even given lip-service. But I have little doubt that it or a very similar policy will be resuscitated as inflation gathers steam. Hence, an understanding of the problems and dangers of guideposts remains timely—indeed, will be more timely a year or two from now than it is today.

I apologize to the reader for some duplication in the guidepost article and the Indian lectures. In presenting the general idea relevant to discussing the specific problem of guideposts, I reproduced verbatim some passages from the Indian lectures.

To remove the duplication from the present publication would have made the guidepost article unreadable by itself or necessitated complete rewriting. Accordingly, I have let the duplication stand as the lesser evil.

Inflation:

Causes and Consequences[1]

CHAPTER ONE Like an old-fashioned preacher, delivering a Sunday sermon, I can provide the audience with texts for my talks. The text for tonight's talk is, "Cherchez la monnaie." The text for tomorrow's talk is, "The cure may be worse than the disease."

By inflation, I shall mean a steady and sustained rise in prices. In this lecture, I shall deal primarily with open inflation, which is to say, an inflationary process in which prices are permitted to rise without being suppressed by Government price controls or similar techniques. In the second lecture, I shall consider at considerable length the problems of suppressed inflation.

It is widely asserted that inflation is inevitable

[1 These two lectures were delivered in Bombay, India, in 1963 and published in book form by Asia Publishing House for the Council For Economic Education, Bombay (1963).]

in a country that is trying to force the pace of development. The argument generally runs something like this. A country that is trying to force the pace of development places heavy pressure upon the available resources. The pressure upon the resources means an increase in demand which can be met only by a rise in prices. In consequence, it is said, the process of development will surely force a rise in prices. This argument, however, confuses *physical* magnitudes with *money* magnitudes. The pressure on resources during the course of development affects relative prices. It tends to make the prices of those things for which the demand is particularly great in the course of development high compared with the prices of other things. It need not, however, affect the absolute price level.

Everything depends on how the real resources, which are employed in the course of development, are acquired. If the real resources are acquired by Government, for example, through taxes or through borrowing from the public, or if the real resources are acquired by private enterprises and individuals by using their own savings for the purpose of investment, there will be no pressure of monetary demand. There will be a shift of demand away from certain things towards other things, and this will produce the shift in physical resources required. On the other hand, if the printing press, or any of its more sophisticated modern variants, is used to try to acquire resources, then, of course, there will tend to be inflation and price rise. The view that development makes inflation inevitable is misleading and arises from confusing physical magnitudes in the economy with monetary magnitudes.

The experience of India in the past 10 years [1952-1962] provides an almost text-book illustration of this elementary point. Consider the two Five Year Plan periods. According to official estimates, the net national product in constant prices rose by 18 per cent in the first Five Year Plan period [1951-1956] and by 21 per cent in the second Five Year Plan period [1956-1961]. The difference between these two numbers is decidedly smaller than the error of estimate of either one of them. Moreover, there is some reason to believe that the increase in real output in the Second Plan period is overstated because of defects in price indices used to deflate national product. Roughly, therefore, we may say that output rose by about the same percentage in the first Five Year Plan period and in the second Five Year Plan period. Yet, in the first period, prices fell; in the second, prices rose. In the first period, the price index that is implicit in deflating the national product fell by 12 per cent; the wholesale price index fell by 16 per cent; the consumer price index fell by 5 per cent. Whichever index you look at, prices fell appreciably. In the second Five Year Plan period, the implicit price index rose by 17 per cent; the wholesale price index rose by 34 per cent; and the consumer price index by 29 per cent. Whichever index you look at, prices rose substantially.

Why was there this difference between the two plan periods? One does not have to look far to find the answer. In the first Five Year Plan period, the stock of money rose by decidedly less than output. One can use alternative definitions of money but it will make no difference which definition one uses. Currency in public circulation—the kind of stuff people carry round in their pockets—rose by 13 per cent; currency plus demand deposits rose by 11 per cent; currency plus demand deposits plus time deposits rose by 15 per cent. The stock of money as defined in any of these ways rose by decidedly less than the 18 per cent increase in output. In consequence, prices fell. In the second Five Year Plan period, the stock of money rose more than output. Again, if we take each of the above definitions of money: currency alone rose by 25 per cent; currency plus demand deposits by 33 per cent; currency plus demand deposits plus time deposits by 53 per cent. The stock of money rose more than output; hence prices rose.

There is one interesting feature about the above figures worth noting. In both periods, the price movement was larger than the discrepancy between the movement in money and the movement in real output. In order to simplify the comparison, let us stick for the moment to the money supply as defined by the Reserve Bank, namely, currency plus demand deposits. In the first Five Year Plan period, it rose by 11 per cent, real output rose by 18 per cent and the difference is 7 per cent. This is the amount of decline in prices that would have occurred if people had continued to hold the same amount of money expressed in terms of their income throughout the period. While this difference is 7 per cent, prices in fact—and again to keep the discussion simple I shall stick to just one index number, the implicit price index—fell by 12 per cent, or by more than the 7 per cent decline in the stock of money relative to output. In the second Five Year Plan period, money supply rose by 33 per cent, output by 21 per cent; the difference is 12 per cent. Prices, according to the implicit price index, rose by 17 per cent and by much more according to the other indices. In other words, movements in the velocity of circulation of money exaggerated the effect of the behavior of the stock of money itself.

This phenomenon of prices changing by more than the difference between the change in output and the change in money stock is often observed and is not special to these particular periods in India. The reason is not far to seek. When prices are going down, money becomes a more desirable way in which to hold assets; its value is increasing day by day; hence people have a strong tendency, if they expect the price decline to continue, to hold a larger fraction of their wealth in the form of money. On the other side of the picture, when prices are going up, money becomes a less desirable form in which to hold assets. In consequence, people tend to economize on their money balances; velocity tends to increase. How much velocity will change depends on whether the fall in prices or the rise in prices is anticipated. Generally, when inflation has started after a period of roughly stable prices, people initially do not expect prices to continue rising. They regard the price rise as temporary and expect prices to fall later on. In consequence, they tend to increase their monetary holdings and the price rise is less than the rise in the stock of money. Then, as people gradually become wise to what is going on, they tend to readjust their holdings. Prices then rise more than in proportion to the stock of money. Eventually people come to expect roughly what is happening and prices rise in proportion to the stock of money.

The tendency for changes in velocity to reinforce changes in the money supply on some occasions and to counter-act them on others has two very important implications. The first is that in an inflation whose prevalence is becoming widely recognized the effect of a change in the stock of money on prices may be a multiple of the change in the stock of money. The second is that, while inflation or, in the contrary case, deflation, is produced by changes in the stock of money per unit of output, the relationship is not mechanically precise. It is not always the same under all circumstances and it cannot be predicted with precise accuracy.

I have been citing Indian experience because you are most familiar with it. Numerous other examples can be cited to demonstrate that inflation is not inevitable in the course of economic development, that it has little or nothing to do with the pressure on real resources, but rather with monetary institutions and the monetary policies which are followed. Let me cite a few such examples. One of the most dramatic is from my own country. It goes back nearly a century to the 15 years following the Civil War in the United States, the years from 1865 to 1879. In that period, there occurred one of the largest and longest continuous price falls on record. If one looks at the whole record of history, price rises are much more prominent than price declines and it is very unusual to find a decline of the kind that occurred in the United States in those years. Prices were a little bit more than cut in half in 15 years. They fell at the rate of something over 5 per cent a year.

During the Civil War itself (1861-65), Government resorted to printing money in order to finance the war—the famous "greenbacks"—with the result that by the end of the war, the price level had more than doubled. The United States wanted to return to the gold standard at the pre-war parity. In order to do this, prices had to be cut in half to bring them into line with prices in the rest of the world. And they were in fact cut in half. The decline owed little to deliberate policies followed by the Government. It was the result rather of an extraordinarily high rate of economic growth in that 15-year period. By all the statistical evidence available, that 15-year period saw a more rapid rate of economic growth than almost any other period in the whole history of the United States. According to the estimates which Simon Kuznets has constructed of income in the United States since 1869, the decade of the 1870's shows a higher rate of growth than any decade from 1869 to 1959. Kuznets himself thinks, and I agree with him, that his estimates overstate the rise in the early decade. But whatever index you look at, whether the expansion of railroads, increase in traffic on railroads and canals and so on, shows that period to have been a period of very rapid growth. Output considerably more than doubled; and since the stock of money rose only a trifle, prices were cut in half.

I do not cite this example to suggest that declines in prices promote economic growth. I cite it rather because it is such an extreme example to contradict the widely believed notion that a price rise is somehow inevitable, or, if not inevitable, at any rate highly desirable, in order to promote economic growth. In the American case, I do not believe that the decline in prices produced economic growth. On the contrary, it was the economic growth, which had its origin in very different sources, which produced the decline in prices. Neither do I mean to suggest that this experience is a model for anybody to follow. The fall in prices created real difficulties. It stimulated political discontent and controversy; there was a long recession from 1873 to 1879 and so on. Very likely, the economic growth would have been the same if a monetary policy had been followed which would have meant stable prices, and other difficulties would have been less. Yet the fact remains that economic growth was entirely consistent with falling prices.

Other less dramatic examples are ready at hand. In the United States from 1879, when the U.S. went back on gold, to 1896, prices fell at the rate of something like 2 to 3 per cent a year. From 1896 to 1913, prices rose at the rate of something like 2 to 3 per cent a year. Yet these two periods show almost precisely the same rate of economic growth as judged by the growth in national product. Again, in the same period from 1870 to 1890 or 1895, prices were falling in the United Kingdom; from 1890 or 1895 to 1913 prices were rising. Yet the estimates of real national output constructed some years ago show that the rate of increase in output was faster during the period of falling prices than during the period of rising prices. In more recent times, since the end of the second World War, countries like Italy and West Germany have had very rapidly rising outputs with roughly constant or mildly rising prices. Since something like 1953 or 1954, Greece has had a very rapid rate of economic growth with highly stable prices. In the early years after the war, Japan had a substantial price rise and also a substantial rise in output. Since then, the rise in output has continued but prices have been roughly stable.[2]

I hasten to add that examples can also be cited when rises in prices went along with expansion of output. What I am arguing is not that falling prices are inevitable in the course of economic expansion but only that rising prices are not inevitable, though they may occur. For example, in addition to the cases in the United States and the United Kingdom that I have given, there is the great period of the price revolution in Europe in the 15th and 16th centuries, to which I shall return in another connection. That was a period when the pace of economic development quickened throughout Europe, along with a steady and long continued rise in prices. Or again, to take the recent postwar experience, over the past 10 years or so, Israel has been experiencing a rate of price rise of roughly 10 per cent a year—not a negligible rate of price rise by anybody's calculation. Yet it has also experienced a rate of rise in real income of the order of something like 10 per cent a year. So clearly, while inflation is not an inevitable accompaniment of development, neither does it necessarily prevent development. The basic forces making for economic growth are much more fundamental than the question of whether prices are rising or falling.

May inflation not be desirable? This question I want to turn to, but before doing so, I should like to spend a bit more time examining analytically the causes of inflation because the emphasis I have just been placing on the stock of money as the culprit is widely regarded as old-fashioned and out of date. Most modern writers today attribute inflation to very different kinds of causes. They say it is the result of attempted investment exceeding desired savings; or of a wage push on the part of employees; or of a profit push on the part of employers and entrepreneurs; or of the inability to increase the output of food as

[2 Since this was written (1963), Japan's output has continued to grow rapidly, but prices have also started to rise fairly rapidly.]

rapidly as the increase in output of other things; and so on in infinite variety and diversity. Now these explanations may, in one sense, be correct. If any of these factors produces a rise in the stock of money, it will produce inflation. But if it does not produce a rise in the stock of money, it will not produce inflation.

The reasons why these explanations are so popular are not far to seek. There are, I think, two main reasons. The first is the natural tendency to confuse what is true for the individual with what is true for the society as a whole. The most interesting and important thing about economics as a science is precisely that almost everything that is true for the individual is false for the society and almost everything that is true for the society as a whole is false for the individual. One individual can affect the price of hardly anything he buys. Yet, all individuals together make the price what it is. In the particular case of inflation, to each individual separately, the price rise is not in any way connected with the fact that somehow or other a printing press has been turning out those loose pieces of paper we like to carry around in our pockets. The individual entrepreneur raises his prices because, on the one hand, his costs have gone up and, on the other, he finds he can still sell his product at higher prices. And so to each one of us separately, a price rise comes from a higher price on some other commodity. We never see the fact that that higher price in turn is ultimately the result of the creation of more money. That is one reason. A second and equally important reason is that, so far as the printing of money is concerned, in modern days the Government has a near-monopoly. This is a little exaggerated, and I shall qualify it later, because private banks do have some possibility of creating money; but in the main, it is true that in modern countries, including India, the Government can control the quantity of money if it wishes to do so. Nobody likes to blame himself for bad things that occur. Though many people like inflation because it helps them personally, nonetheless almost everyone thinks it is a bad thing on the whole and nobody likes to admit that he is responsible for inflation. It is far easier for Government to attribute inflation to the profiteers, or the bad trade unions that insist on pushing up the wages, or the intractability of agricultural producers who are unable to expand food than it is for Government or government officials to say, *mea culpa.*

Though these are the two main reasons why inflation tends to be attributed to everything except money, there is a third supplementary reason which has been especially important in the past 20 years or so. That is something that happened purely in the intellectual sphere, namely, the Keynesian revolution in economic thought in the 1930's, which led many economists to reduce the role assigned to money. The reason why I think that it is not really a basic explanation is because the emphasis on non-monetary explanations is not a new thing. One can go back one or two thousand years and more and find that every time there is inflation, two explanations are offered. One explanation is that the amount of money has increased. The other explanation is that something special has happened: wage-earners have pushed up their wages; profiteers have been active; there has been a blockade of the country and as a result supplies could not come in; and so on and on.

As I have already noted, these two separate explanations are not necessarily contradictory. The non-monetary factors may, on some occasions, be the cause of the monetary expansion. For example, when people argue that attempted investment in excess of desired savings is the cause of inflation, that may be the correct description at a second remove. If the attempted investment is by Government and if Government attempts to finance that investment by printing money, then it is true that the desire to make attempted investment greater than the savings that the public at large will voluntarily make is a cause of inflation. It is a cause of inflation because it produces an increase in the money stock. Or again in some countries—this is not so pertinent in India —the trade unions may in fact push up wage rates sufficiently to create unemployment. If the Government is committed to a full employment policy, it may in response thereto expand the money supply by printing more money for Government expenditures or for other purposes. In that case, it is true that the upward push in wages produced inflation, not because it was necessarily inflationary but because it happened to be the mechanism which forced an increase in the stock of money.

One thing is clear from the historical record. The actual sources of monetary expansion have been very different at different times and in different places. Hence, if a theory of inflation is going to deal not with the expansion of the stock of money but with what brought it about, it will be a very pluralistic theory which will have many possible sources of inflation. For example, in the early days, when actual coin was the medium of circulation, inflations tended to be produced by such devices as sweating and clipping. I am sure you know what that means. You take a bunch of gold coins and you put them together in a bag and then you rattle them around as much as you can so that dust comes off. You then take out the gold coins and the dust that is left is your profit from sweating. Or else you take a little scissors or a little knife and clip around the edge a tiny bit so that the coin looks all right and then you pass it on. Each person who gets the coins proceeds to do the same thing and as a result in the course of years, coins get lighter and lighter and prices get higher and higher. A modern technological invention has largely put an end to that particular source of inflation, the invention being the milling of coins. In addition, the use of pieces of paper, bank notes, instead of actual coins, has also reduced opportunities for that kind of inflation. Another source of expansion in the nominal stock of money has been what the history books always refer to as "crying up" or "crying down" the nominal value of money. Again, a major source of inflation in the past has been discovery of new sources of gold or of silver, or technological changes which have increased the possibility of extracting silver or gold from ores. Printing money to pay for war has always been one of the major sources of inflation. Full employment policy is, however, a modern invention for producing inflation.

Whenever these or other factors have led to a substantially greater expansion in the stock of money than the current rate of increase in output, they have led to inflation. If you are going to regard them as causes, you will, as I said, be fated to have many explanations. I know of no exception to the proposition that a substantial rise in prices is always accompanied by a substantial rise in the stock of money, and conversely. On many occasions, I have challenged people to cite an exception. I have as yet found no exception. But there have been many confirming examples; some of them extremely dramatic. Let me cite two that will illustrate how important the quantity of money is by comparison with everything else. After the Russian revolution of 1917, as you know there was an enormous inflation in Russia when a new currency was introduced by the new Government and printed in large quantities. It depreciated until it became almost valueless. It was a hyperinflation. All the time, there was some currency circulating which had been issued by the pre-revolutionary Government, by the Czarist Government. The Czarist Government was out of power; nobody expected it to return to power. Yet the value of the Czarist currency remained roughly constant in terms of goods and rose very sharply in terms of the Bolshevik currency. Why? Because there was nobody to print any more of it. It was fixed in quantity and therefore it retained its value. Another story has to do with the American Civil War. The North overran the place in the South where the Southerners had been printing paper money to finance the war. The South had to move its headquarters. In the course of doing so, it could not print any money. As a result of this interruption, prices temporarily ceased rising. I conclude that if you want to analyze the process of inflation, "Cherchez la monnaie."

Why should money be so critical a factor in price level behavior? Why should it occupy such a central role in the process? The key to an answer is the difference between the *nominal* quantity of money, the quantity of money expressed in terms of rupees, dollars, or marks or what have you, and the *real* quantity of money, the quantity of money expressed in terms of the goods and services it will buy or the number of weeks of income it is equal to.

People seem to be extraordinarily stubborn about the real amount of money that they want to hold and are unwilling to hold a different amount, unless there is a real incentive to do so. This is true not only over time but over space. Let me give a few striking figures I have picked up in the course of my travels the past few months. I shall refer only to currency in circulation, excluding deposits, since currency is more comparable among the countries I want to deal with.

In India, the amount of currency that is held by people amounts to roughly seven weeks' income. That is to say, if you calculate the aggregate income received by all Indians during a seven weeks' period, the resulting sum is roughly equal to the amount of currency that is held by all the people and all the business enterprises in India. I know from past experience that this result seems surprising. If you ask people individually, "Do you hold seven weeks' income in the form of currency?", you will seldom find someone who says yes. Yet somehow on the average all the people of India hold seven weeks' of income in the form of currency. Part of the explanation is the currency held by business enterprises. I do not know what the rest of the explanation is.

Let us now turn to Yugoslavia, a country that is vastly different in many respects from India. Yugoslavia has a Communist Government and extensive centralized control over economic activity. It has a different kind of agriculture, different social customs and traditions. Yet the people of Yugoslavia hold in the form of currency something like 6¼ weeks' income, remarkably close to the figure for India.

Greece is a royalist country with a king and queen and a very different economic structure from either Yugoslavia or India. Yet its people hold in the form of currency almost the same amount as in Yugoslavia, a little over 6 weeks' income. In Turkey, they hold a little over 5 weeks' income. In the United States, they hold about 4¼ weeks' income in the form of currency. In Israel they hold about 4¼ weeks' income also, although the level of income in Israel is one-third or one-quarter of that in the United States.

Even these relatively small differences are readily accounted for. They are associated with the prevalence of deposit banking in different countries. Deposit banking is most widespread in the U.S. and Israel, next most widespread in Turkey, and least widespread in Greece, Yugoslavia and India. But even if one takes the figures as they stand, they reveal a striking uniformity. Here we have countries with every variety of economic system, with real incomes varying over a range of 15 or 20 to one and yet currency holdings, expressed in terms of weeks' income, vary over a range of decidedly less than 2 to 1.

Given that people are so stubborn about the amount they hold in the form of money, let us suppose that, for whatever reason, the amount of money in a community is higher than people want to hold at the level of prices then prevailing. It does not for our purposes matter why, whether because the Government has printed money to finance expenditures or because somebody has discovered a new gold mine, or because banks have discovered how to create deposits. For whatever reason, people find that although on the average they would like to hold, let us say, the 7 weeks' income that they hold in India, they are actually holding, say, 8 weeks' income. What will happen? Here again it is essential to distinguish between what happens to the individual and what happens to the community. Each individual separately thinks he can get rid of his money and he is right. He can go out and spend it and thereby reduce his cash balances. But for the community as a whole the belief that cash balances can be reduced is an optical illusion. The only reason I can reduce my cash balances in nominal terms is because somebody else is willing to increase his. One man's expenditures are another man's receipts. People as a whole cannot spend more than they as a whole receive. In consequence, if everybody in the community tries to cut the nominal amount of his cash balances, they will on the average be frustrated. The amount of nominal balances is fixed by the nominal quantity of money in existence and no game of musical chairs can change it. But people can and will *try* to reduce their cash balances and the process of trying will have important effects. In the process of trying to spend more than they are receiving, people will bid up the prices of all sorts of goods and services. Nominal incomes will rise and real cash balances will indeed be reduced, even though nominal balances, the number of rupees, are not affected. The rise in prices and incomes will bring cash balances from 8 weeks' income to 7 weeks' income. People will succeed in achieving their objective, but by raising prices and incomes rather than by reducing nominal balances. In the process, prices will have risen by about an eighth. This in a nutshell and somewhat oversimplified is the process whereby changes in the stock of money exert their influence on the price level. It is oversimplified because there is a tendency to

33

overshoot, followed by successive readjustments converging on the final position, but this complication does not affect the essence of the adjustment process.

Let me now turn briefly to the question whether inflation is desirable. I shall have more to say about this question in the next lecture when I talk more systematically about the consequences of inflation. But a number of things can be said first.

Will inflation tend to stimulate development? Two main arguments have been advanced in support of the view that it will. The first argument is that inflation tends to redistribute income and wealth. It is said to redistribute income away from the wage earning classes who are alleged to consume it all, and towards the profit recipients in the community who are alleged both to save a good deal and to invest their savings in productive capital. It is said to redistribute capital away from creditors, people who lend money to other people but are themselves allegedly unproductive and towards debtors, people who borrow, supposedly for productive use. The second argument that is advanced in support of the view that inflation stimulates development is that printing money is a source of revenue to the Government and as such provides the Government with funds that it can use to promote development.

Let us consider each of these in turn. With respect to the redistribution of income and wealth, there is no doubt that there have been some circumstances in the past when such redistribution has been favorable to development. The best documented and the most important is the period in the 15th and 16th centuries of which I spoke earlier. Prof. Earl J. Hamilton, of the University of Chicago, has examined this episode in several books that have become the standard works on the period. The discoveries of gold and silver in the New World produced an inflow of specie into Spain, which spread from there throughout the rest of Europe and indeed the world. Hamilton rather conclusively demonstrates that the resulting rise in prices had its origin in the specie inflow and strongly stimulated economic development presumably by redistributing income and wealth in the way suggested above.

However, the fact that inflation had this influence in one

instance does not mean that it is guaranteed to work in all. The reason inflation had the effects it did in this instance is because it was unexpected. As a result, people clung to traditional prices and traditional levels of interest rates with the result that there was a transfer of income from wage earners to profit recipients and of capital from creditors to debtors. One reason the inflation process was unanticipated is that nobody planned it that way. It was, as it were, an act of God. Somebody found gold and silver; it flowed into Europe and raised prices.

I am exceedingly sceptical that any similar result can be obtained by a deliberate process of expanding the money supply without its degenerating into hyperinflation. If it is done deliberately, many people will know about it and will act so as to prevent the redistribution from taking place. If you announce to the public that you are going to adopt the deliberate policy of increasing prices at the rate of 3 per cent a year everybody will adjust to that announcement. In order to have the redistributive effects favorable to development, you will have to increase prices at the rate of, say, 6 per cent a year. Once people adjust to that rate, you would have to go to a still higher rate and there is no stopping place. So I am very dubious that this allegedly favorable result of inflation can in fact be achieved by a deliberate policy of inflation. The experience of many South American countries suggests that this scepticism is well-founded.

What about the second argument that inflation is a means of raising revenue for Government? It is generally said that there are three ways in which Government can get funds: it can tax people; it can borrow from people; or it can print money. This is a mistake. There are fundamentally only two ways the Government can get resources from the community: by taxes or by borrowings. There is no third way. The printing of money is either borrowing or it is taxation. To the extent to which money can be printed without raising prices, the Government gets resources by borrowing. There is no difference between a promise to pay in the form of a two-rupee note and a promise to pay in the form of a bond except that the bond pays interest and the two-rupee note does not. The notes outstanding are non-interest bearing obligations of the Government. If the public is willing to hold a larger volume of such notes without a rise in the price level, this means that the public is willing to lend more to Government at a zero interest rate. On the other hand, if the printing of money raises prices, then the resources are obtained by Government by taxation.

The particular kind of tax levied by inflation is a tax on cash balances. Consider for a moment a literal tax on cash balances. Suppose the Government were to pass a law saying that everybody will have to pay a tax equal to 5 per cent of the average amount of cash he has on hand throughout the year. That tax would be like a tax on cigarettes, or playing cards, or kerosene, or sugar, or anything else. However, it would be an extremely difficult tax to collect. How can you find out what average amount of cash people have on hand? If you were to make the tax apply to the cash on a particular date, people would adopt all sorts of devices to have as little cash as possible on that date. An easier way to collect the tax is to issue pieces of paper called rupee notes at a rate which will produce a 5 per cent per year increase in the total volume of notes over and above the amount that can be absorbed without a rise in prices. In that case, prices will rise by 5 per cent a year. In order for an individual to keep his *real* cash balances constant, he must use part of his income to add 5 per cent a year to his nominal money balances in order to make good the 5 per cent decline in the value of each piece of money as a result of the price rise. Indeed, if you want to you can look at this process as an explicit tax on cash, interpreting the extra pieces of paper that people have to have on hand in order to have the same level of real cash balances as vouchers given by Government to certify that the tax has been paid.

Like any other tax, the tax on cash balances which is imposed by inflation has side effects; only in this case, the side effects are extremely important. For example, suppose a high tax is imposed on movies. As a result, fewer people will go to movies; production of movies will decline, some actors and others will be unemployed. The people who are unemployed are affected by the tax, but the loss to them does not yield any revenue to Government. It is a side effect. In the same way, if a tax is imposed on cash balances through inflation, there will be side effects. Prices will rise; people who did not anticipate the price rise will be hurt; other people will gain. It is often argued that wage and salary classes and middle class individuals with fixed incomes are hurt by inflation. Whether this is true or not is not relevant to my purpose here. My point is only to distinguish between such an effect and the revenue obtained by Government. Insofar as such people are hurt by inflation, the Government does not benefit in its role as tax collector, though it may in its role as an employer. What happens is that some people are hurt and other people gain. The people whose incomes are fixed find their real income going down; their employers find their incomes going up. There is a transfer between private people that does not yield an iota of resources to the Government as tax revenue. This point needs emphasis because the side effects are in this case especially widespread and especially serious. Nonetheless, they do not alter the statement that the revenue obtained by the Government arises out of a tax on cash balances.

The tax on cash balances differs from most taxes in two important respects. The first respect is that the Government has an implicit agreement with private groups to share the proceeds of the tax. The private groups in this case are the commercial banks which create demand deposits that, in the main, are also non-interest bearing loans. I say in the main, because interest is occasionally paid on demand deposits, but even when it is, the rate is much lower than can be earned on other assets. When the Government creates money, it indirectly provides banks with reserves which enable them to expand their deposits. Consequently the Government shares the tax proceeds in the first instance with the commercial banks. It does not necessarily follow that banks benefit on net from inflation. On the contrary, in most countries rapid inflation has been harmful to banks. The reason is because they in turn have been forced to distribute their share of the proceeds to others. Usury laws which limit the rates of interest that banks can charge have forced them to disgorge their gains and more than their gains to borrowers who are in a position to get loans from the banks at rates of interest well below the yield they can earn on the funds. In India, under current conditions, the sharing ratio is roughly three to one: three to the Government and one to the banks. This is a very high ratio. In most countries of the world, the fraction of the return obtained by the government from inflation is considerably less than 75 per cent.

The other special feature, besides the sharing arrangement, which inflation has as a tax is that it is the only tax I know of that can be levied without specific legislative approval. The monetary agencies of the Government, the Central Bank and the Treasury, can generally—and this is true not only of India but of most other countries—impose this tax without having to go to the legislature for permission to do so. That is why this tax is so often resorted to under pressure of governmental difficulty in raising funds. And that is also why it is so dangerous a tax.

How productive a tax is this tax on cash balances? A few figures will give a good indication. The outstanding amount of government money in India is roughly of the order of Rs. 2,200 crores.[2a] The Government's share of a 1 per cent tax per year would, therefore, be about Rs. 22 crores a year. A 10 per cent tax, i.e., a rate of price rise of 10 per cent per year for a considerable period, a very sizeable price rise indeed, will yield the Government Rs. 220 crores per year or about 1½ per cent of the national income. These figures somewhat overestimate the probable yield because people will tend to reduce the real amount of money they hold since the tax will make it more costly to hold money. However, these figures can nonetheless serve as an indication of the order of magnitude of the yield. Clearly, these are not negligible yields. Inflation is likely to be a fairly productive tax.

Finally, it is not clear that inflation is always a bad tax. That depends on circumstances and alternatives available. I would not want to say that it is always worse than all alternatives. Most people regard all taxes as an evil, even though they regard some of the things that are done with the funds as a good. But if this is so, one must choose among evils. In time of war, for example, when all sorts of tax resources are stretched to their utmost, inflation may not be less bad than the very bad alternatives available.

I have covered quite a lot of ground in this talk. The main points can, however, be summarized in a few brief propositions:

[2a A "crore" is a term used in India which stands for 100,000.]

(1) Inflation is always and everywhere a monetary phenomenon.
(2) Inflation is not inevitable in the course of development.
(3) Inflation is not likely under current conditions to promote development, unless it accelerates, in which case it can be only a temporary panacea.
(4) As a tax on cash balances, inflation may be less bad than some other alternatives on some occasions, but it has very undesirable side effects.

Questions and Answers

Q: You say that inflation is not inevitable in the course of development. Yet you also say that full employment can lead to inflation. But full employment can only come from development. Are you not therefore involved in a contradiction?

A: I did not say that full employment led to inflation. I said that a full employment *policy* led to inflation. That is quite a different thing. A full employment policy is likely to mean that you do not have full employment, because a full employment policy tends to be an open invitation to everybody to try to push up wage rates here, there, and elsewhere. The rises in wage rates lead to unemployment. In trying to counter the unemployment, the Government is likely to increase the money supply and this tends to produce inflation. However, there is widespread opposition to inflation. Hence, Government tends to go less far in this direction than would be necessary to offset completely the rises in wage rates, assuming that to be possible. As a result, a full employment policy tends to mean less than full employment. A prime example is provided by the experience of Britain these past few years, and this is not an isolated case.

I must go on to say that I do not agree with your assertion that full employment can only come from development. The fact is that you can have full employment at any level of stagnation and any level of poverty or any level of wealth. Conversely, you can have development without full employment.

39

I have been using the word "full employment," as if it were a well-defined term. It is far from that; it is almost impossible to define full employment in a way that is logically precise, and yet corresponds to what we have loosely in mind. The reason is partly that we really do not want full employment, but the opposite. What almost all of us would like is a kind of world in which we could have all the good things in life without working any more than we wanted to. Employment is a means, not an end.

Q: Can you envisage a development program taking place in an underdeveloped country if investment is pegged to available savings?

A: Investment must be pegged to available savings; where else can the resources come from? Has investment ever been made with anything other than available savings?

Q: I mean can development occur with savings at the current level and without a policy for greatly increasing savings?

A: Of course it can occur without such a policy. The outstanding examples of economic development have occurred precisely when there has not been a policy for increasing savings, but when there has been an incentive for people to save and invest. As a matter of description, development is a process in which there are widespread incentives to individual people to do something to promote production in the future rather than simply to consume in the present. Given those incentives, people will use their own resources to produce and to save and they will save more than they otherwise would in order to invest. It is this that has produced economic development.

Consider the example from U.S. history that I referred to in the lecture, the period from 1865 to 1879. There was no explicit policy whatsoever to promote savings, or, for that matter, anything else. Most of the political argument at the time was about the greenback issue. Yet, or maybe therefore, development was extremely rapid.

A more recent example is furnished by Japan during its great period of expansion. There was a very rapid increase in investment. Where did it come from? From the savings of individuals in Japan, who were induced by the prospect of a high return on their investment to save and invest.

The savings may of course be made abroad. There may be foreign investment. In the United States in the period I cited, there was a large inflow of capital, mostly from Britain. This too was stimulated by the high earnings that could be made on the capital. In Japan, there was very little foreign capital; it was almost all domestic. The important thing is that what is needed to encourage savings and investment is not a policy of increasing savings through compulsion but a policy of giving individuals an opportunity to use their own resources in a way that will promote their own objectives. Not only can development occur without a deliberate governmental policy of increasing savings, so far as I know development has never in any free country been produced or accompanied by such a policy. The belief that such a policy is necessary in India may be correct but it cannot be derived from experience. Acceptance of the belief is a pure act of faith.

Q: Isn't it true that a little inflation, like a little pregnancy, is a difficult thing. Once started, you can't stop it?

A: No, it is not true. There is a vast difference between a little inflation and a little pregnancy. You are seldom in doubt whether you have a little pregnancy. You are very often in doubt whether you have a little inflation. For example, in the United States in the past 7 years or so prices have risen by something like 1 per cent a year according to official index numbers. A price committee was established under the chairmanship of a colleague of mine at the University of Chicago, Prof. George Stigler, to investigate the index numbers and the measurement of prices. They came to the conclusion that with the best intent and will in the world the price index numbers of the kind used in the United States have an upward bias and that very probably if the price indexes showed that prices were rising at 1 per cent a year, they might really be stable or even falling a little. In consequence you cannot even be sure whether you have a little inflation.

Equally important, there are many examples in history when you have had several decades of generally rising prices or of generally falling prices without the price rise accelerating or the price decline turning into a collapse.

Q: You referred to the price fall in the first plan and a price rise in the second plan, and you ended with the proposition that inflation is basically a monetary phenomenon. In the first plan, the emphasis was on agricultural production and because or in spite of the plan there was a substantial increase in agricultural production. In the second plan, the major emphasis has been on long gestation projects and on heavy industry, and food production did not rise to the same extent or with as much rapidity as in the first plan. In view of these two basic facts: the increase in food production and the emphasis on long gestation projects, would you still consider that inflation is basically a monetary phenomenon?

A: Yes, indeed. One swallow doesn't make a spring and never will. There are many other differences between the two plans. For example, one took place in the years from 1951 to 1956, the other from 1956 to 1961. If you add up the final digits in these dates, the sum of these digits will be less for the first Five Year Plan than for the second. Should I attribute the difference in price behavior to this difference between the two plans?

When I was in India several years ago, I wrote a memorandum in which I argued that the emphasis on heavy projects with a long gestation period was a serious mistake. I still believe it was a mistake, but that doesn't mean it produced inflation. If these projects had been financed by taxes or by borrowing from the public at large they would have had the same effect as they did in wasting resources and slowing up the rise in the standard of life of the people, but there would have been no price rise. The reason there was a price rise in the second Plan period was because the stock of money rose more than output. It may be that the additional money printed was used to pay for long gestation projects, but the price rise would have been roughly the same, if the same amount of money had been printed for other purposes.

What you are doing is generalizing from a single instance. Here you have a particular contrast between the two periods and you associate that with a different contrast, namely the differential behavior of prices. That is a perfectly valid way to derive hypotheses. You look at some facts and try to ask what explains the observed difference. But you cannot test hypotheses that way. To test hypotheses, you must examine other occasions where there is the same difference in price behavior and see whether there is also the same difference in emphasis on heavy gestation projects or food output; and conversely, you must examine other occasions where there is the same difference in the latter respects and see whether such a difference is always associated with a like difference in price behavior. For example, can we say that the contrast between the fall in prices by about a third in the United States from 1879 to 1896 and the rise in prices by a third from 1896 to 1913 was associated with a difference in the relative production of food or with emphasis in the later period on projects with a long gestation period? Not at all. The reason for the difference in price behavior was because of new gold discoveries after 1890 plus the development of the cyanide process as a commercially feasible way to extract gold from low grade ore. As a result, there was an increased rate of gold production. The stock of money rose more rapidly all over the Western world and prices everywhere rose. Try your hypothesis out on still other occasions and see whether you can associate declining prices with a relative increase in food production and rising prices with a relative decrease. I think you will find you cannot do so. One must be chary about jumping to a conclusion on the basis of one case.

Q: Just to say that the rise in the supply of money causes the rise in prices is not sufficient. We can't stop there. We must explain what causes the Government of India to increase the stock of money and then we will come to the real causes of inflation, those which make the Government increase the stock of money.

A: Why must it increase the stock of money? Why can't it

raise taxes? Why can't it borrow? There is nothing about the physical factors in the world that makes the Government increase the stock of money. The volume of resources in the community is not increased by printing pieces of paper. If the community can afford the projects through the tax of inflation, it can afford them through other taxes.

I quite agree with you that it is desirable to look beyond the increase in the stock of money and ask what caused it. But as I pointed out in the lecture, the fact is that very many different things have, on different occasions, produced a rise in the stock of money. On some occasions, the rise in the stock of money has been produced by discoveries of precious metal; on other occasions, by the printing of money to pay for a war, or by a commercial banking system with fractional reserves which has expanded rapidly and in this way has in effect printed money for private purposes. I quite agree that, if you are going to analyze any particular episode, you want to go beyond the increase in the stock of money and ask, what factors, in that particular episode, account for the rise in the stock of money. But this does not alter the fact that inflation is a monetary phenomenon and that you will find yourself avoiding a lot of common mistakes by first asking, what happened to the stock of money and why.

Q: To stop by saying that inflation is a result of printing money is not a sufficient theory.

A: No theory of anything is sufficient. We are imperfect human beings with incomplete understanding and the important thing is that we must economize on our small minds by getting at the essential elements. It will do no good to obfuscate the issue by saying oh no, inflation is not produced by changes in the stock of money but by any one of a million and one things which may give rise to an increase in the stock of money. I must confess that I cannot see much difference between us.

Q: Does population increase have any effect on inflation?

A: Only if it alters the ratio of the stock of money to output. Now how may it do that? Increasing population tends to mean an increase in real output. Thus, if the stock of money were constant, it would mean declining prices. Hence any increase in population means that the stock of money can rise more than it otherwise could without producing inflation. Historically, for example, increasing population is one factor that has helped make possible an increase in the stock of money without prices necessarily rising. Beyond this, increasing population, so far as I know, has not systematically been associated with increases in the stock of money or with inflation.

Q: In your conclusions, you say that inflation is not likely to promote development. Yet I do not recall your dealing with that in the lecture.

A: I think I did deal with it, but I did not express it in precisely those terms. In the lecture I referred to the effect of inflation in redistributing income and wealth: redistributing income from the wage-earner or the fixed income class to the profit earner or variable income class; redistributing wealth from the creditor to the debtor. The reason people think those redistributions are favorable to development is because they think they promote investment by shifting income from non-investors to investors. I pointed out that in the cases where this had happened in the past, it has almost always been because inflation had been unanticipated. Under modern circumstances, the same result is unlikely because a deliberately planned inflation for this purpose is likely to set up private anticipations which will defeat any such redistribution. In addition, under current conditions the very Government that with one hand prints the money will with the other hand undo through social welfare measures any possible favorable effect on investment from redistribution.

I do not mean to say that if redistribution would promote investment, that would make it a desirable policy. I don't myself regard it as a desirable policy. I think the right amount of saving and investment is the amount that people want to make. I see no virtue in impoverishing some people and enriching others in order to get some arbitrarily determined increase in the amount of investment or saving. I was merely trying to explain why it was that many people had argued that inflation would stimulate economic development.

This lecture is mostly about the consequences of inflation which in turn will bring me to the question of the appropriate governmental monetary policy in India's present position. As said earlier, the brief text of the lecture is, "The cure may be worse than the disease."

Two distinctions are basic to any discussion of the consequences of inflation. The first distinction is between a steady inflation, one that proceeds at a more or less constant rate, and an intermittent inflation, one that proceeds by fits and starts, with a sharp burst of inflation, then a period of deflation perhaps because drastic measures are taken to stem the prior inflation, then another burst of inflation, renewed attempts to slow it down, and so on. The second distinction, which is perhaps even more important, is between an open inflation, one in which prices are free to rise without governmental price controls, and a suppressed inflation, one in which the Government attempts to suppress the manifestations of the inflationary pressure by controlling prices, exchange rates, and other magnitudes.

Let me first discuss the difference between steady inflation and intermittent inflation. To separate the issues, I shall assume both of these to be open inflations and then go on to discuss the problem of open versus suppressed inflation. Consider first a steady inflation. By steady, I do not mean precisely steady, but rather an inflation that proceeds at a more or less constant rate year after year, so that prices rise by, say, 3 per cent in one year, 5 per cent in another, 2 per cent in another, but never by an amount that is very far from the average rate. For the present purpose, what that average rate is does not matter, provided it is steady and provided it is relatively moderate—say up to 10 per cent per year or so. Such a steady inflation will soon be widely anticipated. The public at large will come to expect prices to rise at more or less the average rate. As a result, all sorts of economic arrangements will take into account the expected future price rises. Wage contracts will be drawn up so as to allow for periodic rises or so as to be linked to a cost of living index number. Other kinds of long-term contracts will have similar provisions. The rate of interest on money loans will be higher than it would otherwise be by enough to cover the expected rise in prices; for example, if prices are expected to rise by 3 per cent a year, the nominal interest rate will be 3 percentage points higher than it would be with stable prices, say 9 per cent instead of 6 per cent.

A straightforward example of an inflation of this kind happens to be provided by Israel. Over the past ten years or so [1952-1962], Israel has had an inflation at an average rate of about 10 per cent a year. This pattern has now come to be pretty well anticipated. Wage contracts incorporate a cost of living escalator clause. Many private loans contain an escalator clause. That is to say, the principal amount is expressed as a certain number of Israeli pounds multiplied by a price index number, or a particular price, or an exchange rate. Interest rates on money loans which do not have such escalator clauses are 12 to 15 per cent or even higher since everybody knows that the actual return will be less than the nominal rate because the value of the principal will deteriorate. Almost everything is escalated. There are only two major exceptions. One exception is the exchange rate which is not explicitly escalated but which has in fact been changed frequently—whereas it once stood at $3 to the Israeli pound, it now [1963] stands at 3 Israeli pounds to the dollar.[3] A second thing which has not been fully escalated is civil service salaries. Because of political pressures, there has been a tendency to hold these salaries down and this has had the excellent effect that it has induced many of the ablest people not to work for the Government but to seek careers in the private sector.

In a steady and hence anticipated inflation, the kinds of adjustments just described mean that there is little redistribution of income or wealth. The major effects of inflation are those that would be expected to follow from a straightforward tax on cash

[3 In 1968, it is roughly 3½ Israeli pounds to the dollar, and the recent rate of price increase has been less than it was earlier.]

balances rather than from the kind of unanticipated inflation to which I shall come in a moment.

The major effects are:

(1) By making it expensive to hold money, the inflation leads people to hold smaller cash balances than they otherwise would. This is not a good thing because it leads people to waste scarce economic resources in trying to keep down the size of their cash balances, to spend more time than is worthwhile from the point of view of productivity in figuring very closely their cash position, so as to avoid keeping extra cash over a period of time.

(2) Scarce resources are wasted in all kinds of paper work that is necessary for the escalation processes. Everything may be escalated but bookkeepers still have to change the numbers on the books and people have to calculate what adjustment is necessary.

(3) It tends to inhibit the spread of a money economy because money is something which is gradually losing its value so that people are trying to hold relatively little of it. This establishes a strong inhibition against the money economy spreading to those areas of the economy where it does not already exist.

With moderate degrees of inflation and for a country like Israel, which is almost wholly monetized, none of these defects is serious or very important, *provided the inflation is allowed to be open*. I think that Israel would do better to follow a monetary policy that does not involve such an inflation. But I do not think that in their circumstances the burden imposed on the community is very great. For India, I think the cost of a similar policy might be somewhat larger. One reason is that the non-money economy in India is large and the future progress and development of India depend greatly on extending the monetary nexus to a larger and larger part of the economy. Interposing any serious obstacles to this process can only slow down India's development. Another reason is that the average Indian citizen is less sophisticated about financial matters, so the adjustment would be less complete.

Intermittent inflation, one that proceeds by fits and starts, is a very different thing. People are slow to recognize changes from one direction to the other. If they have experienced inflation for a time, they tend to expect it to go on. They make all sorts of adjustments in the expectation that inflation will continue. When the brakes are put on and inflation is slowed down, these adjustments turn out to produce a misallocation of resources and unemployment. There are long lags in adjustment that produce confusion and a waste of resources.

One of the clearest examples of this kind of process occurred some years ago in Brazil. First Brazil experienced a very rapid inflation. Then the Government made an heroic attempt to stop prices from rising by curtailing the printing of money. Initially wages and prices continued to rise for a time and Brazil experienced continued moderate inflation together with a large volume of unemployment and lack of use of resources. There was a specious resemblance to the phenomena described by the so-called cost-push theory of inflation. Indeed, much of the appearance of validity in theories which assert that wages autonomously push up prices comes from precisely the kind of experience I am describing. In an economy adjusted to continuous price inflation, if the stock of money stops rising as rapidly as it did, the tendency is for wages and prices to continue to rise for a time because people still expect such an outcome. The result is unemployment. If the growth of the money stock continued to be restrained, the unemployment would in time be eliminated. After a while, people would adjust their expectations and come to recognize that prices will not in fact continue to rise. However, that is not what generally happens. Instead, government officials say, "Ah, look, we have been stepping on the brake and nonetheless prices have continued to rise and unemployment has been growing. We must do something about it." And so they turn on another burst of inflationary pressure. People's expectations of rising prices are justified. A ratchet process is set in train by successive abortive attempts to curb inflation. The result of this process is an extremely wasteful use of resources. To a minor extent India had just such an experience during the first Five Year Plan when prices first rose and then declined. The up and down in prices was most disturbing at the time to India's economic development.

Under such circumstances, the most valuable quality on the part of a businessman becomes his ability to forecast the changes in prices and to adjust rapidly to them. This becomes more important than his ability as an organizer or as a manager or as a person who can see where there are profitable opportunities. The result is that some of the most valuable and scarcest resources in the economy are diverted into activities that are socially unproductive. Another effect is that you do have sharp redistributions of income and wealth. In the expanding phase, when prices are going up very rapidly, you have the kind of redistribution I spoke about in my first lecture, away from the fixed income groups and toward the variable income groups, away from creditors and toward debtors.

A still more important adverse effect on economic development arises from the different speed of adjustment in different industries and different parts of the economic fabric. Prices are more variable in some parts of the economy than they are in others and there tends to be a strong tendency for resources to be drawn into those parts, even though, in a period of relatively stable prices or with steady rises in prices, that would not occur. The result is a serious misallocation of resources.

The conclusion is very clear. A steady inflation, while not desirable, is not inconsistent with economic development provided the inflation is open and moderate. Such an inflation is not likely to have much effect, either favorable or unfavorable, on economic development. Intermittent inflation, proceeding by fits and starts, is seriously adverse to economic development. It produces a misallocation of resources and arbitrary redistribution of income and wealth.

Let me turn now to the second distinction—between open and suppressed inflation. That distinction is far more important in terms of the consequences of inflation for the economic efficiency of the country than the distinction between inflation and deflation.

The most dramatic example I know to suggest the importance of the distinction is the contrast between the experience of Germany after the first World War and after the second World War. This happens to be one of those beautiful examples that history turns up for us from time to time in which experience is almost in the nature of a controlled experiment. After the first

World War, Germany had an open inflation of extremely large magnitude. It is difficult for us to contemplate the kind of inflation Germany experienced at that time because it is so extreme. A student of mine, Phillip Cagan, wrote a doctoral dissertation on hyperinflation in different countries, which has become something of a classic. He had the problem of how to define hyperinflation. He defined it as beginning when prices started to rise at the rate of more than 50 per cent a month. In the German hyperinflation after World War I there were periods when prices rose not 50 per cent a month but doubled every week and some occasions on which they were doubling every day. Indeed, it got to the point that firms started to pay their employees their wages three times a day—after breakfast, lunch, and dinner, so that they could go out and spend them before they lost their value. Some people think that's where the term the "velocity of circulation of money" came from. You will agree that that was really a whopping inflation. It went on for something like three years.

The inflation did untold harm to Germany. The impoverishment of the middle classes, the redistribution of income, unquestionably helped to lay the groundwork for Hitler's emergence later. But looked at from the purely technical point of view of its effect on production, the astounding thing is that until the last six months of the inflation, total output in Germany never declined. Indeed, Germany was one of the few countries in the world that did not experience a great depression in 1920-21, when prices in the gold standard part of the world dropped by 50 per cent. Total output remained up. Why? Because the inflation was open, i.e., prices were allowed to rise freely and hence the price system could still be used to allocate resources. Of course, after a time people started to use all sorts of escalation devices, to link their contracts to the value of the mark in the foreign exchange market, which was also a free market price, and so on. However, the price system could work even under those handicaps.

After the second World War, Germany had an inflationary potential. By our usual standards, it was substantial. If prices had been allowed to rise freely immediately after the war, the price level would probably have quadrupled. That is a large price rise. But it is negligible by comparison with the price rise after the first

World War which has to be described in terms of factors like 10^{10}. There was however an important difference. The price rise after the second World War was not allowed to take place. It was suppressed. Ordinarily, it is extremely difficult to suppress a price rise of that magnitude, to enforce price control when the market price would be four times the controlled price. But there were certain specially favorable circumstances from the point of view of enforcing price control in Germany at that time. Germany was occupied by the armed forces of Britain, France and the U.S., and the occupation forces enforced price control. The result was that output in Germany was cut in half. The price system was not allowed to function. People were forced to revert to barter. Somewhere Walter Eucken in an article describing this period tells the story of people who worked in a factory making pots and pans. They would work there for two or three days and then they would be given their pay in the form of aluminum saucepans. They would take these saucepans and spend the rest of the week scouring the countryside trying to find some farmer who would be willing to trade a few potatoes or other produce for the saucepans. That is not a very efficient way to organize resources. It was so inefficient that something had to be done and something was done. People developed their own forms of money. Cigarettes came into use as money for small transactions and cognac for large transactions—the most liquid money I have ever come across. But even with this expedient, the effect of suppressed inflation was to cut output in half from the level at the immediate end of the war. In 1948 as you know, the so-called German miracle began. It was not a very complicated thing. It amounted to introducing a monetary reform, eliminating price control and allowing the price system to function. The extraordinary rise in German output in the few years following this reform was not due to any miracle of German ingenuity or ability or anything like that. It was the simple, natural result of allowing the most efficient technique people have ever found for organizing resources to work instead of preventing it from working by trying to fix prices here, there and everywhere.

Though this is the most dramatic example, numerous other examples can be cited of a less extreme kind. In the immediate postwar period, I visited Europe. I spent some time in Britain and in France. Both countries at that time had widespread price controls. But there was an important difference. The people of Britain were relatively law-abiding, the people of France were not. The result was that Britain was being strangled by the law-obedience of her people and France was being saved by the black-market.

The reason suppressed inflation is so disastrous, as these examples suggest, is that the price system is the only technique that has so far been discovered or invented for efficiently allocating resources. If that is prevented from operating, something else must be substituted. What do we substitute? It is always some kind of clumsy physical control, physical allocation. India currently provides a striking example in its system of exchange control and import licences.

In the past five or six years [1957-1963], India has experienced a price rise of something between 20 and 40 per cent. In the main, this price rise has been open, though there have been some price controls. However, there has been one important glaring exception—the price of foreign exchange. The official price of the dollar or the pound sterling in terms of the rupee is precisely the same today [1963] as it was five years ago.[4] If the price of the rupee was anywhere close to being right then, it cannot be right now. And of course it is not right. The effect has been to encourage people to try to import goods because they are artificially cheap, and to discourage them from trying to export goods because the amount of rupees they can get for the foreign exchange proceeds of exports will buy less at home than before. Imports and exports are highly sensitive areas. Even moderate changes can have very large effects. The result has been, as you know better than I, a very serious foreign exchange crisis. India at first allowed her foreign exchange reserves to run down, until today reserves are very small. In addition, direct controls over imports have been increasingly tightened and all sorts of special measures have been taken to subsidize and encourage exports. Certain categories of imports have been banned entirely. With

[4 The rupee was devalued in June, 1966.]

respect to other categories, import licences have been given on a more and more limited scale. And even so, the exchange rate has been able to be maintained only because of very large additional grants of foreign aid.

Since the Government of India has not been willing to allow the price of foreign exchange to ration it among different uses, it has had to use direct controls and direct allocations instead. But these techniques are extremely wasteful and inefficient. It is all very well to talk in the newspapers or in public speeches about banning essential imports. But how do you find out what imports are essential? What is the criterion for essential imports? It is no good simply looking at the first stage. Here is some copper. Is it essential? Its subsequent use must be traced to see where it goes. It is necessary to see what substitutes are available for it or for the products made with it, to determine whether it is easy or hard to find domestic substitutes. And even if all that were known, there still is no criterion of what is essential. Which element of the people's consumption is it appropriate to cut down and which element to expand?

Consider the corresponding question for an individual. Suppose you say to someone, "Your income has suddenly been reduced, for whatever reason, by 10 per cent. You have got to cut down your consumption. What are your essential items of consumption?" Everyone who thinks at all deeply about the issue will conclude that that is a foolish question and that it deserves a foolish answer. What people actually do, when they are faced with the problem of cutting down their expenditures is not to cut out whole categories of expenditure but to cut a bit here, a bit there, and a bit there. All expenditures are equally essential. If they weren't, people would not make them at the margin. If an extra paisa spent on toothpaste isn't worth as much to an individual as an extra paisa spent on a newspaper, he had better spend less on toothpaste and more on newspapers. The result is that the person who must cut down expenditures will not say, "Well, I guess I will cut out buying any clothes for the next ten years and save my money in that way." What he will in fact do is to spend a little less on clothes, a little less on food, a little less on housing and so on.

Exactly the same principle applies to a nation. It has a wide range of imports. Which are essential? None of them. Which are inessential? None of them. The least essential element in the import bundle is a little bit here, a little bit there, and a little bit there. And do you really suppose that you or I sitting at a desk in Delhi, with the best will in the world, have any criterion, any basis, on which to answer this question correctly? What is involved is not that people are incompetent or are trying to do it the wrong way, but that there is no right way to do it. I don't know how many of you have ever seen the books which have to do with the allocation of import licences. I haven't seen the new ones. But when I was here seven years ago I saw the books they had then—and I suspect that they haven't changed much since because conditions were easier then than they are now. There were two fat volumes, filled with line after line of specific detail. One that I remember—because I never could understand what it meant—was a line that said "non-ferrous couplings for iron pipes." And the book specified that permitted imports were to equal such and such a percentage of imports in the base year.

Now, of course, import licences are allocated some way. Since there is no sensible principle on which they can be allocated by direct physical controls, what actually happens is that the structure of import licensing is determined by a mixture of the dead hand of the past and the strong hand of political and financial influence. The first principle everybody uses is to say, "Well, I guess we ought to allow people to import 50 per cent of what they imported in the base year." One thing that is most impressive is that, although many people think of physical planning or centralized planning as forward-looking, farsighted, progressive —in fact, physical planners tend to rely so heavily on past experience that physical planning turns out in practice to be stagnant and backward-looking rather than forward-looking. The reason is that there is nothing else they can do. For the past, the market provided a basis. If you don't have a presently operating market, the best thing you can do is to go to the nearest thing you have which is the market that operated in the past. That is why percentages of base year are used over and over again.

The second major principle used is influence of all kinds,

including corruption and bribery. If something valuable is given away free, people are going to try to get hold of it. An import licence is a valuable asset. There is a widespread market in import licences. The recipient can often sell it for a multiple of the official rupee value of the foreign exchange he is permitted to acquire under it. In this way he can make a splendid profit without doing a thing except getting an import licence. Naturally, there is a strong temptation to try to get import licences by whatever means. Indeed this is one of the most tragic elements in the situation. Though highly unethical and improper in terms of individual ethics, from the social point of view, the process of trying to get import licences by purchase or by bribery performs a valuable social function. It is a kind of weak working of market forces. People who have the greatest need for the imports and can create the most economic value from them are in a position to offer the highest prices. Indeed, this is an example of one of the gravest defects of a centralized controlled economy; it converts into a public virtue what most of us quite properly regard as a private vice. I gave an earlier example when I said that France was being saved by the black-market just after the war. On an individual basis, black-marketing is reprehensible; it involves violating the moral code; yet there is no doubt that in the circumstances created by price control, black-marketing is socially advantageous.

In addition, of course, to relying on the past and on influence, there are largely arbitrary decisions. An excellent example is the decision to ban the import of all motor vehicles into India, a decision that cannot possibly be in India's interest. A personal experience will bring out what seems to me the height of absurdity in this decision. I sold an automobile in the United States before I left for $20, a sum which at the official exchange rate would be Rs. 100 and even at a free market rate no more than about Rs. 150. I have been checking prices in Bombay and I am told that the same automobile in Bombay would fetch something like Rs. 7,500 to Rs. 10,000. Is there any sense at all to India's refraining from availing herself of the opportunity of acquiring transport at so much lower a cost than she is now spending by assembling automobiles here in domestic plants? However, if you have physical allocations, this is the kind of thing you are inevitably driven to.

The effects of exchange control and import licensing are not only arbitrary in the sense that I have just been illustrating, they are actually perverse. If a man gets a licence to import products from abroad, he has an incentive to be very wasteful, to use the wrong criterion—unless he sells the licence. If he uses the licence, he gets the exchange at the official rate. The imported goods then become cheaper, relative to other goods, than they really are from a social point of view. The result, of course, is that the ingenuity of people is devoted not to finding out how they can get the most out of the foreign exchange available, or how they can use imported goods most efficiently, but rather to getting a bigger import licence.

The tendency to waste resources is very widespread under a system of this kind of physical controls. I will just cite one more example in order to get you to try to think about this matter in a realistic context and in many directions. Consider an Indian who has been abroad in the U.S. for some years and who, let us say, has been working and earning some dollars. If he uses those dollars on riotous living by going to night-clubs in New York or Chicago, he will have no problem with exchange authorities or with Customs when he gets back. But if he were so unwise and so foolish as to convert those dollars into useful goods like refrigerators or sewing machines—let alone an automobile—then, when he gets back to India, he is likely to have problems about exchange control, about customs duties, and the like. Again, antisocial behavior is made privately rewarding.

What is the solution? The solution is to convert the inflation from a suppressed inflation to an open one. In the particular case of exchange control, the price that has been suppressed is the price of foreign exchange. The appropriate solution is to stop pegging the price of foreign exchange. Let anybody buy and sell foreign exchange at any price mutually agreeable to buyer and seller. Remove import controls, remove subsidies on exports, and let there be a free market in foreign exchange. In this way, people who can put the scarce foreign exchange to the most efficient use would have an incentive to bid the highest price for it. In this way, everybody, all over the country, would have an incentive to economize on imports, to find domestic alternatives for them. Everybody would have an incentive to try and produce exports for sale. This is, by all odds, the most far-reaching solution and the one that would be most desirable.

An alternative solution, which is not as good, would be to auction off import licences, or, better yet, the foreign exchange that is available for sale. By auctioning off import licences or foreign exchange, you would at least let market forces determine what items are imported. The difficulty with this solution is that it does not provide the appropriate incentive for exports.

Let me note that I am not conjuring a problem out of thin air. This problem will not go away. No country has succeeded in maintaining for long an exchange rate far out of line with the rate that would balance payments in a free market. Devaluation of the rupee is inevitable, sooner or later.[5] The only question is, how soon, by how much, and in what way. India has no alternative. It cannot indefinitely maintain an exchange rate which is far out of line with the rate that would clear the market. On economic grounds, it would be best to adjust the rate as soon as possible so as to eliminate the waste involved in the present arrangement. On political grounds, of course, governmental authorities always try to postpone the evil day, always try to put it off in the hope that some miracle will come along and extricate them from their difficulties. But no miracle will come along.

The question is not only how soon the rupee will be devalued, but also how it will be devalued. The temptation will be to change its value from its present level of Rs. 13 to £1 and Rs. 4.7 to $1, to a more realistic rate, say something like Rs. 20 to the £ or Rs. 7 to $1, and then try to hold it at the new fixed level.[6] That would be another mistake. Even if the new exchange rates are correct when established, once you peg them, there is no assurance that they will indefinitely remain correct. When they become incorrect, India will again be driven to all the ex-

[5 The rupee was devalued in June, 1966, but apparently not by enough to permit the elimination of exchange control.]

[6 This is what was done in June, 1966, the new rate set being 7.5 rupees to the dollar.]

pedients that it has adopted these past few years. A far better solution, as already noted, would be to allow exchange rates to go free and find their own levels, whatever they may be. If India then follows an appropriate monetary policy and maintains relatively stable prices within India, the rupee will also maintain a relatively stable price on the foreign exchange market.

Two major conclusions about Indian monetary policy can be drawn from the discussion in these two lectures. The first and most important conclusion is that a stable and steady monetary framework is desirable for economic development and progress. The simplest way for India to obtain a stable and steady monetary framework would be to plan for a steady rate of rise in the stock of money in India year after year. That would enable the Government to finance roughly Rs. 100 to 120 crores [7] a year of expenditures by printing money. The money it printed would be a non-interest bearing loan from the public. It would not be a tax. On the other hand, if it were decided to impose a tax on cash balances through a price rise, then a larger number should be selected for the annual increase in the quantity of money—8 per cent, 9 per cent. If it were decided to foster a declining price level, a smaller number should be selected. The important thing is to plan and select a policy and let the public know that it is going to be carried out so that the people have a stable monetary background against which plans can be made and expectations can be formed.

If I were choosing among these alternatives, my choice would be an increase in the quantity of money of something like 5 per cent per year indefinitely. That would be very likely to mean relatively stable prices. If economic progress is slower than we hope, it might mean slightly rising prices. If economic progress is more rapid than we expect, it might mean slightly falling prices. In either event, it would be a steady background and a steady policy which could be carried out and which the people could count on.

The second major conclusion is that, if there is any inflation, let it be open. Don't try to suppress the manifestations by price

[7 A "crore" is a term used in India which stands for 100,000.]

control, by rigid exchange rates, or by other methods of a similar nature. These measures do not eliminate the basic source of inflation. They simply prevent the price system from working effectively. They produce waste and misallocation of resources, encourage bribery, corruption, and disrespect for the law. They are a far greater hindrance to economic development than open inflation. This is an attempted cure that is far worse than the disease.

Questions and Answers

Q: Does your estimate of the amount of money the Government could create without inflation refer only to currency notes? What about deposits?

A: It refers to neither currency notes nor currency plus deposits but to Government-created money. There is a tendency to separate the Government and the Reserve Bank of India. For clear thinking about monetary matters, one should always consolidate the Central Bank with the Treasury accounts, on the one hand, and one should never consolidate the Central Bank with the Commercial Banks. Government money consists of currency in circulation plus the deposit liabilities of the Reserve Bank of India. The sum of these two, after some minor technical adjustments, gives the amount of Government money outstanding, which is now roughly of the order of Rs. 2,200 crores. So 5 per cent per year would be about Rs. 110 crores which is the amount of money that the Government could create without raising the total stock of money by more than 5 per cent. If the Government created this amount, Commercial Banks would in addition create some more, because they would have the additional reserves to back a further expansion of their deposit liabilities.

Q: How does the availability of assistance from abroad affect the prospects of inflation?

A: Assistance received from abroad is largely irrelevant to

the subject of inflation. The amount of inflation depends on how much money is printed. The State of Israel has been receiving large assistance from abroad, yet it has also been financing Government deficits by a tax on cash balances, i.e., by printing money. As a result prices have risen at the rate of 10 per cent a year.

What difference does the assistance from abroad make? The difference it makes is in a different respect. It has to do with the relative purchasing power of different monies. Let me see if I can illustrate by example. Let me compare Yugoslavia and Israel. An American dollar, converted into Yugoslavian currency at the official rate of exchange, will buy a great deal more than an American dollar will buy in the U.S. An American dollar converted into Israeli currency at the market exchange rate will buy about the same in Israel as in the United States. Perhaps a little less, certainly not much more. Why? Because Israel has a large source of unilateral transfers to her. As a result, Israel can spend on imports a great deal more than she realizes from exports. As a result, her export prices can be relatively high compared to her import prices. Yugoslavia has no substantial foreign source of unilateral grants of funds. She has been getting American aid of only a rather small magnitude for economic purposes. As a result, Yugoslavia must make her exports pay for her imports. The only way she can do so is by making them financially attractive, which means offering them at relatively low prices at the current exchange rate. So the effect of different volumes of foreign aid is on relative prices in different countries after allowing for the exchange rate. It has nothing directly to do with the problem of inflation. Its only possible connection with inflation is that the availability of foreign resources may lessen the temptation which the Government has to resort to printing money to finance its expenditures. But if experience is any guide, any such lessening of temptation is an effect of the second order of magnitude.

Q: *If we eliminated import licences, would we not have a great shortage of foreign exchange?*

A: You would, if you did not also have a change in the exchange rate. You cannot do part of the thing and not do the whole of it. You cannot be free of import licences and also peg the exchange rate at its present level. This is an impossible combination. If you are going to eliminate import licences, which you should do, you must, at the same time, allow the exchange rate to be free to move in the market. Under those circumstances, it is impossible to be short of foreign exchange. What does it mean —to be short of foreign exchange? To every purchaser there is a seller. If you have a free market in exchange, the amount bought will be equal to the amount sold. What will vary in that case is the price. Of course, I would not for a moment recommend that you should free import licences and try to hold on to your present exchange rates. It would not work.

Q: *If the controls were removed, would there not be much more spending abroad?*

A: What you have now is not too much spending but too much attempted spending. You have too little spending of foreign exchange. The fact of the matter is that you have a limited amount of foreign exchange available to you. You have whatever you can earn from your exports plus the gifts that are made to you or the loans that you get from abroad. This is some amount of foreign exchange. That is all you can spend. At home, the Government can run a printing press and turn out rupee notes. There happens to be no way at the moment in which India can turn out dollar bills. So you have a limited amount to spend.

The problem is that, at the present price, at 4.7 rupees to the dollar, 13⅓ rupees to the pound, people would like to spend more dollars and more pounds than you have available. Also, at that rate, people do not have a sufficient incentive to earn dollars and pounds, to produce goods for export. As a result, at that rate, you have fewer dollars and pounds to spend than you would have if you let the rate go. And, on the other hand, people are trying to spend much more than they would if you let the rate go. As a result, if you let the rate go, you would, in fact, spend more because you would have more to spend. Where would you get more? From the additional exports that it would be in the interests of people to produce and sell. You would spend more than you are now spending, but you would spend less than people are now trying to spend. Why? Because they now know that if they get the dollars they get them at 4.7 rupees. If they had to pay 7 rupees for a dollar, they would be a lot less eager to buy dollars.

Q: How long would it take to adjust things out?

A: Two minutes. It depends on what you mean by adjust things out.

Q: Wouldn't we find ourselves short of foreign exchange?

A: You cannot be short of foreign exchange with a free market. With a free exchange rate there is no such thing as a shortage.

Q: It won't take any time for adjustment?

A: No time. The speculators of the world will come in and provide you with reserves. If tomorrow you were to let the exchange rate go free, the rupee would depreciate. It would depreciate quite substantially. I don't know where it would go. It would probably go too far. Because it would go too far, it would give people in the rest of the world an incentive to buy the rupee and to provide you with a temporary supply of foreign exchange to tide you over the period until your exports started to expand and you started to earn your own foreign exchange.

If you ask what is the period of full adjustment, that is un-definitely long, because, of course, full adjustment means creating the industries that will create the industries that will create the exports 100 and 200 years from now. That's the meaning of a full adjustment. But an adjustment in the sense that anybody who wants to buy foreign exchange can do so and anybody who wants to sell foreign exchange can do so, that will occur at once. Maybe two minutes is a little extreme because if the exchange rate were set free and controls removed after markets had closed, you would have to wait until the next morning.

Q: Would your panacea of a free exchange rate not inter-fere with a desirable distribution of income?

A: It might, but in fact it is far more likely to promote it. The thing that impresses me is the extent to which people stick to myths in the face of the most obvious and glaring empirical evidence. If I look at all the underdeveloped countries and not India alone, where are the ill-gotten gains? Who are the conspicuous spenders? The people who get import licences. Import licences are the single most important source of rapid riches in every country around. The same thing is true for almost any other way in which you suppress inflation. What does the suppression of inflation mean? It means that there are big opportunities for those who can get to the right people at the right time. They get income for rendering a social service that exists only because of the exchange controls.

I am not saying that open inflation is a panacea. On the contrary, I would myself prefer the adoption of a monetary policy, both in your country and mine, which would be consistent with stable prices. What I say is, if you decide to go in for inflation, you will do yourself far less harm by permitting it to be open than if you try to suppress its manifestations. As to the inequality of income, that is really something which should be handled in another way. It may or may not be exacerbated by open inflation. I do not think it will be much affected by an open inflation. It is almost certain to be exacerbated by any widespread attempt to substitute physical controls and licensing and rationing for open inflation, particularly in the foreign exchange market.

Q: Is devaluation the only corrective?

A: No. In principle, there is another way. You could drive down prices in India by thirty or forty per cent. Deflation would be an alternative. What matters is the relation between prices in India and prices in the rest of the world, account being taken of the exchange rate. The question is, if I take a dollar and I convert it into rupees, how much will it buy in India compared with the U.S.? The problem today is that a dollar converted into rupees at the official exchange rate will not buy as much as is necessary in order for India to have balance of payments equilibrium. The amount that a dollar will buy in India can be increased in either of two ways: by a devaluation of the exchange rate or by a reduction of prices in India. However, as a practical matter, I think that no government will in fact try to force a deflation of thirty or forty per cent and I think a government would be most unwise to try to do so.

It was probably a mistake to have the inflation in the first place. That may be. But the fact that you made a mistake does not mean that the best thing to do is to try to go back to where you were before. You had better live with your mistakes. It seems to me far better to adjust the one price—it's not one price, it's a set of prices, rates of exchange for dollars and pounds and other currencies—rather than to try to force down the wages of everybody in the community, the prices of all products in the community and so on.

Q: What is your opinion about the recent gold control orders?

A: The gold control orders are of no great fundamental importance. It seems to me as an outsider looking at it, that it is simply one of those things that always happens. You have a government that is responsible for a state of affairs that is unfortunate. For one reason or another, the correct solution is politically unpalatable. And so the Government tries to look around for gimmicks and gadgets with which it can make a public appearance of attacking the problem while it really does not do so.

Consider your gold situation. Look at the magnitudes involved and you see immediately that this is a drop in the bucket. It is estimated that the smuggled gold coming in is Rs. 30 to 40 crores a year. That is 3 per cent of your annual savings. Moreover, this policy will not stop the smuggling. What brings that gold in? The fact that gold has twice as high a rupee price as the international price at the official exchange rate. As long as you make it profitable to bring in gold, gold will come in. Consequently, the gold control measures are not in fact likely to improve your foreign exchange position.

I may add that, aside from their effectiveness, they seem to me objectionable in principle. If one man wants to work and use the income he gets to buy gold, while a second wants to use it to enlarge or adorn his house, why shouldn't each be free to do what he wants with his own income?

You know, we tried a similar policy for a different reason. In 1933 and 1934, President Roosevelt and the New Deal were trying to raise internal prices. They were trying to depreciate the exchange rate for this purpose. As part of this policy, they planned to change the price of gold. They did not want private individuals in the community to get any so-called profits from the rise in the price of gold. The official price of gold, the price at which gold had been maintained since 1879, was, in early 1933, $20.76 an ounce. By the end of 1933, it had gone up to $32 or $33 and in January, 1934, the price was raised to $35 an ounce. In the middle of 1933, an executive order made it illegal for private individuals to hold gold except for numismatic purposes and for use in the arts. Private individuals were required to turn over their gold to the Government at the original price of $20.76 an ounce although at the time this declaration was made the market price of gold was something like $30 to $33 an ounce.

The dollars outstanding were in two forms. There were gold certificates which were promises to pay gold and, of course, they were useful for nothing, so most of them were turned in. The rest was in gold coins, slightly over $350 millions. Of this part, the gold coin held by the banks was turned over. As for the rest of the gold, only a small fraction of the estimated amount outstanding was turned in. The statisticians of the Federal Reserve Board decided that the reason why such a small fraction was reported as turned in must be because the estimates of the amount of gold outstanding were wrong. Of the estimated amount of gold, $287 million was not turned in. So the statisticians proceeded to revise the estimates of the stock of money from 1933 all the way back to 1914 by subtracting out the hypothetical $287 million of gold which they assumed must have been lost or exported without record. In fact, it is possible to establish beyond a peradventure of a doubt that such a large amount of gold could not possibly have been lost. I won't go into details, but we have made some estimates suggesting that the maximum conceivable amount of loss was about $13 million, not $287 million. What happened, of course, was that the gold simply wasn't turned in, and it has been turning up ever since, here and there. Indeed, four or five years ago, the Treasury of the U.S. declared that all gold coins minted before a certain date—and I may add that none has been minted since—would be regarded as numismatic. In consequence, it is perfectly legal now to hold the gold which people did not turn in at that time. I doubt very much whether your gold measures will have any greater measure of success.

Q: Do you approve of planned economic development?

A: I am not sure I know what planned economic development is. Because the fact of the matter is that this expression is something of a contradiction in terms. If you really have extensive central planning of the kind you now have, you won't have much economic development. And if you have rapid economic development, it will be in spite of that kind of centralized planning.

Q: Doesn't the free exchange market take the heart out of economic planning?

A: It takes the heart out of the wrong kind of planning. There is a right way and wrong way to do most things. Planning is the appropriate use of means for the achievement of objectives. In this country, planning is taken to mean the attempt by a centralized agency to establish a pattern for the economy as a whole and to enforce it by a host of specialized and detailed controls, including Government engaging in certain enterprises and so on. This whole paraphernalia, which in this country goes by the name of planning, is in fact bad planning, because it is almost guaranteed to defeat rather than to promote your objectives.

On the other hand, a Central Government which maintained law and order, provided for the national defence, secured people in the enforcement of private contracts freely entered into, provided a stable monetary framework, fostered the spread of elementary schooling and the improvement of road communication and, for the rest, fostered a free market to enable millions of individuals in this country to use their own resources in accordance with their own objectives—such a government would be engaging in good planning, in planning which was suited to the promotion of economic development in the sense of the improvement of the lot of the ordinary man.

Q: Prof. Friedman is obviously against any kind of centralized allocation of resources. If we abandoned import control, what is to assure that we imported not the requisites to build up a steel plant but Cadillacs and refrigerators?

A: Well, let me ask you whether you are sure that the requisites to build a steel plant are really more essential for your country than Cadillacs and refrigerators?

Q: It might be that if in the last ten years, India had not built up three steel plants, probably you wouldn't have been sorry, but we would have been.

A: I am not sure you would have been. I do not know the precise details of the Indian economic structure. But I know in many a country, a steel plant is a burden upon the community. One case I know for sure is Egypt. It costs Egypt about twice as much each year to produce the steel that comes out of its steel plant as it would to buy the steel in the free market. I have always described the steel plant in Egypt as a modern pyramid with the exception that the maintenance cost is much higher. Maybe India's case is different. Don't misunderstand me. I cannot profess to know whether India ought to have steel mills or not. What I am sure of is that if you do not have steel mills with a free exchange rate and no import controls, then the odds are very heavy that steel mills will be a drain on India and not a source of strength.

You referred to the importing of Cadillacs. I do not know why the import of Cadillacs is worse than the use of the same amount of resources to build fancy houses, or to buy a small Fiat.

Suppose a man imports a second-hand Cadillac at lesser cost in resources than it costs India right now to produce a small Fiat. Is there something wrong with that? The problem of importing Cadillacs involves confusing two wholly different things. Do keep your problems separate.

One problem is the distribution of income and wealth. That problem refers just as much to domestic consumption as it does to foreign consumption. If you allow people to have large incomes and large wealth, it makes no difference from the economic point of view whether they absorb domestic resources or foreign exchange, provided you have a free market so that these two are interchangeable. The problem of inequalities of income and wealth is a very important problem; but it has nothing to do with the problem of import controls. That is a smoke-screen.

On the other hand, you have the problem of having an efficient system for combining your internal resources with imported components, with foreign goods and so on. The most efficient way to do that is through a market system. The present method is certainly a most inefficient one. As a result of the import controls and of the artificial exchange rate, the Indian economy is a protected sheltered economy. Look at what businesses are being established and where investment is going. He would be a courageous man who would say those are the things in which India has a comparative advantage. There is almost no industry in which people do not have an incentive to go, regardless of whether it is appropriate for India to engage in that activity, simply because competition is kept out from abroad. It seems to me patent that India cannot afford to waste her resources. India is facing a desperate problem of trying to improve her conditions and the standard of life of her people in as brief a time as she can. In those circumstances, does it make sense to throw your resources away simply because you insist on having an exchange rate of Rs. 4.71 to the dollar? Where did that come from? What makes that holy? What you are now doing is following a policy which encourages a waste of foreign exchange and a waste of current resources. A system of free exchange rates and free imports would be much more efficient.

Let me say one more thing. I said before that it is important to separate issues. I mean that in a more general way. I personally happen to be in favor of a free market in a wide range of its manifestations. But suppose you are not. Suppose you are in favor of centralized allocation of priorities in Delhi, of government nationalization of enterprises and so on. Nonetheless, if you are going to do that, do it efficiently. Don't throw away tools that are at hand. If you want to allocate imports, it is not for the purpose of maintaining the exchange rate at 4.7 rupees to the dollar. I cannot believe any central planner would regard that as a relevant objective. In consequence, if you are going to do this kind of central planning, you will find it much easier to do so if the exchange rate comes closer than it now does to reflecting the real value of a rupee in terms of foreign money. I believe it would be well-nigh impossible to give a rational justification in terms of the economic logic of central planning for the kind of system of allocation of exchange India is now using.

Q: The exchange has to be fixed at some rate. It can't go on fluctuating. Do any other countries do that?

A: Of course countries do it now and many countries have done it in the past. Canada had such a floating rate from October, 1950 to May, 1962. The reason she departed from it recently was because it was such a good thing that the Government tried to exploit the floating rate by speculating in the exchange market. It thereby got itself involved in a box from which it could get out only by pegging the exchange rate.

Let me urge you to get some historical perspective. Do you realize that the system of exchange controls, import licences and the whole complex paraphernalia connected therewith is one of the few really modern inventions in economic policy? The word inconvertibility of money used to have a very different meaning from that which it now has. It used to mean that you could not take paper money to a government and get a specified amount of gold or silver in exchange. Until the year 1934, so far as I know, inconvertibility of money never meant that it was illegal for a citizen of one country to transfer the currency of his country to a citizen of another country at whatever terms were mutually acceptable.

In 1934, a German financier by the name of Hjalmar Schacht invented, or maybe I should say perfected, a system of exchange control and import licences. That was the beginning of the use of the term inconvertibility in the modern sense, to mean that it was illegal for a citizen of a country to exchange his currency for that of a foreign country except with the permission of a government agency and at an officially determined rate.

The policy India is following is simply the Schachtian policy. For some thousands of years before Mr. Schacht, the world got along perfectly well in a situation in which anybody could buy or sell currency at any price he had to pay or could get. It is a striking sign of how easily we lose perspective and become provincial, that a recent and highly exceptional set of arrangements should seem to so many the only way things can be done.

Q: Wasn't Schacht the Finance Minister under Hitler?

A: Of course. The policy he perfected was adopted to make Germany self-sufficient and to prepare for war, and also, incidentally, to facilitate the expropriation of the persecuted Jews and prevent them from getting their capital out of the country. It is not entirely clear that it was the most effective policy even for that. It is certainly not a policy that is designed to make a country strong, prepare it for peace, and mete out justice and equity to all its inhabitants.

Why the American Economy

is Depression-Proof [1]

CHAPTER TWO   The United States is currently [1954] in an economic recession. This recession started sometime in the middle of 1953, around June or July, and has been proceeding steadily, ever since. So far, the recession has been relatively mild. Unemployment is only in the neighborhood of four million out of a total labor force of more than sixty million, and industrial production, which is an extremely sensitive index whose movements exaggerate the movements of output as a whole, has declined only about 10 per cent. The decline in gross national product to date is attributable almost entirely to expenditures on inventories: the sum of expenditures on private consumption, governmental activities, construction, and equipment has shown no significant decline. As to prices, a decline in wholesale

[1 This lecture was delivered in Stockholm in April, 1954 and published in Nationalekonomiska Föreningens Forhandlingar.]

prices antedated by a considerable period the onset of the recession. In recent months this decline has, if anything, been proceeding at a slower pace, if it has not been halted or reversed. Retail prices have moved little either way. Interest rates have declined considerably and stock prices, after an initial substantial decline, have more recently recovered. In general, the recession has all the hallmarks of the usual cyclical recession of the kind that has occurred with varying regularity in most Western countries during at least the past two hundred years. In the United States, such recessions have lasted about 20 months on the average during the past century, so, in terms of life expectancy, this one is already middle aged.

It was not until something like six or seven months after the onset of the recession that there was anything approaching agreement about its existence—testimony neither to ignorance nor to incompetence but solely to the superiority of hindsight over foresight. Now that the existence of a recession is widely recognized, the crucial question has become its probable duration and severity. Does it, as Colin Clark has predicted, contain the seeds of a major depression of the 1929-33 variety, seeds that can be kept from producing their noxious fruit only by immediate and large scale government action? Or is it, as the President has suggested in his Economic Report, a mild readjustment, a mere growing pain that is destined to fade away after a brief interval?

This question cannot be answered in precise detail. One of the few things that has been firmly established by past research on business cycles is that we do not yet know how to predict the detailed course of business activity. We can describe, as business analysts are wont to do, the detailed movements in inventories, employment, retail sales, interest rates, stock prices, and the like. But we do not know how to use these signs as a sure guide to the precise severity of a particular cyclical movement or to the precise date when it will be reversed.

In this instance, as in so many others in economics, a roundabout method promises to be more productive. Though we cannot get a detailed answer by the direct path of predicting the immediate future, I submit that we can get a meaningful general answer by examining the institutional environment within which the current recession is proceeding and interpreting it in the light of the known past. There have been fundamental changes in institutions and attitudes in the United States since the Great Depression. Changes in the banking structure and in the fiscal structure have basically altered the inherent cyclical responses of the American economy. Changes in general psychological attitudes toward inflation and deflation have basically altered the likely political responses toward economic change. In my view, the combined effect of these alterations in institutions and in attitudes has been to render a major depression in the United States almost inconceivable at the present time. The immediate situation is deflationary; but the longer term outlook remains inflationary. We cannot say just when the present recession will come to an end, but we can say with considerable confidence that it will not degenerate into a major depression. In developing this thesis, I shall discuss matters that may seem far removed from the present situation. I hope I can persuade you that they offer a much firmer basis for judging this situation than do the facts of the moment. Let me turn first to the changes that have occurred in the banking structure of the United States.

1. Changes in Banking Structure

As you know, the American banking structure is very different from that which exists in most other countries. It is composed of some 15,000 independent banks, about a third chartered by the Federal government, the rest by the forty-eight states. About half the banks, including almost all the large ones, are members of the Federal Reserve System, which performs the functions of a central bank. This unit banking system has had great advantages in flexibility, competition, and enterprise. But it has also lent itself to banking panics and widespread bank failures, most recently, of course, in the early 1930's.

Three major changes have occurred in this system since the great depression: first, the establishment in 1934 of the Federal Deposit Insurance Corporation; second, a growth in the importance of government obligations among bank assets; third, a loosening of the links between gold and domestic monetary conditions. These changes have transformed the banking system to an extent that is not generally recognized.

a. ESTABLISHMENT OF FEDERAL DEPOSIT INSURANCE CORPORATION

In my view, the federal insurance of deposits is by all odds the most important of these changes in its effects on the cyclical characteristics of the American economy. Indeed, I venture to suggest that it produced a more basic change in American banking institutions than did the much more widely heralded establishment of the Federal Reserve System in 1913. Federal deposit insurance has made bank failures almost a thing of the past. A bank no longer fails when it has been badly managed and its assets fall short of its liabilities. The F.D.I.C. takes over its bad assets, or assumes responsibility for them, and arranges a merger of the "bad" bank with a "good" bank. The statistical record of yearly bank failures requires three to four digits up to 1934; one digit suffices for recent years. The result has been that depositors in insured banks have suffered negligible losses, although nominally only deposits less than a specified sum are insured. The Federal Reserve System was never more than a "lender of last resort"; it gave depositors no protection against bad banking, and, partly as a consequence, was unable even to perform its proper function of protecting them against bad central banking. The F.D.I.C. has in effect converted all deposit liabilities of private banks into a Federal liability. It has thus eliminated the basic cause for runs on banks of the kind that occurred in 1931 to 1933, as well as at earlier periods. Such runs represented attempts by bank depositors to convert liabilities of private banks—deposits —into liabilities of the Federal government—currency. Both deposits and currency are now in effect Federal liabilities.

b. CHANGE IN STRUCTURE OF ASSETS

Federal deposit insurance was deliberately enacted to protect bank depositors. Without intention or design, a change has occurred in the structure of bank assets that has in part duplicated the effect of deposit insurance. The change I refer to is the increased importance of government obligations among bank assets, a change that has occurred in most other Western nations as well. In 1929, commercial and savings banks owned government obligations equal in value to around 15 per cent of their deposit liabilities to the public; today [1954] they own government obligations equal in value to more than half of their deposit liabilities to the public.[2] More than half of the deposits of the public are thus government liabilities at one remove, in the sense that the bank assets corresponding to them are government liabilities. For this half, Federal deposit insurance simply gilds the lily and makes them a government liability twice over. The high ratio of government obligations has the further consequence that it greatly reduces the potential effects of changes in private demand and supply for credit on the quantity of money. The private lending activities of banks are no longer the dog; they are threatening to become the tail.

I cannot forbear a minor digression at this point. For a long time I have been a proponent of 100% reserve banking. Under this system, the depositary activities of banks would be separated from their lending and investing activities, and the depositary institutions would serve as pure warehouses of funds. For every dollar of deposits, they would be required to hold a dollar of currency or its equivalent. Those of us who favor this scheme are accustomed to being labelled "unrealistic"; to being told that we are proposing a reform that has no chance of adoption and would require utterly impractical changes in the banking system if it were adopted. Yet, ironically enough, a completely unnoticed effect of the changes in bank assets I have described has been to take us half the way to complete adoption of the plan. For the essence of the plan is precisely to make all money, whether currency or deposits, a direct liability of the government issued under uniform arrangements. Generals are not the only ones who fight wars that are past.

[2 By early 1968, government obligations again amounted to about 15 per cent of deposit liabilities.]

c. Changed role of gold

The third change in the banking structure that I want to call to your attention is the role played by gold. The removal of gold from public circulation in 1934 was the first step in a successive loosening of the links between gold and the internal supply of money. The monetary role of gold in the United States today is largely nominal. The Federal Reserve has almost twice as large a gold reserve as it legally requires; and even this understates its leeway for there can be little doubt that if the reserve ratio were ever to approach the legal minimum, the minimum would be lowered.[3] The fixed U.S. buying price for gold, rather than being the kingpin of its monetary structure, is in the same class as the fixed buying price for domestically produced wheat: gold is a storable commodity for which there is a rigid support price. The only difference is that the support price is offered to foreign as well as domestic producers, so that the gold program is also part of our foreign economic aid.[4]

d. Significance of the changes

The combined effect of Federal Deposit Insurance, the higher ratio of government obligations to other assets of banks, and the dethroning of gold, is to eliminate as a practical possibility anything approaching a collapse of the American banking structure. Insurance rules out an internal drain or banking panic; the importance of government obligations reduces the sensitivity of the stock of money to internal private credit changes; the dethroning of gold reduces its sensitivity to changes in external conditions. It is hard to see how under these circumstances any sharp *decline* in the stock of money could occur except through deliberate action by the monetary authorities to bring one about. This is very different from the situation prior to 1933, when it would have required deliberate action by the monetary authori-

[3 It has by now been completely removed. First, the requirement was changed from 25 per cent of both Federal Reserve notes and deposits to 25 per cent of Federal Reserve notes, then in March, 1968, completely removed.]

[4 The fixed price for gold was abandoned in March, 1968.]

ties to prevent a decline in the stock of money. I hasten to add that none of these changes rules out sharp increases in the stock of money.

2. Importance of Changes in the Banking Structure

Granted that a substantial change has occurred in the American banking structure, how important is this change for the avoidance of a major depression? From the 1930's until almost the present, economists tended to deprecate the role of monetary factors and of the banking system—a tendency Swedish economists avoided to a larger extent than most others but from which, if I may judge from recent Swedish writings on inflation, they have by no means been entirely free. Postwar experience has forced a considerable revival in the attention paid to monetary factors. Easy money policies were adopted in most countries after the war. And every country that adopted an easy money policy also experienced inflationary pressure and did so whether its governmental budget was yielding a surplus or deficit. On the other hand, the adoption of a tighter monetary policy accompanied every successful attempt to stop inflation.

These events produced a healthy reaction against the view that money doesn't matter. But this reaction has not yet gone far enough. The fashionable view at the moment is to grant that monetary measures are vitally important in preventing inflation but to argue that they are of minor importance in preventing depression. Monetary policy, it is said, is like a string. You can pull it but you can't push on it.

This view is based in large measure on the belief that monetary measures were tried in the great depression and found wanting. And this belief—which seems to me completely mistaken —in turn derives partly from accepting the protestations of monetary authorities at their face value rather than looking at what they in fact did; partly from looking at the effect of policy on the liabilities of the central bank rather than on the total stock of money. In the United States—and the experience of the United States is not atypical—the total stock of money in the hands of the public declined by more than a quarter from 1929 to 1933. The subsequent expansion in the stock of money was not out of proportion to the expansion in money income. Far from being testimony to the irrelevance of monetary factors in preventing depression, the early 1930's are a tragic testimony to their importance in producing depression. This is a point to which I shall return.

I do not myself believe that the string-analogy is valid. If it were, one would expect to find that major depressions had occurred despite favorable monetary conditions. Yet so far as I know, there is no such example on record. Certainly, in the United States, about which I can speak with most confidence, there has been no major depression that has not been associated with and accompanied by a monetary collapse. Let me run briefly over the record; it is most instructive.

Perhaps the best starting point is the major depression that began in the late 1830's and continued through the early 1840's. Statistical records are too meagre for this period to permit detailed comparisons with later depressions. Such records as there are, together with qualitative and descriptive evidence, suggest that it was comparable in severity and duration with the great depression that came not quite a century later—though of course the lesser importance of industry and of the market made its social and human consequences quite different. This depression followed hard on the political battle over the Second Bank of the United States which ended in the spectacular demise of the Bank. The initial effect of the battle was to produce widespread inflation of the currency and a speculative boom. The ultimate result was a drastic deflation of the currency, disorganization of the banking system, and numerous bank failures.

The next depression of comparable magnitude was the long-drawn out period of hard times during the 1870's. This was the period when vigorous efforts were being made to return to the gold standard at the former parity after the greenback inflation of the Civil War. The effort was crowned with success when specie payments were resumed in 1879, but at the cost of a decade of more or less steady deflationary pressure, and of the longest continuous contraction in the recorded annals of American business cycles. Resumption, which meant the cessation of the deflationary pressure, ushered in a period of expansion.

The 1890's produced an even more pronounced depression than the 1870's; it was probably less severe than the 1930's but this is by no means unambiguously clear. It was a period of great monetary agitation when the burning political issue was whether silver or gold should be the monetary standard, agitation that reached its highest emotional peak with Bryan's famous "cross of gold" speech. The United States almost went off gold; J. P. Morgan and associates were called upon by the Treasury to help and were widely given the credit for keeping the dollar on gold, though it seems clear that Dame Fortune, who produced a good harvest in the United States and a poor harvest abroad, deserves much of the credit. A banking panic was a striking feature of the depression and bank failures were numerous.

The stream of gold from South Africa undermined the economic basis for the political agitation and ushered in a period of monetary expansion, which produced a rise of over a third in the American price level from 1898 to the outbreak of World War I. This period was punctuated by a banking panic in 1907, but the accompanying depression was nothing like so severe as that of the 1870's or 1890's. It did however produce renewed pressure for banking reform, pressure which eventuated in the establishment of the Federal Reserve System in 1913.

The Reserve System was established just in time to serve as the channel for wartime inflation. Doubtless there would have been inflation in any event during World War I. However, without the newly established central banking system, the inflation probably would have been less severe during the war than it was, and almost certainly would have come to an end by early 1919. As it was, the Reserve system, more by default than by design, continued to add fuel to the inflationary fire on a large scale for more than a year after the government ceased calling on it to do so to finance its expenditures. When the System woke up to what it was doing in 1920, it put on the brakes sharply, producing a contraction in the supply of money and the sharp if brief depression of 1921, so adding yet another to our list of depressions accompanied or occasioned by monetary contraction.

The final exhibit in this chamber of horrors that I shall discuss is the 1929-33 depression, which is also in many ways the most interesting and instructive. From 1929 to 1931, the Reserve system was largely passive. It allowed the stock of money to decline by about 10 per cent and banks to fail in a steady if not spectacular stream. Yet by spring 1931, there were signs of revival: if one examines the statistical records of the early months of that year and closes one's eyes to what followed, they bear all the earmarks of the typical turning point of a cycle. Had the decline come to an end in 1931, it would have been entered in statistical annals as a severe recession but certainly not a major depression comparable to the depressions of the 1840's, 1870's, and 1890's. But the decline did not come to an end. In the autumn of 1931, England went off the gold standard. The Reserve authorities became frightened that there would be a drain of gold from the United States. Although their gold reserves greatly exceeded legal requirements and were extremely high by any absolute standard, they succumbed to something approaching panic and proceeded to take strong deflationary measures, putting up the bank rate more sharply and suddenly than at any previous time in their history—and this after two years of economic contraction. The result in my view was to nip a putative revival in the bud and to initiate a new and sharper contraction. Up to this point, deposits in commercial banks had fallen by about 10 per cent. In the next year and a half they fell by over a third. Bank failures increased at an alarming pace and the sorry tale was not completely told until the official closing of all banks in the banking holiday of March, 1933. True, the Reserve system reversed its policy in early 1932 and undertook moderately expansionary measures; but by then it was too late. Measures of this magnitude might easily have saved the day in 1931; by 1932 they were utterly inadequate to stem the raging flood of deflation that the Reserve system had unleashed.

A major motive in establishing the Reserve System was to prevent banking panics of the kind that had been recurrently experienced. The system completely failed to do so. The panic of

1933, when it came, was of the same company as the panics of 1837, 1873, 1893, and 1907. The existence of the Reserve system did make one difference. It postponed the panic until after a shamefully large fraction of the banks had failed, whereas in the bad old days, a panic occurred before any large number of banks failed and was indeed the device for preventing the failure of a few banks from spreading to the rest of the system. It was this experience, as I have already noted, that brought the Federal Deposit Insurance Corporation and an effective end to banking panics.

There is no gainsaying the fact illustrated by these episodes: major depressions and monetary contraction or collapse go hand in hand. But, it will be asked, which is the hen and which the egg? May not the monetary collapse be the inevitable result of severe depression rather than a cause thereof? And if this is so, may not the only effect of the change in the American monetary structure be to remove a manifestation of severe depression rather than to prevent the severe depressions themselves? The episodes I have outlined give, I believe, a reasonably clear answer to these questions. Many of the events that produced monetary contraction or collapse were clearly independent of the particular state of business when they occurred. If they did not produce the severe depression, they were certainly not produced by it, and their simultaneous occurrence would have to be explained by sheer coincidence. The political agitation about the Second Bank of the United States in the 1830's and its ultimate failure is perhaps the clearest example. The deflation of the 1870's is another. And I believe that the Federal Reserve action in the fall of 1931 is a third. This final case is particularly instructive because it is almost a controlled experiment. The countries of the world that like Britain and Sweden went off gold in 1931 and engaged in monetary expansion at home, one and all saw contraction end in late 1931 or early 1932. The countries that, like the United States and France, stayed on gold and engaged in monetary contraction, saw contraction continue until 1933 or even 1934.

The conclusion seems inescapable: monetary contraction or collapse is an essential conditioning factor for the occurrence of a major depression. To avoid misunderstanding, let me say explicitly that I do not mean to assert that all cyclical fluctuations are monetary in origin. Far from it. The usual run of cyclical fluctuations have occurred under a wide variety of monetary institutions and conditions, and have been accompanied by no standard behavior of the stock of money or other monetary indexes.[5] Monetary factors doubtless play a role in such fluctuations but I believe that we do not yet know what role. Nor do we as yet in my view have any alternative explanation of such fluctuations: we are here in an area where we simply do not know the answers. My proposition is much more limited. It is that we must distinguish between minor recessions and major depressions and that it takes a monetary contraction or collapse —a monetary mistake—to convert a minor recession into a major depression. Though not directly connected with my present theme, a similar proposition seems to me valid for expansions: it takes monetary measures to convert minor expansions into inflationary booms.

If this conclusion is valid, it means that the structural change in the American banking system is alone enough to rule out a major American depression. But it is not the only institutional change that works in this direction. It is strongly reinforced by changes in the American fiscal structure, to which I now turn.

3. The Fiscal Structure

During the last few decades, the size of governmental activity has grown sharply relative to the economy as a whole. In the 1920's, government expenditures, both national and local, amounted to less than one-eighth of the national income; they now [1953] amount to more than one-quarter.[6]

This increase in the role of government is fundamental for the long run trend of the American economy and for the prospects

[5 The research I have done since indicates a much more regular behavior of the stock of money in the course of the "usual" cycle than this sentence suggests. See Chapter Four, "The Lessons of Monetary History."]

[6 By 1968, they amounted to more than one-third.]

of political freedom. It is not fundamental for its cyclical behavior. From the cyclical point of view, the change in the character of both expenditures and receipts is more important than the change in their size.

On the expenditure side, the two most important changes have been the introduction, first, of a broad program of social security benefits, in particular, of unemployment insurance, and second, of a farm program designed to support the prices of agricultural products. The effect of these and similar programs is that a decline in general business automatically raises government expenditures: people become unemployed and start drawing unemployment benefits; agricultural prices tend to fall—though this link is much looser than the unemployment link thanks to the importance of variations in weather at home and in production abroad—and so support payments tend to increase. Conversely, an expansion of business in general reduces these expenditures. These programs thus make for high expenditures in depression; low expenditures in prosperity. Let me hasten to emphasize that here as with the banking changes discussed earlier I am simply describing the effects of these changes on the cyclical prospects of the economy, not evaluating or approving them in general. In particular, the farm support program has tended to become a means of permanently subsidizing agriculture rather than of preventing seriously depressed conditions. And the disadvantages in other directions of such a program for either purpose seem to me enormously to outweigh any advantages it may have for cyclical stability.

On the income side, the important changes have been mostly in the personal and corporation income tax: these have come to account for a much larger share of total tax receipts, the personal income tax has been made much more progressive, and methods of collecting the tax have been radically reformed. The reason these developments are important for cyclical purposes is that they have greatly increased the sensitivity of tax payments to changes in economic conditions. Let national income rise and liabilities for some taxes, like property taxes, will be affected little if at all; for other taxes, like excise taxes, they will rise with income but generally by a smaller percentage. Income tax liabilities, on the other hand, are almost sure to rise with income and to rise by a larger percentage. Similarly, when national income falls, income tax liabilities fall even more sharply. And the more progressive the income tax, the sharper the rise or fall in tax liabilities for a given rise or fall in income. Increased reliance on income taxes and their greater progressiveness have therefore combined to make *tax liabilities* more responsive to changes in business conditions than at an earlier date. But there is a slip between tax *liabilities* and tax *payments,* and it is here that the third change mentioned, in methods of collection, has been important. Prior to World War II, the income tax for any year was collected entirely after the end of the year. There was a lag of over a year on the average between the receipt of income and the payment of taxes on that income. During World War II, collection at source was introduced for wages and salaries, and prepayment for other personal income. And more recently, corresponding changes have been made for corporations. The result has been to reduce to very small proportions indeed any lag between the receipt of income and the payment of tax on that income.

Under the existing fiscal system any decrease in national income is accompanied, or followed with only a brief lag, by a sharper decrease in tax receipts and by a rise in expenditures on unemployment benefits, farm price supports, and the like. The changes in taxes and in expenditures reinforce one another and together are by no means negligible in size. Roughly speaking, a decline of say $10 billion in national income means a combined effect on the government budget of some $3 to $4 billion. This is the amount by which any budget surplus is reduced or a budget deficit increased. And this occurs without any legislative or executive action whatever. The strictly automatic changes in the government budget in this way offset directly from 30 to 40 per cent of any change that would otherwise take place in national income.

The reduced importance attached to monetary policy that I referred to earlier has been accompanied by an increase in the importance attached to fiscal policy. In consequence, many economists are likely to regard this change in fiscal structure as even more important than the contemporaneous changes in the monetary structure. Whatever one may conclude about the relative importance of these two sets of changes, there can be no disagreement that the fiscal structure is now an exceedingly important and powerful "built-in stabilizer."

4. Psychological Climate of Opinion

The structure of institutions is important, but so also are the ideas and attitudes of the men who run them. The golden mean is universally sought but seldom attained. Men tend to overdo things; to react from having gone too far in one direction by going too far in the opposite direction. So it has been in attitudes toward inflation and deflation.

Before the Great Depression, the men who guided our economic institutions, and the responsible body of public opinion, were much more concerned about the dangers of inflation than of deflation. The origins of this attitude go back to the birth of the nation. Monetary experience during the American Revolution gave the nation at its outset a horror of unrestrained inflation that led to the inclusion of provisions in the American Constitution to prevent—or so it was thought—the issuance of fiduciary money by the Federal government. It is one of the ironies of history that Salmon P. Chase who, as Secretary of the Treasury, was responsible for the decision to issue greenbacks during the Civil War, later, as Chief Justice of the Supreme Court, ruled that their issuance violated these constitutional provisions.

The War of 1812, with the doubling of prices, confirmed and strengthened the fears engendered by the hyperinflation of the Revolution. Whatever weakening was produced by the great depression of the 1840's—and it was little because so much of the blame was rightly attributed to the preceding inflationary frenzy —was more than reversed by the Civil War inflation. The rest of the nineteenth century, with its generally downward pressure on prices and its several really severe depressions worked strongly in the opposite direction, as is evidenced by the political strength that the free silver and greenback parties attained. The effect was less than might have been expected, however, thanks partly to the near-self-sufficiency of much of the society, partly to the flexibility of the economy that enabled the deep depressions to manifest themselves mainly in monetary magnitudes. In any event, this change in attitudes was in turn reversed, and the earlier biases reinforced, by the fifteen years of generally rising prices that preceded World War I, the sharp inflation during and immediately after the War, and the ten years of prosperity that followed the sharp but brief slump of 1921. By 1928, more than three decades had passed since a really deep and long-continued depression; these decades had seen generally rising prices and had been punctuated by the wartime episode in which prices more than doubled in a few years. Is it any wonder that men viewed inflation as the chief threat to their prosperity?

This attitude, with its emphasis on "hard-money" at all costs, was surely a major factor explaining the actions of the Federal Reserve authorities that I have already discussed, as well as other governmental actions during the recession and depression. Being more afraid of inflation than of deflation, men over-did their reactions to any events that seemed to them to threaten inflation, and in the process produced a serious deflation.

The deflation changed all that. It took place in an economy in which agriculture had become of minor importance, and in which rigidities had greatly increased. Widespread unemployment and human misery understandably pushed depression into the front rank of the evils to be avoided at all costs. Even today, despite 20 years of nearly continuous price rise, despite widespread political agitation about rises in the cost of living and the dangers of inflation, the real fear of the public at large is of depression. Even the objections to inflation are indirect evidence: again and again one finds that the chief criticism of inflation is the assumption that what goes up must come down, so inflation now must produce a depression later.

We have swung from the one extreme to the other. And just as deflation resulted from going too far in trying to avoid inflation, so now inflation is likely to result from going too far in trying to avoid depression. The reaction to the current recession is striking evidence for this view. The recession is to date exceedingly mild, yet it has been watched over and reported about with the care and in the tones of an anxious mother whose child has been given only a 50-50 chance to live. Never in its history has the Federal Reserve system shifted so rapidly and completely from a tight money policy to an easy money policy. Pressure for tax cuts and for public works to stimulate purchasing power came hard and fast on the first slight faltering in the pace of economic advance and have multiplied since, even though purchasing power is still near an all time peak. Even so staunch a champion of financial orthodoxy as the Democratic Senator George of Georgia has recommended a sharp rise in the amount of income which is exempt from tax.

It is sometimes argued that the return of the Republican party to power alters the prospects substantially. The Republicans are the traditional defenders of "sound money"; they made much political capital out of the charge that the Democrats had destroyed the value of the dollar. Does it not follow that they are more likely than the Democrats to follow deflationary policies? I believe that precisely the reverse is true. A serious depression in their first term in power in over 20 years would be the end of the Republican party as a serious force on the national scene—certainly for the foreseeable future. It is the one outcome that they must avoid at all costs. Their incentive to avoid depression is therefore even greater than the Democrats' would have been. And this incentive is a far better clue to their likely behavior than the political slogans that were available to embarrass their opponents.

Indeed, in the light of this incentive, the President and his Council of Economic Advisors deserve unreserved tribute for political courage and economic wisdom. The easy and politically attractive path is to take precipitate and drastic action. This would steal the opponents' thunder and be applauded by the bulk of economic and business opinion. The claim that the Republicans had avoided a serious depression by their action would be one of those claims that could never be shown to be wrong. When their actions produced subsequent inflation, that could always be explained by special circumstances of the morrow. They have instead chosen the much harder course of trying to restrain vigorous actions designed to forestall the depression that is not yet here; of trying to reconcile the public to a minor recession that still has some time to run.

5. Prospects for the Future

I can perhaps best summarize the implications of my argument by outlining what seem to me the prospects for the American economy for the next few decades.

Our present monetary and fiscal institutions are so constructed that anything more than a minor economic recession is extremely unlikely, even if, or especially if, no explicit action is taken by Congress or the Administration. But unless the recession is *exceedingly* minor, explicit action will be taken. The widespread general fear of depression would lead Congress to force such action on any Administration whatever its political complexion. Political considerations render a Republican legislature and Administration particularly likely to take explicit action. The present recession and the political reaction to it are a clear example of these tendencies. If my basic premise is sound, such additional action will be unnecessary. Even more, it will be positively harmful. Contractions in the United States have averaged about 20 months in length over the past century or so, and this average includes the long contractions that were produced by monetary mistakes. Judging by this record, the present recession is probably more than half over,[7] so that any actions that are taken are not likely to have much effect until after recovery has already begun. But even if they should, their effects are almost certain to last well beyond the onset of recovery. It is one thing to reduce taxes; it is another thing to raise them again. Public works once undertaken will turn out to have lives of their own not closely linked to the life of cyclical movements. Other public activities entered into in an atmosphere of approval for any kind of government spending will not rapidly be reversed. The result is that measures taken to stem a supposed depression will serve

[7 It ended in August, 1954.]

to stimulate the succeeding recovery and to convert it into another round of inflation.

This inflation will not get out of hand; the same built-in stabilizers that would prevent a depression from getting out of hand will also prevent a runaway inflation. Sooner or later another recession will come along. After all, we have been having such recessions for hundreds of years and we doubtless shall continue to have them for some time. When it does, the same process is likely to be repeated.

The prospect is therefore a period of recurrent bouts of inflation produced by overreaction to the temporary recessions that punctuate the period. How long will this period last? How serious will the inflation be? Will overreaction to recession and a spurt of inflation begin with the present recession? These questions seem to me to admit of no easy answer. Much depends on accidents of timing and politics, both internal and external.

Economists have known—at least intermittently—for over a century and a half two propositions: first, that by printing enough money you can produce any desired degree of activity; second, that the ultimate result is destruction of the currency. The American public has learned the first proposition. It once knew, but has now forgotten, the second. Only experience is likely to teach it once again.

Questions and Answers

Professor Erik Lundberg: I thank Mr. Friedman for this survey. He has taken us back to the earliest recognizeable cycles, in the 1830's and 1840's, and not only brought us up to the present but even taken us some decades into the future. This is really a background for a discussion of our present situation. I think we have never before in our society had such a broad background for a discussion about business cycles.

One problem that we are very interested in in Sweden is the international repercussions of even minor recessions in the American economy. It is often said that a sneeze in the United States brings pneumonia to other parts of the world, and we have had some experiences of that. This time the 10 per cent decline in industrial production does not seem to have influenced the economy of the outside world very much. That may be accidental because of the raw material policy in the United States and some other factors, but still it is a problem.

I should like to ask Professor Friedman in this connection whether it is not possible to consider another alternative to the prospects than the one he described. He thought that we should expect recessions now and then in the United States, though a general inflationary tendency would prevail. Is it not possible, against the background of the economic experiences in the 1930's and the prevailing thought in many academic circles in the United States, that a new kind of stagnation period might come back? I am not thinking of a stagnation on a low level of activity as in the 1930's but of a relative stagnation with 10–15 per cent lower industrial production and national income than would be possible at a full employment use of the labor force.

Professor Friedman had a very good explanation of how some recessions have been deepened by monetary factors. But does it really explain the stagnation of the American economy in the second half of the 1930's, when interest rates were kept rather low and no monetary forces prevented increased activity and better use of capacity? Is it not possible, from this point of view, that USA might have a second period of stagnation for some years with say the present 10 per cent lower rate of economic activity than would be possible? I understand that professor Friedman has good arguments for the opinion that this is not very likely, but even this possibility has to be considered. In case of an inflationary tendency prevailing in Sweden and other countries, then the dollar shortage will be a serious problem.

Professor **Milton Friedman:** As I see it, I have to reply on three points: 1) What will be the effect on international trade of the present recession in the United States or of similar recessions? 2) Is it possible that the United States might have a period of stagnation? 3) What would be the international effect of such a period?

On the first question, I think that there is a tendency to generalize too readily from the relation between American income and American imports during the 1948-1949 movement, when a minor decline in

American income was accompanied by a much larger percentage decline in American imports. But one swallow does not make a summer, and the present experience seems to be quite different. I do not pretend to be an expert on these matters, but it seems to me highly uncertain that the relation between American income and American imports is so close, or so regular, as is widely held today. If the recession in the United States is no larger than I have suggested, it ought not to produce any difficulties.

It is a historical fact that before World War II cyclical movements in the United States were wider in amplitude than cyclical movements in most other countries. Thus one could argue that the United States was a source of instability. It is now almost a decade since the end of World War II, and the governments of many European countries have devoted considerable efforts to building storm-shelters against the supposed instability of the American economy, yet in the postwar period the American economy has shown less instability than most European countries.

I cannot pretend to give a precise answer to the question of the effects on international trade of future recessions in the United States or of a period of stagnation. It seems to me, however, that no foreign trade policy is reasonable if it can be destroyed by a minor quiver of the American economy. After all, it seems rather unreasonable to construct systems for relations among countries which have the property that if either country moves one per cent from some undefined norm the relation will be destroyed. Furthermore, I believe that the major problem in international trade is not so much to prepare for the effect of an American recession as to construct a structure of relations among nations that has more flexibility than the present highly rigid structure. Let me suggest that the appropriate system for this purpose is a system of freely floating exchange rates like the present Canadian system.[8]

I come to the second question that Professor Lundberg raised: can one rule out completely the possibility of a temporary stagnation in the American economy? I do not think one can rule this possibility out completely, but I am almost certain that the odds are very strongly against such an outcome. Given the psychological environment that I have described, any threat of a long continued period of unemployment is almost certain to produce a reaction on the part of the government, whatever party may be in power. So I find it exceedingly hard to con-

[8 A floating rate instituted in October, 1950, was terminated in May, 1962, when Canada fixed a new parity at which it has been pegging the Canadian dollar since.]

ceive of circumstances under which you could have any kind of stagnation. I think that the "stagnation" during the latter half of the 30's—if a five to ten year episode can be so termed—is the exception and not the rule and is the thing to be explained. And I think the explanation is not hard to find. The stagnation was partly a consequence of the extremely severe and serious depression that preceded it, partly a consequence of the effect of trying to institute far-reaching social and economic changes of the kind that were brought in during the New Deal at the same time as the country was recovering from such a depression, and partly a result of monetary changes in 1937. So I think the circumstances that produced this period were peculiar to it, cannot be expected to continue beyond it and give no reason to anticipate stagnation in the future.

Överingenjör **Oscar Wiberg:** I am very thankful for your very clear description of the economic development during one century and a half.

I would like to ask one question: Does the Federal Reserve System in America increase the interest level during an inflation and decrease it during a depression? I think the interest level is the instrument to balance the monetary system. In itself, the monetary system is unstable, like a pyramid turned upside down, and small disturbances can cause deviations in both directions, inflation or deflation.

Professor **Milton Friedman:** As I interpret it your question is a double one: 1) Does the American Federal Reserve System try to increase interest rates during a period of inflation and decrease them during a period of depression? 2) Is that an effective policy for controlling business conditions?

In recent years, the Federal Reserve System has operated in this fashion. During the period up to the spring of 1951 the monetary policy of the Federal Reserve System—like the monetary policy of so many other countries—was dominated by a belief that it was necessary to keep interest rates down under all circumstances. Since 1951 the Federal Reserve System has behaved in an extremely flexible fashion. It first kept the money market tight and produced a substantial rise in interest rates. In the spring of last year (1953), it reversed its actions and has since produced a substantial decline in interest rates.

On the second question, I believe very strongly that changes in monetary conditions have a significant effect on business conditions, though the interest rate by itself is largely a symbol of certain consequences rather than the immediate moving force. But it does not follow that discretionary actions by monetary authorities are an effective or desirable technique for promoting economic stability. Clemenceau once made the statement that war is too serious a matter to be left to generals. I think that economic stability is too serious a matter to be left to central bankers. At least for the United States—I do not want to speak about other countries—the outstanding characteristic of the record I ran over briefly in my talk was that the monetary authorities repeatedly did the wrong thing. I think the major requirement for the American economy is to establish a system in which the monetary authorities cannot make mistakes.

Fil. kand. **K. M. Savosnick:** I just want to ask a technical question in order to make sure that we have not misunderstood you. I think we all want to know what you mean by a recession as distinguished from a depression. From your speech one could gather that the period 1929-1931 should be termed a recession and the period 1931-1933 a depression. Could you tell us in terms of the 1954 economy how much unemployment the 1929-1931 recession would mean today?

Professor **Milton Friedman:** That is a very important and relevant question. Clearly, there is in principle a continuum between an exceedingly minor movement in employment and an exceedingly severe movement. Yet I think that if one looks at the historical movements in the United States, most of them fall rather sharply on one side or the other, though there are a few in the middle that it is hard to classify. The 1929-1931 movement is one of these borderline cases as you point out.

Now let me try to answer your question as explicitly as I can by indicating certain broad limits. Under present conditions, the civilian labor force in the United States numbers well over 60 million. The unemployed currently number something under four million. If that figure remains below, say, 5 million, I would call the recession very mild. That is the kind of thing we had in 1948-1949. At the depth of the great depression of the 1930's, 10-15 million were unemployed out of a much smaller labor force. A comparable level of unemployment today would be of the order of about 15 million or more. These are the two extremes. As to what the level of unemployment we had in 1931 would mean in terms of today's labor force, I am afraid I cannot give a precise answer. I believe that the answer would be something like 7-8 million, but I am not sure.

To some extent, I have evaded your question, but that is because there is no sharp answer to it. One can easily distinguish the two extremes, but then there are these rather fuzzy borders. Under present circumstances I would be very much surprised if we should have over 5 to 6 million unemployed.

Professor **Erik Lundberg**: When you told us that central banks have made many mistakes and are going to make many more mistakes I am sure that I interpret you correctly if I say that this does not mean that you would advise us to let the finance ministers lead the monetary policy instead? You have some other kind of policy in mind, and we should be very much obliged to get even a loose idea of what it is. In Sweden we think of the finance minister, the central bank and other institutions as the main actors of economic policy, but I have a notion that you prefer more or less automatic stabilizers, such as floating exchange rates and flexible rates of interest. What would such arrangements mean in an economy like Sweden's with trade unions, agricultural organizations and so on determining wages and prices? Is it necessary to make far-reaching changes in our institutions in order to make markets work and prevent people who are responsible for economic policy from making mistakes?

Professor **Milton Friedman**: I really do not want to talk about Sweden. I am, of course, an expert on Sweden. I have been here just a week, and that seems the right length of time, for if I stay any longer I shall disqualify myself when I find out all the things I do not know. But even though I am an expert on Sweden in that very limited sense, I believe I had better limit my comments to the American economy. For the United States, I would certainly agree that the finance minister or Secretary of the Treasury, as we call him, is not a very good substitute for the central bank.

I want to emphasize, as I was saying before, that in my view the Federal Reserve System has on the whole been a mistake. I do not attribute this to ignorance or incompetence or malice on the part of the people who have run the Federal Reserve System. If one looks over the list of names of the people who are or have been in charge of the Federal Reserve System, as members of its board of governors or in other important policy-making positions, one is impressed by how able, experienced, and public-spirited a group they are. It simply seems to me that their task is one in which mistakes are bound to be made from time to time, and such mistakes, under the kind of a system we have had, are likely to be exceedingly serious even with the best intentions in the world. With as much ability as one could reasonably hope to get from individuals, the results are not likely to be very happy. So simply substituting one person or group of persons for another is not a satisfactory solution. The desirable solution is rather to reduce as far as possible the necessity or possibility of discretionary action.

For the United States, my own favorite gadget to eliminate discretionary actions of central bankers is to have a highly automatic monetary and fiscal system closely connected one with the other. I would like to see 100 per cent reserve banking. This would essentially make all money in the society a direct government liability and would eliminate the existing situation in which government-created money can serve as a reserve for the creation of a larger volume of private deposits. It would also separate sharply the depositary activities of the banks from their lending and investing activities. I would like to see the monetary authorities have no discretion about the size of the stock of money. The particular arrangement I favor is one in which the stock of money automatically goes up when the government has a deficit by the amount of the deficit, and automatically goes down when the government has a surplus by the amount of the surplus. Under this system, the built-in stability of the fiscal system that I described in my talk would also operate on the monetary system.[9] As to international arrangements, I would favor a system of floating exchange rates with no government intervention through exchange equalization funds and the like. This would eliminate discretionary action in this area as well.

I cannot pretend to say whether the system so briefly summarized would be consistent with your institutions in Sweden. I have a feeling that general descriptions of these institutions and similar ones in other countries tend to overrate the importance of non-market forces and to underrate the importance of market forces. In the Swedish society, for example, the picture an outsider would gather of the determination of wage rates from much published material must, I feel sure, be a false picture. That picture would portray some people sitting in a room together, deciding that the wage rates must go up by 5 per cent, and then centrally distributing the increase among various trades and industries. It seems incredible that this should be a correct description. There must be some indirect channels whereby market forces of supply of and demand for the particular types of labor in particular markets make themselves felt, and the overall increase must, one feels, be built up, at least in considerable part, from these particular changes without explicit design rather than the other way around.

[9 I have since come to the conclusion that an even simpler arrangement would be preferable, namely one in which the quantity of money increases at a steady rate, year in and year out.]

What Price Guideposts?[1]

CHAPTER THREE   The student of inflation is tempted to rejoin, "I've heard that one before," to exhortations now emanating from Washington. Since the time of Diocletian, and very probably long before, the sovereign has repeatedly responded to generally rising prices in precisely the same way: by berating the "profiteers," calling on private persons to show social responsibility by holding down the prices at which they sell their products or their services, and trying, through legal prohibitions or other devices,

The author has drawn at various points in this paper on his book, *Inflation: Causes and Consequences* (New York: Asia Publishing House, 1963), which contains two lectures that he gave in Bombay, India, in 1963.

[1 Reprinted from George P. Shultz and Robert Z. Aliber (eds.), *Guidelines, Informal Controls, and the Market Place,* University of Chicago Press, 1966, a record of a conference at the University of Chicago.]

to prevent individual prices from rising.[2] The result of such measures has always been the same: complete failure. Inflation has been stopped when and only when the quantity of money has been kept from rising too fast, and that cure has been effective whether or not the other measures were taken.

The first section of this paper explains why the attempts to hold down individual wages and prices have failed to stop inflation. Direct control of prices and wages does not eliminate inflationary pressure. It simply shifts the pressure elsewhere and suppresses some of its manifestations.

Inflation is always and everywhere a monetary phenomenon, resulting from and accompanied by a rise in the quantity of money relative to output. This generalization is not an arithmetical proposition or a truism, and it does not require a rigid relation between the rates of rise in prices and in the quantity of money. The precise rate at which prices rise for a given rate of rise in the quantity of money depends on such factors as past price behavior, current changes in the structure of labor and product markets, and fiscal policy. The monetary character of inflation, as the second section points out, is an empirical generalization backed by a wide range of evidence which suggests that substantial changes in the demand for money seldom occur except as a reaction to a sequence of events set in train by changes in the quantity of money. It follows that the only effective way to stop inflation is to restrain the rate of growth of the quantity of money.[3]

[2] In a market economy, prices of particular goods and services, including labor services, are always changing relatively to one another, some rising, others falling, some rising rapidly, others slowly, and so on. When rises predominate, in some sense which allows for the relative importance of the items whose prices are considered, there is inflation; when declines predominate, there is deflation. This definition is purposely vague because there is no unique way to measure the "average" behavior of prices; different indexes often give different answers not only about the size of any price change, but even about its direction. These differences are sometimes very large and are important for many purposes. In the context of this paper, however, they are not. We shall restrict attention to cases in which the general tendency for prices to rise is so clear and widespread that it would be reflected in just about every broadly based index number.

[3] As Robert Solow pointed out in his comments on this paper at the conference, the argument of the other sections of this paper (sections I, III, and IV) is almost entirely independent of my generalization about the central role of the quantity of money in the inflationary process. The words inflationary pressure can

Given inflationary pressure, rises in recorded or quoted prices and wages can be suppressed to some extent. The less severe the inflationary pressure, and the more vigorous and effective the enforcement of price controls, the greater the extent to which the manifestations of inflation can be suppressed. As the third section points out, such suppressed inflation is far more harmful, both to efficiency and freedom, than open inflation, and the more effective the suppression, the greater the harm. It is highly desirable to avoid inflation but if, for whatever reason, that is not feasible, it is far better that inflation be open than that it be suppressed.

The final section of the paper asks what harm, if any, will be done by the guideposts. Even granted that compulsory price and wage controls cannot stop inflation and can do great harm, may not some measure of voluntary compliance by businessmen and union leaders ease the tasks of other instruments of policy and enable businessmen and union leaders to display their sense of social responsibility? In my opinion, the answer is clearly in the negative. Compliance with the guideposts is harmful because it encourages delay in taking effective measures to stem inflation, distorts production and distribution, and encourages restrictions on personal freedom.

Entirely aside from their strictly economic effects, guidelines threaten the consensus of shared values that is the moral basis of a free society. Compliance with them is urged in the name of social responsibility; yet, those who comply hurt both themselves and the community. Morally questionable behavior—the evading of requests from the highest officials, let alone the violation of legally imposed price and wage controls—is both privately and socially beneficial. That way lies disrespect for the law on the part of the public and pressure to use extralegal powers on the part of officials. The price of guideposts is far too high for the return,

---

be interpreted to mean an aggregate nominal demand in excess of the value of prior (or potential) output at prior prices. Whether this excess nominal demand reflects a change in the quantity of money, as I believe it generally does, or a change in velocity produced, for example, by changes in fiscal policy or investment demand, as others may believe, the analysis of the effects of price and wage guidelines or controls is precisely the same.

I am indebted to Mr. Solow for making this point explicit at the conference.

which, at most, is the appearance of doing something about a real problem.

I. Why Direct Control of Prices and Wages Does Not Eliminate Inflationary Pressure

An analogy is often drawn between direct control of wages and prices as a reaction to inflation and the breaking of a thermometer as a reaction to, say, an overheated room. This analogy has an element of validity. Prices are partly like thermometers in that they register heat but do not produce it; in both cases, preventing a measuring instrument from recording what is occurring does not prevent the occurrence. But the analogy is also misleading. Breaking the thermometer need have no further effect on the phenomenon being recorded; it simply adds to our ignorance. Controlling prices, insofar as it is successful, has very important effects. Prices are not only measuring instruments, they also play a vital role in the economic process itself.

A much closer analogy is a steam-heating furnace running full blast. Controlling the heat in one room by closing the radiators in that room simply makes other rooms still more overheated. Closing all radiators lets the pressure build up in the boiler and increases the danger that it will explode. Closing or opening individual radiators is a good way to adjust the relative amount of heat in different rooms; it is not a good way to correct for overfueling the furnace. Similarly, changes in individual prices are a good way to adjust to changes in the supply or demand of individual products; preventing individual prices from rising is not a good way to correct for a general tendency of prices to rise.

Suppose that there is such a general tendency, and suppose that some specific price (or set of prices), say, the price of steel, is prevented from rising. Holding down the price of steel does not make more steel available; on the contrary, given that other prices and costs are rising, it reduces the amount that producers can afford to spend in producing steel and is therefore likely to reduce the amount available from current production. Holding down the price of steel does not discourage buyers; on the contrary, it encourages consumption. If the suppressed price is effectively enforced and not evaded by any of the many channels that are available to ingenious sellers and buyers some potential buyers of steel must be frustrated—there is a rationing problem. Chance, favoritism, or bribery will have to decide which buyers succeed in getting the steel. Those who succeed pay less than they are willing to pay. They, instead of the steel producers, have the remainder to spend elsewhere. Those who fail will try to substitute other metals or products and so will divert their demand elsewhere; the excess pressure is shifted, not eliminated.

The situation is precisely the same on the labor market. If wages are tending to rise, suppressing a specific wage rise will mean that fewer workers are available for that type of employment and more are demanded. Again rationing is necessary. The workers employed have less income to spend, but this is just balanced by their employers having larger incomes. And the unsatisfied excess demand for labor is diverted to other workers.

But, it will be said, I have begged the question by *starting* with a general tendency for prices to rise. Can it not be that this general tendency is itself produced by rises in a limited number of prices and wages which in turn produce sympathetic rises in other prices and wages? In such a case, may not preventing the initial price and wage rises nip a wage-price or price-price spiral in the bud?

Despite its popularity, this cost-push theory of inflation has very limited applicability. Unless the cost-push produces a monetary expansion that would otherwise not have occurred, its effect will be limited to at most a temporary general price rise, accompanied by unemployment, and followed by a tendency toward declining prices elsewhere.

Suppose, for example, a strong (or stronger) cartel were formed in steel, and that it decided to raise the price well above the level that otherwise would have prevailed. The price rise would reduce the amount of steel people want to buy. Potential purchasers of steel would shift to substitute products, and no doubt the prices of such substitutes would tend to rise in sympathy. But there is now another effect. Steel producers would hire fewer workers and other resources. These would seek employment elsewhere, tending to drive down wages and prices in other industries. True, wages and prices might be sticky and decline only slowly, but that would only delay the downward adjustments and only at the expense of unemployment.[4]

A textbook example is provided by John L. Lewis and the United Mine Workers. Coal mining hourly earnings rose by "163 per cent from 1945 to 1960. Bituminous coal mining employment dropped from 284,000 to 168,000. By way of comparison, in the same period, manufacturing production hourly earnings rose . . . 122 per cent and manufacturing employment rose."[5] High coal prices undoubtedly put upward pressure on the prices of oil and gas; but the high unemployment put downward pressure on other prices.

The only example I know of in United States history when such a cost-push was important even temporarily for any substantial part of the economy was from 1933 to 1937, when the NIRA, AAA, Wagner Labor Act, and associated growth of union strength unquestionably led to *increasing* market power of both industry and labor and thereby produced upward pressure on a wide range of wages and prices. This cost-push did not account for the concomitant rapid growth in nominal income at the average rate of 14 per cent a year from 1933 to 1937. That reflected rather a rise in the quantity of money at the rate of 11 per cent a year. And the wage and cost-push had nothing to do with the rapid rise in the quantity of money. That reflected rather the flood of gold, initiated by the change in the United States price of gold in 1933 and 1934 and sustained by the reaction to Hitler's assumption of power in Germany.

The cost-push does explain why so large a part of the growth in nominal income was absorbed by prices. Despite unprecedented levels of unemployed resources, wholesale prices rose nearly 50 per cent from 1933 to 1937, and the cost of living rose by 13 per cent. Similarly, the wage cost-push helps to explain

[4] Note that even for such a temporary effect, it is not enough that there exist monopolies of business and labor; it is necessary that monopoly power increase; otherwise, relative prices will already have become adjusted.

[5] Yale Brozen, "Guide Lines and Wage Laws: How Should Wage Changes Be Determined?" Unpublished paper, p. 8.

why unemployment was still so high in 1937, when monetary restriction was followed by another severe contraction.

The popularity of the cost-push theory of inflation, despite its limited applicability, stems I believe from two sources: first, the deceptiveness of appearances; second, the desire of governmental authorities to shift the blame for inflation.

One of the fascinating features of economic relations is the frequent contrast between what is true for the individual and what is true for the community. Time and again the one is precisely the opposite of the other. Each individual takes for granted the prices of the things he buys and regards himself as having no effect on them; yet, consumers as a whole greatly affect those prices by the combined effects of their separate actions. Each individual can determine the amount of currency he carries around in his pocket; yet, all individuals together may have nothing to say about the total amount of currency to be carried around; that may be determined by monetary authorities, the individuals being free only to shuffle it around and transfer it from one to the other. Indeed, it is precisely this contrast between what is true for the individual and for the community that underlies many, perhaps most, common economic fallacies. They arise from invalid generalization from the individual to the community.

The widespread belief in the cost-push theory of inflation is a striking example. To each businessman separately, inflation tends to come in the form of increasing costs, and, typically, he correctly regards himself as having to raise the price at which he sells because his costs have risen. Yet, those cost rises may themselves reflect an increase in demand elsewhere and simply be part of the process whereby the demand increase is transmitted; and his ability to raise his price without a drastic decline in sales reflects the existence of excess demand. The monetary expansion and the associated increase in money demand take place through mysterious, widely dispersed, and largely invisible channels. The cost and price increases are their visible tracks.

In a recent elementary economics textbook, Alchian and Allen have given a vivid illustration of how a price rise produced by a demand increase can make itself felt to almost all the participants in the process as a cost-push:

Pretend that for some reason people's desire for meat increases. . . . Housewives reveal an increased demand by buying more meat than formerly at the current prices in the meat markets. . . . [T]he increased demand takes its toll of inventories. . . . [The] butcher will buy more meat than usual the next day in order to restore his inventory from its abnormally low level. . . . Just as butchers use inventories, so packers . . . also rely on inventories. . . . [A]ssume that the first day's change in demand was within that inventory limit and therefore was met without a price increase.

Packers restore inventories by instructing their cattle buyers . . . to buy more cattle than usual. But with all the packers restoring their inventories in this manner, the number of cattle available for sale each day are inadequate to meet the increased total demand *at the old price.* . . .

[T]he buyers will begin to raise their offers . . . until the price rises to the point where the packers will not want to buy more meat . . . than is available from the cattlemen. . . .

[T]he packers experience *a rise in costs* . . . [so] the packers must charge a higher price to butchers if they are to continue as profitable meat packers. . . . The butchers, in turn, post higher prices to the housewives. When housewives complain about the higher price, the butcher in all innocence, honesty, and correctness says that it isn't his fault. The cost of meat has gone up. . . . And the packers can honestly say the same thing.[6]

To almost all participants, therefore, a rise in price produced by increased demand appears to take the form of a rise in costs that enforces a higher price.

The interpretation of inflation as a reflection of cost-push is greatly fostered by governmental authorities. In modern times, the government has direct responsibility for the creation and destruction of money; it determines what happens to the quantity of money. Since inflation results from unduly rapid monetary expansion, the government is responsible for any inflation that occurs.[7] Yet, governmental authorities, like the rest of us, while only too eager to take credit for the good things that occur, are most reluctant to take the blame for the bad things—and inflation

[6] Armen A. Alchian and William R. Allen, *University Economics* (Belmont, Calif.: Wadsworth Publishing Co., 1964), pp. 105-7.

[7] To repeat in a specific context the point made earlier, note that precisely the same argument would hold if, as many believe, it is fiscal policy rather than monetary policy that accounts for the excess demand.

generally is regarded as a bad thing. Their natural tendency is to blame others for the inflation that governmental policies produce —to castigate the rapacious businessman and power-hungry labor leader rather than point to the government printing press as the culprit.

The 1966 *Annual Report* of the Council of Economic Advisers is an amusing and distressing example. It has a 31-page chapter on "Prospects for Cost-Price Stability" that so far as I have been able to determine has only two passing references to "monetary policy" and does not even contain the word "money" —a treatment of money strictly comparable to the way a rigid Puritan writing a book about love might have handled "sex." In the page and a half section on "Determination of the Price Level," there is no mention of the government's role until the last of eight paragraphs where the main emphasis is on the government's role as a customer and on governmental measures that directly affect costs. The one sentence in this section on the government's role in affecting aggregate demand is simply: "Fiscal policies help determine the over-all size of markets" (p. 65). Similarly, in the Council's explicit discussion of monetary policy elsewhere in the report (pp. 44–52), there is no reference at all to inflation or price level, although there is a passing reference to "spending." The careful reader of this 186-page report will have to wait until page 176, in a historical chapter on experience under the Employment Act, to find the first explicit recognition that there is any relation between monetary policy and inflation!

II. Inflation Is a Monetary Phenomenon

Yet, the central fact is that inflation is always and everywhere a monetary phenomenon.[8] Historically, substantial changes

[8 The word money is used in at least three different senses: (1) as in "money balances" when the reference is to the pieces of paper we carry in our pocket or the credits to our account on the books of banks—this is the sense in which I shall use it; (2) as in "making money" when the reference is not to a counterfeiter but to a recipient of income; and (3) as in "money markets" when a reference is to "loans" or "credit," paper claims that cover a vastly broader range of instruments than those we designate "money" in the first sense. Confusion among these meanings underlies much misunderstanding about the role of money in prices have always occurred together with substantial changes in the quantity of money relative to output. I know of no exception to this generalization, no occasion in the United States or elsewhere when prices have risen substantially without a substantial rise in the quantity of money relative to output or when the quantity of money has risen substantially relative to output without a substantial rise in prices. And there are numerous confirming examples. Indeed, I doubt that there is any other empirical generalization in economics for which there is as much organized evidence covering so wide a range of space and time.

Some confirming examples are extremely dramatic and illustrate vividly how important the quantity of money is by comparison with everything else. After the Russian Revolution of 1917, there was a hyperinflation in Russia when a new currency was introduced and printed in large quantities. Ultimately, it became almost valueless. All the time, some currency was circulating which had been issued by the prerevolutionary Czarist government. The Czarist government was out of power. Nobody expected it to return to power. Yet, the value of the Czarist currency remained roughly constant in terms of goods and rose sharply in terms of the Bolshevik currency. Why? Because there was nobody to print any more of it. It was fixed in quantity and therefore it retained its value. Another story has to do with the United States Civil War. Toward the end of the war, the Union troops overran the place where the Confederates had been printing paper money to finance the war. In the course of moving to a new location, there was a temporary cessation of the printing of money. As a result, there was also a temporary interruption in the price rise that had been proceeding merrily.

The fact that inflation results from changes in the quantity of money relative to output does not mean that there is a precise, rigid, mechanical relationship between the quantity of money and prices, which is why the weasel-word "substantial" was sprinkled

---

in economic affairs. In particular, confusion between the first and third has led to great overemphasis on the "credit" effects of governmental monetary policy rather than the effects on the quantity of money. Hence, the statement that inflation is a monetary phenomenon is sometimes interpreted not as I do in the text but as indicating that inflation reflects changes in credit markets.]

in my initial statement of the proposition. First, over short periods, the rate of change in the quantity of money can differ and sometimes by appreciable amounts from the rate of change in nominal income or prices because of other factors, including fiscal policy. Second, and more important, changes in the quantity of money do not make their effects felt immediately. It may be six months or a year or a year and a half before a change in the quantity of money appreciably affects nominal income or prices. Failure to allow for this difference in timing is a major reason for the misinterpretation of monetary experience. Third, and most important of all, there is a systematic and regular difference between changes in money and in prices in the course of an inflationary episode that is itself part of the very process by which monetary changes produce changes in prices.

The typical life history of an inflation is that the quantity of money per unit of output initially increases more rapidly than prices. During this period, the public does not anticipate price rises, interprets any price rise that occurs as temporary, and hence is willing to hold money balances of increased "real" value (i.e., corresponding to a larger volume of goods and services) in the belief that prices will be lower in the future. If the quantity of money continues to increase faster than output, however, prices will continue to rise, and sooner or later the public will come to anticipate further price rises. It then wishes to reduce its money balances not only to their former real value but to an even smaller level. Cash has now become a costly way to hold assets, since its purchasing power is decreasing. People therefore try to reduce their cash balances. They cannot, as a whole, do so in nominal terms (i.e., in terms of dollars), because someone or other must hold the amount in existence. But the *attempt* to do so bids up prices, wages, and nominal incomes. The result is to reduce "real" balances. During this stage, therefore, prices rise more rapidly than the quantity of money, and sometimes much more rapidly. If the rate of rise of the quantity of money stabilizes, no matter at how high a level, the rate of price rise will ultimately settle down also. The total price rise may bear very different relations to the rise in the quantity of money per unit of output depending on the size of the monetary expansion. In moderate inflations, as for example the rise in prices in the United States by a third from 1896 to 1913, prices and money may rise by about the same percentage. In really substantial inflations, such as have occurred in recent decades in many South American countries, the price rise will generally be several times the monetary rise; in hyperinflations, the price rise will be many times the monetary rise.

The United States today is in the early stages of such an episode. From 1961 to 1965, the quantity of money per unit of output rose more rapidly than prices—the typical initial reaction. From early 1965 to early this year [1966], the monetary rise has been accelerated, and the price rise has accelerated even more rapidly as anticipations of inflation have become widespread. As of now, if the rate of monetary growth were stabilized at the high level attained in 1965, the rate of price rise would continue to accelerate for a time. Even if the rate of monetary growth were sharply reduced, prices would continue to rise for a time under the combined influence of earlier monetary growth and changing anticipations.[9]

Why should money be so critical a factor in price level behavior? Why should it occupy such a central role in the process? The key to an answer is the difference, already referred to, between the *nominal* quantity of money, the quantity of money expressed in terms of dollars, and the *real* quantity of money, the quantity of money expressed in terms of the goods and services it will buy or the number of weeks of income it is equal to.

People seem to be extraordinarily stubborn about the real amount of money that they want to hold and are unwilling to hold a different amount, unless there is a strong incentive to do so. This is true over both time and space.

Let me illustrate with currency in circulation alone, which is more comparable among countries and over time than a broader definition of money, including deposits. In the United States, the amount of currency held by the non-banking public amounts to

[9 The rate of monetary growth was sharply reduced from April, 1966, to December, 1966. Prices did continue to rise, at first at as fast a rate as earlier, then after a lag of 5 or 6 months, at a slower rate. The slower rate ended about 6 months after rapid monetary expansion was resumed. See Chapter 5, "Current Monetary Policy."]

roughly four weeks' income. I know that this result seems surprising. When I ask people separately whether they have as much as four weeks' income in the form of currency, I have rarely had anyone say yes. Part of the explanation is that about one-fifth of the currency is held by businesses such as retail stores. The main explanation, I am sure, is that there are a small number of people who hold very large sums in this form while the rest of us hold more moderate amounts. In any event, that is what the figures show. The fascinating thing is that the corresponding number was not very different a century ago. In 1867 people on the average held about five weeks' income in the form of currency, compared to today's four weeks' income. In the interim this number has gone as low as 2¼ weeks' income in 1929, as high as 8½ weeks' in 1946. That is a substantial range, it is true, but those are long periods spanning major changes in circumstances.

This range, moreover, contains the figures for most countries in the world. In Israel, the amount held is about the same as in the United States, a little over four weeks' income; in Japan and Turkey, about five weeks' income; in Greece and Yugoslavia, about six weeks' income; in India, about seven weeks' income. Again, these are not negligible differences; yet, they are small compared to the differences among the countries in wealth, economic structure, political forms, and cultural characteristics.

Even these relatively small differences over time and space can be largely explained by a few major factors, of which the prevalence of deposit banking is perhaps the single most important.

Given that people are so stubborn about the amount they hold in the form of money, let us suppose that, for whatever reasons, the amount of money in a community is higher than people want to hold at the level of prices then prevailing. It does not for our purposes matter why, whether because the government has printed money to finance expenditures or because somebody has discovered a new gold mine or because banks have discovered how to create deposits. For whatever reason, people find that although on the average they would like to hold, let us say, the four weeks' income that they hold in the United States, they are actually holding, say, five weeks' income. What will happen?

Here again it is essential to distinguish between the individual and the community. Each individual separately thinks he can get rid of his money and he is right. He can go out and spend it and thereby reduce his cash balances. But for the community as a whole the belief that cash balances can be reduced is an optical illusion. The only way I can reduce my cash balances in nominal terms is to induce somebody else to increase his. One man's expenditures are another man's receipts. People as a whole cannot spend more than they as a whole receive. In consequence, if everybody in the community tries to reduce the nominal amount of his cash balances, on the average nobody will do so. The amount of nominal balances is fixed by the nominal quantity of money in existence and no game of musical chairs can change it.

But people can and will try to reduce their cash balances and the process of trying has important effects. In the process of trying to spend more than they are receiving, people bid up the prices of all sorts of goods and services. Nominal incomes rise and real cash balances are indeed reduced, even though nominal balances, the number of dollars, are not affected. The rise in prices and incomes will bring cash balances from five weeks' income to four weeks' income. People will succeed in achieving their objective, but by raising prices and incomes rather than by reducing nominal balances. In the process, prices will have risen by about a fifth. This in a nutshell and somewhat oversimplified is the process whereby changes in the stock of money exert their influence on the price level. It is oversimplified because there is a tendency to overshoot, followed by successive readjustments converging on the final position, but this complication does not affect the essence of the adjustment process.

Emphasis on the key role of the quantity of money leaves open the question of what produced the changes in the quantity of money. Hence, if an analysis of inflation is to deal not only with the change in the quantity of money but with what brought it about, it will be a very pluralistic theory. Historically, the actual sources of monetary expansion have been very different at different times and in different places.

In United States history, the most dramatic inflations have been wartime inflations—those associated with the Revolution, when prices skyrocketed and the declining value of the money produced the phrase "not worth a continental," and with the War of 1812, the Civil War, and the two world wars, in all of which prices roughly doubled. In these episodes, the increase in the quantity of money was produced mainly by the printing of money to pay for governmental wartime expenses.

But even these episodes are not wholly to be explained in that fashion. In the final year of the World War I inflation (1919–20), when prices rose at their most rapid pace, the government budget was in surplus, and the rapid increase in the quantity of money was being produced for private, not governmental, purposes.

The two main periods of peacetime inflation in the United States were in the 1850's and from 1896 to 1913. Both were parts of worldwide movements. The first resulted from the gold discoveries in California, the second from the development of a commercially feasible cyanide process for extracting gold from low-grade ore plus gold discoveries.

There is a widespread belief that inflation is somehow related to government deficits. This belief has a sound basis. The existence of deficits tempts governments to finance them by printing money (or the equivalent, creating deposits), hence deficits have often been the source of monetary expansion. But deficits per se are not necessarily a source of inflation. As already noted, the federal budget ran a surplus during 1919–20 when prices rose rapidly; similarly, there were extremely large surpluses immediately after World War II, when prices also rose rapidly. On the other side, the budget was in deficit during 1931–33, when prices fell sharply. Deficits can contribute to inflation by raising interest rates and so velocity; for the rest they are a source of inflation if and only if they are financed by printing money.

The same considerations apply to other alleged sources of inflation. Increasingly strong trade unions can be a source of inflation if by their actions they produce unemployment and if a government committed to full employment expands the quantity of money as part of a policy of eliminating unemployment. This particular chain of events has often been alleged but, as already noted, seldom observed in the United States. More generally, a full employment policy can be a source of inflation if it produces undue monetary expansion.

III. Suppressed Inflation Is Worse than Open Inflation

The distinction between inflation and deflation, important as it is, is less important than the distinction between open inflation, one in which prices are free to rise without governmental price controls, and suppressed inflation, one in which the government attempts to suppress the manifestations of the inflationary pressure by controlling prices, including prices not only of products but also of factor services (i.e., wage rates, rents, interest rates) and of foreign currencies (i.e., exchange rates).

Open inflation is harmful. It generally produces undesirable transfers of income and wealth, weakens the social fabric, and may distort the pattern of output. But if moderate, and especially if steady, it tends to become anticipated and its worst effects on the distribution of income are offset. It still does harm, but, *so long as prices are free to move,* the extremely flexible private enterprise system will adapt to it, take it in stride, and continue to operate efficiently. The main dangers from open inflation are twofold: first, the temptation to step up the rate of inflation as the economy adapts itself; second, and even more serious, the temptation to attempt cures, especially suppression, that are worse than the disease.

Suppressed inflation is a very different thing. Even a moderate inflation, if effectively suppressed over a wide range, can do untold damage to the economic system, require widespread government intervention into the details of economic activity, destroy a free enterprise system, and along with it, political freedom. The reason is that suppression prevents the price system from working. The government is driven to try to provide a substitute that is extremely inefficient. The usual outcome, pending a complete monetary reform, is an uneasy compromise between official tolerance of evasion of price controls and a collectivist economy. The greater the ingenuity of private individuals in

112

evading the price controls and the greater the tolerance of officials in blinking at such evasions, the less the harm that is done; the more law-abiding the citizens, and the more rigid and effective the governmental enforcement machinery, the greater the harm.

A dramatic illustration of the difference between open and suppressed inflation is the contrast between the experience of Germany after World War I and after World War II. This happens to be one of those beautiful examples that history turns up for us from time to time in which experience is almost in the nature of a controlled experiment, because the difference in the character of the monetary phenomena is so great compared to differences in other relevant respects. After World War I, Germany had an open inflation of extremely large magnitude. It is difficult for us to contemplate the kind of inflation Germany experienced at that time because it is so extreme. A student of mine, Phillip Cagan, wrote a doctoral dissertation on hyperinflation in different countries, which has become something of a classic. He had the problem of how to define hyperinflation. He defined it as beginning when prices started to rise at the rate of more than 50 per cent a month. In the German hyperinflation after World War I, there were periods when prices rose not 50 per cent a month but doubled every week and some occasions on which they were doubling every day. Indeed, it got to the point that firms started to pay their employees their wages three times a day— after breakfast, lunch, and dinner, so that they could go out and spend them before they lost their value. That was really a whopping inflation, yet it went on for something like three years.

The inflation did untold harm to Germany. The impoverishment of the middle classes, the arbitrary redistribution of income, and the frantic instability unquestionably helped to lay the groundwork for Hitler's emergence later. Looked at, however, from the purely technical point of view of its effect on production, the astounding thing is that until the last six months of the inflation, total output in Germany never declined. Indeed, Germany was one of the few countries in the world that did not experience a great depression in 1920–21, when prices in the gold standard part of the world dropped by 50 per cent. Total output remained up. Why? Because the inflation was open. Prices were allowed to rise freely and hence the price system could still be used to allocate resources. Of course, after a time people started to use all sorts of escalation devices to link their contracts to the value of the mark in the foreign exchange market, which was also a free market price, and so on. The price system, however, could work even under those handicaps.

After World War II, Germany was under inflationary pressure as a result of an increase in the quantity of money during the war and the fixation of prices. By our usual standards, the pressure was substantial. If prices had been allowed to rise freely immediately after the war, the price level would probably have quadrupled. That is a large price rise. But it is negligible by comparison with the price rise after World War I which has to be described in terms of factors like 10^{10}. The price rise after World War II, however, was suppressed. Ordinarily, it is extremely difficult to suppress a price rise of that magnitude, to enforce price control when the market price would be four times the controlled price. But there were certain especially favorable circumstances from the point of view of enforcing price control in Germany at that time. Germany was occupied by the armed forces of Britain, France, and the United States, and the occupation forces enforced price control.

The result of suppressing inflation was that output in Germany was cut in half. The price system was not allowed to function. People were forced to revert to barter. Walter Eucken in an article describing this period tells the story of people who worked in a factory making pots and pans. They would work there for two or three days and then they would be given their pay in the form of aluminum saucepans. They would take the saucepans and spend the rest of the week scouring the countryside trying to find some farmer who would be willing to trade a few potatoes or other produce for the saucepans. That is not a very efficient way to organize resources. It was so inefficient that something had to be done and something was done. People developed their own forms of money. Cigarettes came into use as money for small transactions and cognac for large transactions—the most liquid money I have ever come across. But even with these expedients, suppressed inflation cut output in half from the level at the immediate end of the war.

In 1948 as you know, the so-called German miracle began. It was not a very complicated thing. It amounted to introducing a monetary reform, eliminating price control, and allowing the price system to function. The extraordinary rise in German output in the few years following this reform was not owing to any miracle of German ingenuity or ability or anything like that. It was the simple, natural result of allowing the most efficient technique people have ever found for organizing resources to work instead of preventing it from working by trying to fix prices here, there, and everywhere.

Although this is the most dramatic example, numerous other examples can be cited of a less extreme kind. In the immediate postwar period, I visited Europe and spent some time in Britain and France. Both countries at that time had widespread price controls. But there was an important difference. The people of Britain were relatively law-abiding, the people of France were not. The result was that Britain was being strangled by the law obedience of her people and France was being saved by the black market.

The reason suppressed inflation is so disastrous, as these examples suggest, is that the price system is the only technique that has so far been discovered or invented for efficiently allocating resources. If that is prevented from operating, something else must be substituted. What do we substitute? It is always some kind of clumsy physical control.

A striking current example is provided by India with its system of exchange control and import licenses. In the past decade, India has experienced a price rise of something between 25 and 50 per cent. In the main, this price rise has been open, although there have been some price controls. There has been, however, one important glaring exception—the price of foreign exchange. The official price of the dollar or the pound sterling in terms of the rupee is precisely the same today [early 1966] as it was ten years ago.[10] If the price of the rupee was anywhere close to be-

[10 The rupee was devalued in June, 1966, but not by enough to permit elimination of exchange control.]

ing right then, it cannot be right now. And of course it is not right. The effect has been to encourage people to try to import goods because they are artificially cheap and to discourage them from trying to export goods because the amount of rupees they can get for the foreign exchange proceeds of exports will buy less at home than before. Imports and exports are highly sensitive areas. Even moderate changes can have very large effects. The result has been a serious foreign exchange crisis. India at first allowed her foreign exchange reserves to run down until today reserves are very small. In addition, direct controls over imports have been increasingly tightened and all sorts of special measures have been taken to subsidize and encourage exports. Certain categories of imports have been banned entirely. For other categories, import licenses have been given on a more and more limited scale. And even so, the exchange rate has been able to be maintained only because of very large additional grants of foreign aid.

The result has been incredible waste and inefficiency, proliferating bureaucracy, and widespread corruption and bribery. In my opinion, the pegging of the exchange rate is the key to India's economic failure. Setting it free, along with the wiping away of the mountains of regulations exchange control has engendered, is the most important single step that India could take to unleash its very real potentialities.

The experience of India could be duplicated manyfold. I cite it only because it happens to be the case with which I am most intimately familiar.

India is a far-off land. But the same process has been getting under way in the United States. As in India, the pegging of exchange rates is the most conspicuous example of the suppression of inflation in the United States, and it has been having the same effects. The changes in tourist allowances; the "voluntary" quotas imposed on the exports of foreign countries to us; the establishment of a cartel agreement among banks to limit foreign loans, an agreement that would be clearly illegal if privately entered into but that is urged in the name of patriotism and is policed by the Federal Reserve System; the so-called voluntary foreign exchange program for business enterprises, administered by the Department of Commerce and constituting an extralegal exchange control arrangement—these are but a sample and a foretaste of what suppressed inflation implies.[11]

A perhaps even more illuminating foretaste is furnished by the recent developments in connection with copper, which combine internal price restraint with control of exchange rates. The posted American producer price of blister copper is being kept, by pressure from Washington, at about 36 cents a pound, well below the world price.[12] The result, of course, is that it is profitable to export copper. Accordingly, the export of copper without a license has been prohibited and full-fledged governmental export control of copper has been introduced. Needless to say, not even the government can live with such a price discrepancy when the United States must import copper. The United States government has therefore made a deal with Chile involving Chile's selling us copper at 36 cents a pound in return for our giving them a development loan of $10 million at highly favorable terms.[13] A bit of quick arithmetic yields a gross price of copper, including the value to Chile of the soft loan, of between 40.6 and 41.6 cents a pound, or almost precisely Chile's current export price of 42 cents a pound.[14] Such shenanigans to conceal the United States government's evasions of its own guidelines would be as humorous as they are ludicrous if the episode were not such a disheartening harbinger of what currently looks like the wave of the future. Again, in a futile effort to hold down the price of copper, the United States government sold 200 million tons of copper from its stockpile at the price of 36 cents a pound it has been trying to peg. Since the market price of scrap plus the cost of converting it was at the time about 50 cents a pound, this amounted to splitting a melon of $56 million with the users of copper lucky enough to buy from the government at the fixed price.

[11 In January, 1968, the President replaced the "voluntary" program to restrict foreign investment by business enterprises by a compulsory program prohibiting any such investment without government permission. At the same time, he requested Congress to enact laws penalizing tourism by U.S. residents.]

[12 The domestic posted price of copper has since been raised.]

13 See *Wall Street Journal*, January 31, 1966.

14 I am indebted to David Kleinman for calling this episode to my attention and for the calculations referred to. Since this was written, Chile has raised her export price sharply.

The United States had widespread experience with the results of price and wage controls during World War II, and New York City's housing difficulties are a current reminder of their long-reaching effects, since New York is the only city in the land that still has rent controls as a heritage of the war. The memory of this experience leads government officials to disavow any intention of imposing explicit price and wage controls. But voluntary controls are no improvement, except as they are more readily evaded. Let them be abided by, and the consequences will be the same.

IV. What Harm Will Be Done by the Guideposts?

Even granted that legally imposed and vigorously enforced wage and price ceilings covering a wide range of the economy would do enormous harm, some may argue that the enunciation of guideposts, their approval by businessmen and labor leaders, and voluntary compliance with them, or even lip service to them, is a palliative that can do no harm and can temporarily help until more effective measures are taken. At the very least, it may be said, it will enable businessmen and labor leaders to display their sense of social responsibility.

This view seems to me mistaken. The guideposts do harm even when only lip service is paid to them, and the more extensive the compliance, the greater the harm.

In the first place, the guideposts confuse the issue and make correct policy less likely. If there is inflation or inflationary pressure, the governmental monetary (or, some would say, fiscal) authorities are responsible. It is they who must take corrective measures if the inflation is to be stopped. Naturally, the authorities want to shift the blame, so they castigate the rapacious businessman and the selfish labor leader. By approving guidelines, the businessman and the labor leader implicitly whitewash the government for its role and plead guilty to the charge. They thereby encourage the government to postpone taking the corrective measures that alone can succeed.

In the second place, whatever measure of actual compliance

there is introduces just that much distortion into the allocation of resources and the distribution of output. To whatever extent the price system is displaced, some other system of organizing resources and rationing output must be adopted. As in the example of the controls on foreign loans by banks, one adverse effect is to foster private collusive arrangements, so that a measure undertaken to keep prices down leads to government support and encouragement of private monopolistic arrangements.

In the third place, "voluntary" controls invite the use of extralegal powers to produce compliance. And, in the modern world, such powers are ample. There is hardly a business concern that could not have great costs imposed on it by antitrust investigations, tax inquiries, government boycott, or rigid enforcement of any of a myriad of laws, or on the other side of the ledger, that can see no potential benefits from government orders, guarantees of loans, or similar measures. Which of us as an individual could not be, at the very least, seriously inconvenienced by investigation of his income tax returns, no matter how faithfully and carefully prepared, or by the enforcement to the letter of laws we may not even know about? This threat casts a shadow well beyond any particular instance. In a dissenting opinion in a recent court case involving a "stand-in" in a public library, Justice Black wrote, "It should be remembered that if one group can take over libraries for one cause, other groups will assert the right to do it for causes which, while wholly legal, may not be so appealing to this court." Precisely the same point applies here. If legal powers granted for other purposes can today be used for the "good" purpose of holding down prices, tomorrow they can be used for other purposes that will seem equally "good" to the men in power—such as simply keeping themselves in power. It is notable how sharp has been the decline in the number of businessmen willing to be quoted by name when they make adverse comments on government.

In the fourth place, compliance with voluntary controls imposes a severe conflict of responsibilities on businessmen and labor leaders. The corporate official is an agent of his stockholders; the labor leader, of the members of his union. He has a responsibility to promote their interests. He is now told that he must sacrifice their interests to some supposedly higher social responsibility. Even supposing that he can know what "social responsibility" demands—say by simply accepting on that question the gospel according to the Council of Economic Advisers—to what extent is it proper for him to do so? If he is to become a civil servant in fact, will he long remain an employee of the stockholders or an agent of the workers in name? Will they not discharge him? Or, alternatively, will not the government exert authority over him in name as in fact?

V. Conclusion

Inflation being always and everywhere a monetary phenomenon, the responsibility for controlling it is governmental. Legally enforced price and wage ceilings do not eliminate inflationary pressure. At most they suppress it. And suppressed inflation is vastly more harmful than open inflation.

Guideposts and pleas for voluntary compliance are a halfway house whose only merit is that they can more readily be abandoned than legally imposed controls. They are not an alternative to other effective measures to stem inflation, but at most a smokescreen to conceal the lack of action. Even if not complied with, they do harm, and the more faithfully they are complied with, the more harm they do.

Nonetheless, we should not exaggerate either the problem or the harm that will be done by false cures. Prices will almost surely rise in coming months. We shall probably continue to experience inflationary pressure on the average over the coming years. The price rise, however, will be moderate. A major war aside, I cannot conceive that the monetary authorities will permit the quantity of money to rise at a rate that would produce inflation of more than, say, 3-to-10 per cent a year. Such inflation will be unfortunate, but if permitted to occur reasonably openly and freely, not disastrous. And, despite all the talk, prices and wages will be permitted to rise in one way or another. The guideposts will be more talked about than they will be voluntarily complied with or enforced by extralegal pressure. Hypocrisy will enable effective evasion to be combined with self-congratulation. Debasing the coin of public and private morality is unfortunate, but in moderate doses not disastrous. The greatest harm will continue to be done by the measures taken to peg exchange rates. It is well to keep in mind Adam Smith's famous comment, "There is much ruin in a nation,"—to avoid overstating a good case, not to condone bad policy.

Monetary Policy

PART TWO Part One on inflation makes it clear that the quantity of money plays a major role in determining the course of prices in the long run, and the ups and downs of the economy in the short run. For the United States, the quantity of money is currently controlled by the Federal Reserve System. The System can, within wide limits, make the quantity of money and its rate of growth whatever it wishes. While the System *can* do this, it has generally not expressed its operating objective in terms of the quantity of money, but rather in terms such as interest rates, free reserves, or other indicators of credit conditions. In consequence, it has often let the quantity of money move in whatever way was necessary to foster these other objectives.

At the apex of the Federal Reserve System is the Board of Governors, consisting of 7 men named by the President of the United States for overlapping 14-year terms. In recent years, the Board has adopted the admirable practice of meeting several times a year with small groups of academic economists, varying in composition, to hear their opinions about both the broader aspects of monetary policy and the current economic situation. The first two items in this section are memoranda which I prepared for two of the meetings of this kind in which I have participated. The memoranda were prepared at the request of the Board and on topics suggested by the Board.

The first memorandum deals mostly with a very broad survey of the lessons offered by past experience that are relevant for current monetary policy. Because it was prepared for a group of people intimately familiar with the details of monetary and banking arrangements, it is highly concise and much of it may be too cryptic for some readers. Nonetheless, I have left it and the subsequent memorandum exactly as they were prepared (except for correcting typographical errors), for two reasons. First, it seemed to me it would be instructive to many readers to see examples of the kind of memoranda that the Federal Reserve considers in formulating its decisions—though I need hardly say that this is a very limited and may be a highly unrepresentative sample. Second, the memoranda contained predictions and I wanted to avoid any temptation on my part to color with hindsight the imperfections of my foresight.

The second memorandum is essentially a continuation of the first, covering the period between the two meetings at which the memoranda were presented. Though I have attended additional meetings since, I have prepared no additional memoranda. Instead, I have included in this section three columns from *Newsweek* (to which I have contributed economic comment since September, 1966). These carry the record closer to the present. They will, I believe, be more meaningful to the reader who has read the two Federal Reserve memoranda than they could have been to the readers of *Newsweek* who did not have this background.

The views expressed in these items are entirely my own. The willingness of the members of the Federal Reserve Board to read, to hear, and to discuss in considerable detail the views expressed is a tribute to their eagerness to explore fully all aspects of their task and does not imply either agreement or disagreement.

The final two items in this section are on a very different level. They deal not with current policy but with more fundamental matters. The first of them, "Should There be an Independent Monetary Authority?" discusses whether it is desirable to have an institution like the present Federal Reserve System which has a considerable measure of independence from both Congress and the Executive and which has enormous powers that can be exercised at its discretion, subject to no very clearly defined Congressional mandate. This is both a political question —whether the granting of such powers to an independent authority is consistent with a democratic political structure—and an economic question—whether the granting of such powers will promote economic progress and stability. On both scores, my answer is in the negative: on both scores, rules seem to me preferable to authorities.

The final item, though included in this section on monetary policy, deals with the factual basis underlying policy, rather than directly with policy itself. Control of the quantity of money— of the number of dollars of currency and deposits available to be held by the public—is important because, and only because, there exists a relatively stable demand on the part of the public for money to hold—where money must this time be expressed not in dollars but in "real" terms, in terms of the amount of goods and services the money will command. A great deal of scientific work has been done on the characteristics of the demand for money in recent years. The final paper was an attempt to explain to an audience of non-economists what Anna Schwartz and I had learned in our studies of this subject.

The Lessons of U.S. Monetary

History and Their Bearing

on Current Policy [1]

CHAPTER FOUR   I have interpreted my assignment as twofold: first, to summarize briefly the conclusions relevant to monetary policy that I have drawn from the monetary history of the United States; second, to interpret the present monetary situation of the United States in light of those conclusions. For many of the conclusions, *A Monetary History of the United States,* by Anna Schwartz and myself, contains full documentation, and the necessary qualifications.[2] Other conclusions come from the continuing statistical research Dr. Schwartz and I have been doing since the publication of *A Monetary History.* Since much of this is unpublished, I give somewhat fuller,

[1 Memorandum prepared for consultant's meeting, Board of Governors, Federal Reserve System, October 7, 1965. I am indebted to Anna Schwartz for invaluable assistance in preparing this memorandum.]

[2 Princeton University Press, for the National Bureau of Economic Research, 1963.]

though still necessarily scanty, documentation for such conclusions. Needless to say, both sources are heavily indebted to the scholarly work of others on money, which has fortunately been experiencing very much of a boom in both quantity and quality.

I. The Lessons of Monetary History

I shall summarize these lessons under three headings: (a) the relation between money and other economic magnitudes; (b) major generalizations about policy episodes; (c) lessons about tools and policy criteria.

A. RELATION BETWEEN MONEY AND OTHER ECONOMIC MAGNITUDES

1. *The rate of change in the quantity of money* (per cent growth or decline per year) is closely correlated with the rate of change in (a) nominal income, (b) real income, and (c) prices. The correlation is higher for nominal income than for either prices or output separately. The correlation holds both for cyclical movements and for periods longer than the usual business cycle. It holds for any of a number of definitions of the quantity of money. Both the closeness of the correlation and the functional relation between money and the other magnitudes appear to have remained the same over the past century.

1.1. *Long periods.* The evidence for periods longer than the usual business cycle is summarized in Figures 1 and 2. In both figures, rates of change are plotted for two definitions of money: M_1 = currency plus adjusted demand deposits; $M_2 = M_1$ plus time deposits in commercial banks. Reasonably accurate figures for M_1 are available only since 1915; for M_2, for the whole period since 1869. To eliminate intra-cyclical effects, the rates of change plotted on these figures are computed from average values covering a cyclical phase (either a whole expansion or a whole contraction, as dated by the National Bureau). It is worth emphasizing that the money series and the income series are

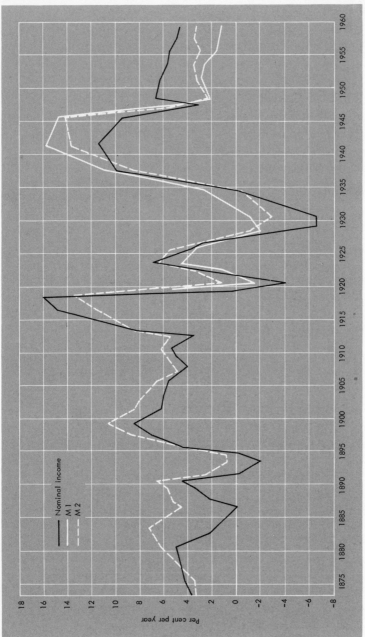

Figure 1. Rates of Change Computed from Phase Averages: M_2 and Nominal Income, 1870-1961; M_1, 1910-1961. Phase bases are averages of logarithms of data, with initial and terminal turning points weighted by ½, intervening observations by unity. Rates of change are the slopes of a least squares line fitted to groups of three successive phase bases, with observations weighted inversely to their variances. (*Source*: M_2, 1867-1946, and M_1, 1914-46, Friedman and Schwartz, *A Monetary History*, Table A-1, cols. 7 and 8, pp. 704-718; thereafter, *Federal Reserve Bulletin*. Nominal Income, *A Monetary History*, source notes to Chart 62, facing p. 678.)

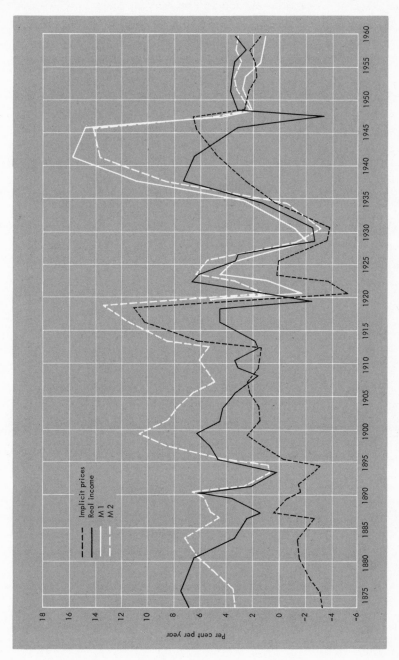

Figure 2. Rates of Change Computed from Phase Averages: M_2, Implicit Prices, and Real Income, 1870-1961; M_1, 1918-1961. (*Source:* Same as for Figure 1; source cited there for nominal income is also source of real income and implicit prices.)

statistically completely independent of one another; they were constructed by different investigators from wholly different sets of basic data.

The relations shown in Figure 2 reflect influences running both from money to prices and output and from prices and output to money. During the pre-Federal Reserve period, 1879-1915, gold flows assured that the money stock changed so as to keep prices in the U.S. adjusted to prices elsewhere; the money stock was, in a fundamental sense, the dependent variable. However, this was not true prior to 1879 or in the 1920's and 1930's, when we know, from our historical analysis, that the money stock was, in a fundamental sense, the independent variable.[3]

1.2. *Cycles.* The evidence for cyclical periods is summarized in the three panels of Figure 3, which shows the rate of change per month in the quantity of money (M_2) during individual cyclical expansions or contractions plotted against the corresponding rate of change in bank clearings (1879-1919) or debits (1919-61) outside New York, as an index of nominal income (Panel A); an index of physical output (Panel B); and an index of wholesale prices (Panel C). For the briefer period for which M_1 is available, the scatter (not given here) is very similar.[4]

Like the secular relation, this one too shows no sign of having changed over the past century.

The brevity of the periods encompassed by individual cyclical phases gives much play to both erratic perturbations and errors of measurement. Hence the relations shown by Figure 3 are considerably looser than those shown by Figures 1 and 2.

2. *Instability in the rate of change in the quantity of money* is highly correlated with instability in the rate of change in

[3] The unusually large discrepancies in the 1940's in Figure 2 undoubtedly reflect largely deficiencies in the price indexes produced by wartime price control and postwar decontrol.

[4] The scatter for expansion is around a higher level regression line than that for contractions in each of the panels, primarily because this Figure does not allow for the characteristic tendency of monetary changes to precede the other economic changes. The rate of change in money therefore tends to be underestimated during expansions and overestimated during contractions; the former shifts the scatter for expansions to the left; the latter, the scatter for contractions to the right.

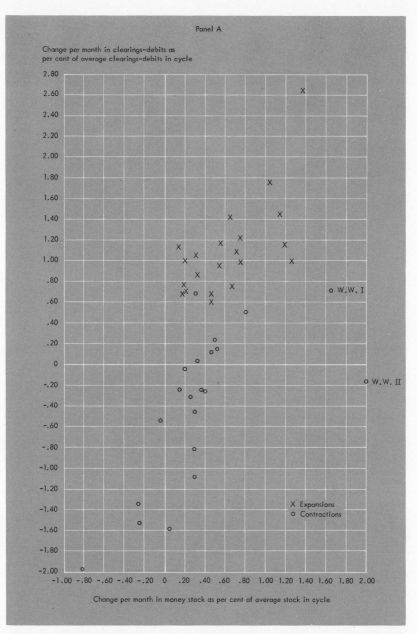

Figure 3. Relation between Cyclical Changes in General Business and Changes in M_2 During Reference Expansions and Contractions, 1879-1961. (*Source:* Computation of change per month as per cent of reference cycle average follows Burns and Mitchell, *Measuring Business Cycles,* pp. 176-177. Money figures, same as for Figure 1. Wholesale prices, *A Monetary History,* source notes to Chart 62, facing p. 678. Clearings-debits and Moore index (an average of 3 trend-adjusted indexes of business activity), Forty-Fourth Annual Report of NBER, June 1964, p. 16.)

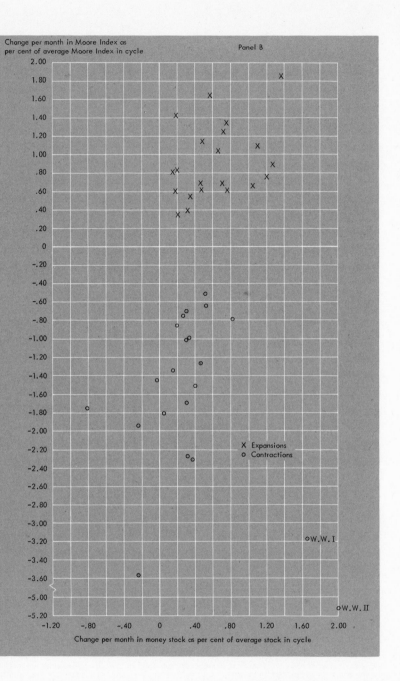

Change per month in Moore Index as
per cent of average Moore Index in cycle

Panel B

X Expansions
o Contractions

o W.W. I

o W.W. II

Change per month in money stock as per cent of average stock in cycle

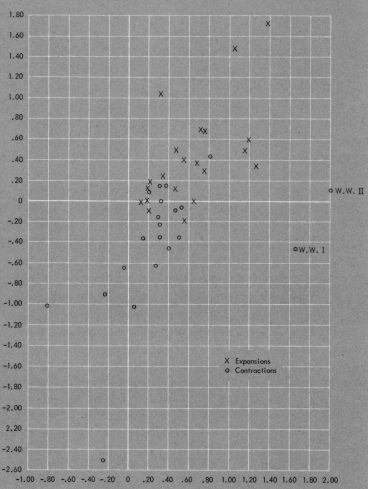

Panel C

Change per month in Index of Wholesale Prices
as per cent of average Index in cycle

X Expansions
o Contractions

Change per month in money stock as per cent of average stock in cycle

133

nominal income, as documented in Figure 4, which shows moving standard deviations of the rate of change for both the quantity of money and nominal income. This is a particular manifestation of the relations summarized in point 1.

3. *Timing of monetary changes.* Over cyclical periods, peaks and troughs in the rate of change in money tend to precede in time the dates designated by the National Bureau as cyclical peaks and troughs and also, though by a much smaller margin, peaks and troughs in the rate of change in nominal income. The leads are so long, relative to the Bureau dates, that the average cyclical pattern of money could be described as inverted, i.e., as showing a declining rate of change during cyclical expansions, a rising rate of change during cyclical contractions. However, evidence for individual cycles demonstrates that interpreting the money series as conforming positively with a lead fits the data far better than interpreting the series as conforming invertedly. For example, the dispersion (as measured by the standard deviation) of the leads and lags is uniformly and substantially lower when the money series is treated as conforming positively.

4. *Direction of influence in cyclical periods.* As for secular periods, there are influences running both from money to business and from business to money. A number of pieces of evidence combine to suggest that the influences running from money to business are highly important in all cyclical fluctuations and dominant in major ones (for a summary of evidence on this and the preceding point, see my contribution to NBER Annual Report for 1964).

5. *Interest rates* clearly play an important role in affecting both the quantity of money people wish to hold and the quantity of money available to be held for given amounts of high-powered money; and in transmitting the influence of monetary changes through the credit market. Yet, as an empirical matter, there is a much looser relation between either the level of interest rates or their rates of change, on the one hand, and rates of change in nominal income, output, and prices, on the other, than between

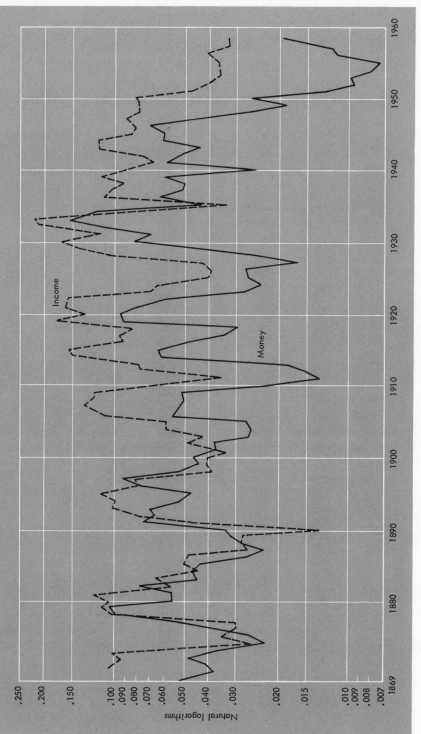

Figure 4. Moving Standard Deviation of Annual Rates of Change in Money, (M_2) 1869-1958, and in Nominal Income, 1871-1958, 4-Term Series. (*Source:* Friedman and Schwartz, "Money and Business Cycles," *Review of Economics and Statistics,* Supplement: Feb. 1963, p. 41.)

the rate of change in the quantity of money and these same magnitudes.[5]

Presumably, the loose relations partly reflect the complex ways in which interest rates interact in the monetary sector, partly the nonmonetary forces affecting interest rates. Whether or not interest rates are regarded as the primary channel through which monetary effects occur, they are a less accurate and stable indicator of the pressure being exerted by monetary magnitudes than is the rate of change in the quantity of money.

6. *Effect of prior price experience.* On a more sophisticated level, recent price experience has an important effect on (1) the precise relation between money and nominal income (i.e., the behavior of velocity); (2) the behavior of rates of interest; (3) the division of a change in nominal income between output and price change. Although these effects are to be expected on theoretical grounds, we have been able to identify them clearly in the observed data only in the past few months, so the results that follow are still highly tentative.

6.1. *Price behavior and velocity.* When prices have recently (i.e., over the past several cyclical phases, say, on the average, five years or so) been accelerating (i.e., rising at an increasing rate, or falling at a decreasing rate), this tends to produce a rise in velocity which reinforces the price acceleration; and conversely when prices have been decelerating. The reason, presumably, is that acceleration of prices leads to widespread ex-

---

[5] To illustrate, here are a few simple correlations between rates of change in various magnitudes based on phase averages for 1878-1961 (like those plotted in Figures 1 and 2):

Variable	Correlation Coefficient of Variable in First Column with Rate of Change in		
	Nominal Income	*Real Income*	*Implicit Prices*
Rate of change in M_2	.88	.70	.79
Call Interest rate	.69	.45	.70
Commercial paper rate	.65	.42	.66
Long-term bond yield	.24	−.12	.47

pectations of a higher rate of price rise, which, in turn, reduces the real quantity of money demanded.

6.2. *Price behavior and interest rates.* When prices have recently been accelerating, there is a delayed effect on rates of interest, which tend to rise subsequent to an acceleration, and to fall subsequent to a deceleration. The reason is that expectations of higher rates of price rise make demanders of loanable funds willing to pay higher rates and suppliers unwilling to lend except at higher rates. The reason for a delay in the effect is that the initial acceleration of prices is associated with a more rapid rate of monetary expansion which, through the liquidity effect, tends to depress interest rates, offsetting the opposite effect of changed price expectations.

This phenomenon, which is hard to extract from U.S. data because of the small amplitude of rates of price change, shows up clearly in international comparisons. Contrary to the naïve expectation based on a stable liquidity preference function in nominal terms, interest rates tend to be highest in countries experiencing the most rapid rates of growth in the quantity of money and in prices, and lowest in countries experiencing the slowest rates of growth in both.

6.3. *Price vs. output change.* When prices have recently been rising at a rapid rate, a larger fraction of any increase in nominal income will take the form of a price rise and a smaller fraction the form of an output rise than when prices have recently been stable or declining or rising at a slow rate. Again, this phenomenon shows up in a gross way internationally in the recessions that have followed attempts to taper off rapid inflations.

7. *International.* U.S. prices have been closely linked with foreign prices, when adjustment is made for exchange rate changes (see Chart 63, pp. 680-81 of *A Monetary History*, and attendant discussion).

8. *Supply of money.* Over long periods, the major factor accounting, in an arithmetic sense, for changes in the quantity of money has been changes in the quantity of high-powered

money (what Brunner and Meltzer call the monetary base).[6] Changes in the public's ratio of deposits to currency and in the banks' ratio of deposit liabilities to reserves in high-powered money have played only a minor and supplementary role.

Cagan has recently demonstrated that over cycles, the two ratios play a much more important role, particularly the deposit-currency ratio. This ratio has had a highly regular cyclical pattern. Cagan concludes that interest rates have played only a minor role in cyclical fluctuations in the rate of change of money. As I understand Brunner and Meltzer's results, they appear to attribute somewhat more significance to interest rates, yet they too find that variations in the monetary base are far more important.

8.1. *Controlling the quantity of money.* The studies by Brunner and Meltzer, Meigs, Dewald, and Cagan have all documented the fact that the links connecting Federal Reserve actions and the quantity of money are sufficiently rigid over short periods so that the Reserve System can, if it wishes, determine the rate of change of the quantity of money within fairly narrow limits and with relatively short lags.

B. MAJOR GENERALIZATIONS ABOUT POLICY EPISODES

9. *Inflationary policies.* Monetary developments in the United States favorable to or producing significant inflation have occurred predominantly in wartime or immediately thereafter.

9.1. *Wartime.* The five major wars in our history (the Revolution, War of 1812, Civil War, World War I, and World War II) have been accompanied by sharp rises in both the quantity of money and in prices—a manyfold rise in the Revolution, roughly a doubling in prices in the other wars. The minor wars (Mexican, Spanish-American, Korean) were accompanied

[6 High-powered money is currency held by the public plus currency held by commercial banks plus deposits liabilities of Federal Reserve Banks. In other words, it is the kind of money that can be used as bank reserves. It is called "high-powered" because for each dollar held by a bank as reserves, the bank can have a number of dollars of deposit liabilities.]

by developments in the same direction but of much smaller magnitude. For wartime itself, the inflation cannot clearly be designated a "mistake." The printing of money was a means of imposing a tax to finance the war and may well have been the least bad of the alternatives readily available for the purpose. My own judgment is that it was generally a desirable component of wartime taxation but (a) was relied on to a greater extent than desirable, (b) perhaps more important, was used inefficiently, a large part of the proceeds going to nongovernmental uses.

9.2. *Postwar episodes.* Postwar inflation was experienced only after World Wars I and II, to a far greater extent after World War I than after World War II (if we roughly correct the price indexes for World War II for the bias introduced by price control). After both wars, the reason was the same: the maintenance by the monetary authorities of artificially low official interest rates, something which was not easily feasible after prior wars because of the absence of an explicit central bank. After both wars, this was a mistake of policy, was recognized as a mistake at the time by many of the leading figures in the Reserve System, and even more widely after the event. It was excused by Treasury pressure, which certainly played a role but after both wars only reinforced the general policy view within the System.

9.3. *Peacetime.* The only peacetime periods showing anythink like comparable price rises were the early 1850's, after the gold discoveries in California, and 1896-1913, as part of a world-wide price rise reflecting gold discoveries and improvement in technical processes for extracting gold. Both involved much slower rates of price rise than did the wartime episodes.

10. *Deflationary policies.* With the exceptions just noted, all other important monetary disturbances in peacetime in the United States have been deflationary—in my opinion, precisely because the wartime episodes produced such fear of inflation as to lead to a peacetime bias in the opposite direction. This historical fact is of the very greatest importance. On the world scene, the reverse is likely true—that major disturbances have been inflationary. These, plus the war episodes, have led to a widespread

belief that the major problem for U.S. monetary policy is the avoidance of inflation. That may well be true for the future, and it is my own belief that it is likely to be, yet it is worth emphasizing that such a conclusion cannot be derived from past U.S. experience; on the contrary, it involves asserting that the future will differ in this respect from the past.

To document this generalization, I shall simply list what seem to me the major disturbances with only brief comments on some of them:

(i) Deflation after War of 1812;

(ii) Sharp deflation in early 1840's;

(iii) Post-Civil War deflation;

(iv) Silver agitation of the 'eighties and, particularly, early 'nineties. Feared as an engine for inflation, it actually produced deflation because it generated fears that the United States would devalue in terms of gold and hence discouraged capital inflows or stimulated capital outflows. Both the devices used to protect the gold standard and the effects of fears of devaluation have their precise counterparts today. In these respects, those years are far more like recent years than are the oft-cited 1920's;

(v) Banking panic of 1907;

(vi) Deflation of 1920-21. Most rapid rate of decline in prices in United States history. Sharpest decline in rate of monetary growth up to that point in United States history. Produced by overreaction by Federal Reserve to prior unduly expansionary policy, and undue delay in reversing monetary deflation;

(vii) Great Contraction of 1929-33 (fuller discussion in point 11 below);

(viii) Recession of 1937-38. Associated with sharp decline in rate of change in quantity of money produced largely by doubling of legal reserve requirements;

(ix) Brief expansion of 1958-60 and recession of 1960-61. Associated with sharpest decline in rate of change in money other than in major contractions (1873-79, early 1890's, 1907-08, 1920-21, 1929-33, 1937-38).

11. *The Great Contraction of 1929-33* has played such an important role in shaping attitudes that it deserves special attention. Five myths in particular have developed about it: (1) that it was a reaction to prior inflationary excesses; (2) that it was imported from abroad; (3) that it reflected the supreme weight attached to the gold standard vs. internal stability; (4) that "you can lead a horse to water but you can't make him drink" or "monetary policy is a string," i.e., that the System made reserves available but the banking system was unwilling or unable to use them; (5) that the System's policy was enforced by a shortage of "free gold" as a result of legal restrictions on the assets that could be used to back Reserve liabilities. All are clearly contradicted by the evidence.

The brute fact is that the severity of the contraction had its origin in the United States, was produced or at least greatly fostered by a monetary policy that permitted the quantity of money to decline by one-third, and that neither the preservation of the gold standard nor any other legal or institutional constraints enforced such a policy. A few remarks on these points are perhaps necessary.

11.1. *Alleged prior inflationary excesses.* The expansion of 1927-29 is unusual for its *deflationary*, not *inflationary* character. The quantity of money including commercial bank time deposits (M_2) grew less during that expansion than in any other cyclical expansion since 1869; currency plus demand deposits (M_1) showed practically no increase at all—the only expansion since our data start in 1915, except for 1958-60 of which this was true. Wholesale prices were unchanged during the expansion—the only expansion since 1894 except for 1958-60 in which wholesale prices did not rise appreciably. And what is true of 1927-29 is true to only a slightly lesser extent of the whole decade of the 'twenties after recovery from the 1920-21 contraction.

Moreover, one fascinating feature of U.S. business cycle experience is that there is no correlation between the amplitude of an expansion and the severity of the succeeding contraction, although there is a high correlation between the severity of a contraction and the amplitude of the succeeding expansion.

11.2 *Alleged importation of contraction from abroad.* The decisive evidence that the U.S. was an exporter and not an importer of deflation is the movement of gold: from 1929 to 1931 the U.S. gained gold. The U.S. gold stock rose by 15 per cent from August, 1929, to August, 1931. We not only sterilized this rise but actually went farther. The quantity of money, as measured by M_2, fell 10 per cent between these dates; as measured by M_1, by nearly 12 per cent. M_2 was 11.4 times the gold stock in August, 1929, 8.8 times in August, 1931; M_1 6.5 and 5.0 times, respectively.

As Governor Harrison [7] said in April, 1931, "it may be said that the United States has prevented the usual or normal effect of gold which has come to it. . . . The evils to the world of continued gold sterilization . . . are so great as to make desirable a careful scrutiny of Federal Reserve open market policy."

Of course, the effects abroad later reacted on the U.S. and intensified the domestic problems but there is no relevant sense in which the U.S. difficulties can be attributed to foreign developments—that shoe is on precisely the other foot.

11.3. *Alleged overemphasis on maintaining gold standard.* As the figures in the preceding paragraph make clear, up to August, 1931, there was certainly no threat to the gold standard. Also, there is no evidence that any leading participants in the formation of U.S. monetary policy thought that there was a threat, and no sign that a possible threat played any role whatever in the formation of U.S. monetary policy. The ratios cited above for August, 1931 (8.8 for M_2, 5.0 for M_1) were lower i.e., higher gold reserves) than in 1914 when the Federal Reserve was set up, when the ratios were 10.8 for M_2 and 7.6 for M_1, drastically lower than in August, 1920, when they were 13.6 and 9.2, and of course, than they are now, 21.6 and 11.7.

The System's reaction to Britain's departure from gold in September, 1931, did reflect the importance attached to remaining on the gold standard and is correctly interpreted as showing the greater weight attached to that objective than to internal

[7 George Harrison, Governor of Federal Reserve Bank of New York, 1929-1940. The title of the chief operating officer of the Federal Reserve Banks was changed from Governor to President in the Banking Act of 1935.]

stability. However, important as the action taken in September, 1931, by the System in response to Britain's departure from gold undoubtedly was, because it was positive and dramatic (sharp rises in the discount rate), it has been attributed even more importance than it deserves. The basic direction of Federal Reserve policy had already been set by that time, and the fundamental mistake already made.

11.4. *Alleged commercial bank unwillingness or inability to use reserves.* Whatever may be the merits or demerits of the excess reserves argument for the later 1930's, it had no relevance to the course of the contraction itself. Excess reserves did not begin to emerge until mid-1932. The problem earlier was to provide reserves to banks that were being forced to contract by a shortage of bank reserves, not to induce the banks to expand when they possessed ample reserves.

11.5. *The alleged "free gold" problem.* This was a rationalization for Federal Reserve policy developed after the event, not a reason for the policy followed, as we demonstrate at length in our *Monetary History.*

11.6. *The decline in the quantity of money.* This decline, the largest in the U.S. record, was produced, in the first instance, by the effects of bank failures and the attendant attempt of the public to convert deposits into currency. But this attempt reduced the quantity of money only because the Reserve System failed to provide sufficient high-powered money to accommodate the changed desires. Had the System done so, as many within the System urged at the time, the failures, even if they had occurred, would not have appreciably reduced the money stock. In addition, the failures would never have risen to the level they did if the System had provided the high-powered money. A major source of bank weakness was the decline in the price of bonds held by banks as a secondary reserve, including U.S. bonds, produced by the desperate attempts of banks to replenish their reserves as they were drawn down by depositors, in a setting in which the total amount of high-powered money was inadequate. The provision of additional reserve funds would certainly have prevented this train of events.

12. *Formation of policy.* In my view, the most important single lesson from history for the formation of monetary policy is the desirability of having quantitative, unambiguous, and widely accepted indicators of monetary conditions and targets of monetary policy. Among the alternatives available, the evidence suggests that the quantity of money, or the rate of change in it, should be either the, or at the least, one of the key indicators and targets. And this is true regardless of whether monetary policy actions are believed to operate primarily through market interest rates and credit conditions or not.

12.1. *"Money" and "credit."* A major source of difficulty in monetary management has been the failure to distinguish between the problems connected with the quantity of money and those connected with conditions on the credit market. The two are undoubtedly interconnected especially in a system like ours where the major component of the money supply consists of the liabilities of lending and investing institutions. Changes in the quantity of money have effects on interest rates and credit market conditions; and conversely, changes in the credit market affect the quantity of money. Yet money and credit are two different magnitudes or sets of magnitudes; for example, the deposit liabilities of commercial banks are the bulk of the stock of money; their assets in the form of loans and investments are a minor fraction of the total outstanding volume of credit.

The reason emphasis on credit conditions has been a source of difficulties is twofold. First, the specific features of credit conditions examined have time and again turned out to be misleading indicators of monetary conditions as judged after the event by consequences. As recent studies by Leonall Anderson and Jules Levine have shown, there often is little relation between credit conditions and the rate of monetary growth. Second, it has so far proved impossible to find a satisfactory objective quantitative measure of credit conditions that would command widespread acceptance by the participants in the formation of monetary policy and be interpreted by all of them alike. This second point is part of a broader issue that deserves separate attention.

12.2. *Vagueness of monetary policy discussion.* In studying the formation of monetary policy in this country, I have been much impressed by the vagueness of the discussion and the extent to which participants talk at cross-purposes. The discussion teems with undefined terms: "ease" and "tightness"; "sloppy market"; "disorderly market"; "redundancy of credit"; "leaning against the wind"; "productive use of credit." Similarly, the policy directives issued to the New York trading desk by the FOMC [Federal Open Market Committee] are qualitative in character: "open market operations shall be conducted with a view to maintaining about the same conditions in the money market as have prevailed in recent weeks, while accommodating moderate expansion in aggregate bank reserves." The staff of the New York trading desk and of the FOMC have therefore constructed a terminology to interpret these instructions. Money market conditions are described in terms of a degree of pressure in the money market. Money market pressure is said to increase when short-term interest rates rise, free reserves decline, and borrowings, reserve deficiencies, and the discount rate increase. Opposite changes are said to reduce market pressure. The effect is unintentionally to delegate the actual formation of the policy to the people who are supposed simply to be carrying out the policy; to give an undue role to inertia; and to make it difficult or impossible after the event to judge whether the actual policy followed was in accord with either what was intended or required.

The most dramatic example, in my opinion, is 1929-33. It seems to me literally true that the monetary collapse of that period would have been impossible if (a) there had existed current figures on the quantity of money published on a periodical basis, even if only semiannually; (b) it had been recognized that the behavior of the quantity of money was at least one among a number of indicators of the state of monetary conditions. It would have been impossible for leading figures in the formation of monetary policy to congratulate themselves, as they did, that the Reserve System was following an "easy" policy if they had been aware that the quantity of money was declining at unprecedented rates, and had regarded this as revelant.

12.3. *Importance of current figures.* It is not, I believe, too much to say that one of the two most important guarantees (the other is FDIC) against the recurrence of a monetary experience such as 1929-33, or even 1920-21, or 1937-38, is simply the availability and regular publication of estimates of the quantity of money, plus the fact that some attention is now paid to this magnitude in the formation of policy, even if only as one among a number of indicators of the state of monetary conditions. The experience of 1959-60 is a recent example.

13. *Tools of policy.* Experience suggests that open market operations are the most effective and sensitive tool of policy available.

13.1. *Reserve requirement changes* have proved to be a crude tool whose short-term effects are hard to predict. The 1936-37 episode is the most striking.

13.2. *Qualitative measures* of credit control, such as discretion in rediscounting, "direct pressure," "moral suasion," and the like, have uniformly been ineffective. If past experience is any guide, the present so-called "voluntary" control of foreign loans, though more specific and perhaps armed with more teeth than earlier ventures, will not have more than a temporary effect.

13.3. *The discount rate* has at times been highly effective (e.g., in January, 1920, and in September, 1931), but it has been a discontinuous and crude tool compared to open market operations.

13.4. *Maximum time deposit* rates have introduced erratic behavior into the division between time and demand deposits. I know of no evidence that they serve any useful positive function whatsoever.

II. Relevance of Lessons of Monetary History to Present Situation

In considering the implications of past experience for current policy, I shall concentrate on the general stance of policy over the past few years, not on the issues associated with week-to-week or month-to-month changes. In addition, I shall concentrate on the quantitative aspect of policy as reflected in the rate of monetary growth, not on structural problems.

14. *Recent behavior of money stock.* The quantity of money as measured by M_2 has been growing for the past three years (August, 1962-August, 1965) at the average annual rate (continuously compounded) of 8.3 per cent per year; as measured by M_1, of 3.7 per cent per year. Both are relatively high rates in the light of past experience, especially the rate of growth of M_2. If we exclude the wartime inflations, the average rate of growth of M_2 was 4.7 per cent per year from the cycle phase 1873-78 to the phase 1960-61; of M_1, 2.8 per cent per year from 1920-21 to 1960-61, and wholesale prices, with the same exclusions, showed no net change over either the longer or shorter period.

The discrepancy between the two rates of monetary growth during the past three years is larger than for any comparable period since 1915 when reliable figures for M_1 first are available. The reason is the successive rises in the maximum rate payable on time deposits. These have made the rate of rise of M_2 higher, and of M_1 lower, than the rate of rise of an economically homogeneous monetary total.

The rate of monetary growth has been relatively stable by past standards. Though I shall argue below that the rate of growth has been somewhat higher than desirable, let me emphasize at the outset that a higher rate than prevailed from 1958 to 1960 was eminently desirable. With respect to the level and even more to the stability of the rate of monetary growth, monetary policy in the past few years has been excellent and deserves much of the credit for the long-sustained economic advance.

15. *Price implication of continuation of present rate of monetary growth.* Past experience suggests that a continuation of the present rate of growth of M_2, or of a somewhat lower rate but with less of a gap between the rate of growth of M_1 and M_2, is not indefinitely sustainable without a price rise. Excluding World Wars I and II and the years immediately thereafter, there

are only three periods since 1879 when M_2 rose at the rate of 8 per cent or more for more than two years: 1879-83, 1898-1902, 1934-36. In the first case, wholesale prices rose 12 per cent, in the second, 21 per cent, in the third, nearly 8 per cent. The only other time when prices rose as much in a comparable period was during the Korean War. Again, excluding the World Wars, the only period since 1915 when M_1 rose at a more rapid rate for more than two years is 1934-37.

Three further points need comment: (1) why there has been so little price rise so far; (2) the danger of acceleration of price rise; (3) the effect on rate of output rise.

15.1. *Why so little price rise so far?* Item 1 points out that the rate of monetary change has been more closely correlated with the rate of change of nominal income than with the rate of change of either prices or real income separately. The relation between the rate of change of money and of nominal income in 1962, 1963, 1964, and, so far as we can tell, 1965 as well, is entirely in line with the long-term relation, as is clear from the following comparison between the actual rates of change in nominal income in these years and the rates of change estimated from a single simple regression fitted to annual data for the 94 years from 1870-1963 using M_2 as the concept of money:

Rate of Change of Nominal Income
(per cent per year) [8]

	Computed from Regression	Actual
1962	5.9	6.9
1963	6.6	5.0
1964	6.4	6.7
1965	7.2	7.6

[8] Concept of nominal income is net national product. Rates of change assume continuous compounding, i.e., differences between natural logarithms of successive annual observations. For 1965, computed by assuming rates of change from 1964 to average of first two quarters of 1965 will continue for rest of year.

The rate of price change, on the other hand, has been less, especially for wholesale prices, than would have been predicted from a simple correlation with the rate of change of money for the same 94 years, as the following comparison shows:

Rate of Change
(per cent per year)

| | Implicit Price Index | | Wholesale Prices | |
	Computed	Actual	Computed	Actual
1962	1.57	1.09	1.55	0.30
1963	1.90	1.28	2.07	−0.30
1964	1.80	1.67	1.92	0.20
1965	2.16	1.70	2.48	1.29

However, item 6.3 points out that the division of a change in nominal income between output and prices has been systematically affected by prior price experience: the lower the earlier rate of price rise, the smaller the fraction of an increase in nominal income absorbed by a price rise. And the prior years, from 1958 through 1961, were years of relatively little price change. Perhaps even more important, they were years when the rate of rise of prices had declined from a higher level and was continuing to decline. This seems like the most plausible explanation for the relatively low rate of price change in 1962-65. To put it in non-statistical terms: by instilling expectations that prices would be relatively stable, the favorable price experience of 1958-61 established a setting in which an unusually large part of increases in nominal income would take the form of output increases.[9]

But this favorable situation is temporary. The decline in the rate of price rise has ceased and has been replaced by an acceleration, which brings us to our next point.

15.2. *The danger of price acceleration.* Points 6.1 and 6.3

[9] Unfortunately, we are not yet in a position to test this explanation quantitatively. So far, our analysis of the effect of prior price behavior has been based on average values for cyclical phases, not data for individual years.

combine to suggest that the cessation of the deceleration of the price rise, let alone its apparent replacement by an acceleration, will tend to mean, first, a larger rate of rise in nominal income for the same rate of rise in the money stock; second, the absorption of a larger fraction of this rise in nominal income by price rises. The two combined spell a real danger of accelerated price rise if the present rate of monetary expansion continues, and the figures just cited show some signs that such a tendency is already under way.

Two qualifications are in order to avoid misunderstandings. First, I am speaking in terms of the next several years, not of a few months, and the suggested outcome is not inconsistent with temporary interruptions. Second, in speaking of an acceleration, I do not mean an indefinite one. On the contrary, to the present rate of monetary expansion indefinitely continued, there corresponds a relatively stable and fairly moderate rate of price rise— to judge from past experience, in the neighborhood of 2 to 4 per cent per year. The point is that this rate is higher than the present rate, and that the process of attaining it would involve initial overshooting and hence a temporarily still higher rate of price increase.

15.3. *The effect on rate of output rise.* The preceding paragraph implies also that continuation of the present rate of monetary growth would mean a slower rate of growth in output than in the past three years. The only way to maintain the rate of growth of output would be to increase still higher the rate of monetary growth, but this would intensify pressures on prices.

16. *Implications for interest rates of continuation of present rate of monetary growth.* Point 6.2 suggests that the continuation of the present rate of monetary growth will also make for higher interest rates, as changed price expectations overcome the liquidity effect of rapid monetary growth. This effect, past experience suggests, will occur later than the price acceleration. Also, because of the many other factors affecting interest rates, one can have less confidence for interest rates than for prices that this effect will dominate.

17. *Implications for balance of payments of continuation of*

present rate of monetary growth. The interest rate effects of point 16 would tend to improve our payments balance on capital account; the price effects of point 15 to worsen it on current account. Point 7 implies that the price effects are likely to dominate. But, of course, what matters is not price behavior in the U.S. alone but the behavior of U.S. prices relative to foreign prices. If (and this is a very big if) prices abroad were to be stable, then the U.S. could not for long continue the present rate of monetary expansion and also maintain the present levels of exchange rates. On the other hand, if prices abroad were to rise more rapidly than in the U.S., the present rate of monetary expansion could continue along with an improvement in the balance of payments. Since what is at question is the monetary policy of other countries, past history can give no definite answer. Its key lesson on this point is that, *so long as exchange rates are fixed,* the money stock must adjust itself sooner or later so as to keep prices in the U.S. in line with prices abroad. There is much leeway for a few years, especially for a country for which foreign trade is as unimportant as it is for the U.S. and which has such large reserves, but there is very little leeway in the course of a decade or so.

18. *Problems in reducing rate of monetary growth.* Given the objectives of stable prices and maintenance of present exchange rates, the preceding paragraphs suggest the desirability of reducing the rate of monetary growth to a level that is indefinitely sustainable without price rises (which past experience suggests would be somewhere around 4 to 6 per cent a year for M_2 and whatever rate for M_1 accompanies this, when there are no disturbances such as changes in maximum interest rates on time deposits). While this does seem to me desirable, it should be emphasized that the immediate effects will be adverse. There is no way of getting rid of the after-effects of the high rate of monetary growth of the recent past. As indicated in point 15.3, these delayed effects are likely to mean a decline in the rate of growth of output—a recession or pause or slowdown or tapering off or whatever word one wants to use—even if the present rate of monetary growth continues. A reduced rate of monetary growth will intensify this effect. Moreover, a larger fraction of monetary

growth will be absorbed by price rises than would have been the case if that lower rate of monetary growth had prevailed all along. Just as the relative stagnation of 1958-61 created conditions favorable to rapid growth in 1962-64 with relatively stable prices, so the recent rapid expansion and the beginning of rising prices create conditions that are unfavorable to rapid growth without price rises in the coming years.

An illustration of the problem may be found in the recent past. It would have been highly desirable in 1959 and early 1960 to have increased the rate of monetary growth. It was highly desirable to do so when it was done in mid-1960. But when it was done, it was not maintained, and in early 1962, there was a shift to a lower rate of monetary growth. There was a corresponding decline in the rate of growth of output during the third and fourth quarters of 1962 and the first quarter of 1963. The subsequent increase in the rate of monetary growth beginning August, 1962, was desirable but was overdone. A moderate reduction in the rate of monetary growth was desirable a year or more ago and it is desirable today. The reduction should not, as has so often occurred in the past, be overdone. However, even if it is not overdone, the initial effects will be adverse, as in 1962, and more adverse than the ultimate effect will prove to be if that rate is sustained (this is the import of point 6). These initial effects will create great pressure for a reversal of policy, and the pressure will be much harder to withstand if the reduction in the rate of monetary growth has been overdone.

My conclusion is, therefore, that applying the lessons of the past to the present situation calls for a moderate reduction in the rate of monetary growth. In principle, the best procedure would be to make the reduction by steps to the rate around which it is desired to hold it at least for some time. However, we are probably sufficiently close to the desired rate that it would be adequate to make the reduction in one step. A partial compromise would be to choose as the new target a rate close to the top of the desirable range of 4 to 6 per cent for M_2.

Current Monetary Policy [1]

CHAPTER FIVE The present note deals with the period from August, 1965, to April, 1966, the latest month for which data are available as this is written, and is primarily in the nature of an addendum to and updating of an earlier memorandum [see preceding essay].

1. Recent Behavior of the Money Stock

As the following table shows, the rate of growth of the money stock has sharply accelerated since August, 1965, most notably for the narrower definition of money.

As I pointed out in the earlier memorandum, "the discrepancy between the two rates of monetary growth during the past three years is larger than for

[1 Of the four items in this chapter, the first is a memorandum prepared for Consultant's Meeting, Board of Governors, Federal Reserve System, June 15, 1966; the next three are columns published in *Newsweek* Magazine.]

	Annual Rate of Change (continuously compounded) from	
	August, 1962 to August, 1965	August, 1965 to April, 1966
M_1 (Currency plus demand deposits adjusted)	3.6	7.6
M_2 (M_1 plus time deposits in commercial banks)	7.9	9.5

any comparable period since 1915 when reliable figures for M_1 first are available. The reason is the successive rises in the maximum rate payable on time deposits." Apparently, the further rise in the maximum rate in December, 1965, had a less drastic effect than earlier rises, so the two rates of growth have converged sharply.

By this criterion, monetary policy, which was relatively easy from 1962-65 compared with past experience, has become easier still.

In addition to becoming easier, monetary policy has been much more erratic. In the earlier memorandun, I emphasized the relative stability in the rate of monetary growth. The period since then shows a very different behavior. A very rapid rate of rise toward the end of 1965 was followed by a drastic tapering off and, indeed, absolute decline in the weekly figures in early 1966. Another spurt at a very high rate followed. Recently, the weekly figures show another absolute decline, but in light of the recent erratic behavior of the money stock, this can as yet not be regarded as more than another temporary perturbation.[2]

2. Price Implications of Behavior of Money Stock

In the earlier memorandum, I stated that "past experience suggests that a continuation of the present rate of growth of M_2, or of a somewhat lower rate but with less of a gap between the

[2 In fact, it was the early stage of a sharp reduction in the rate of monetary growth. See next item.]

rate of growth of M_1 and M_2, is not indefinitely sustainable without a price rise." After pointing out that one reason why the price rise up to that time had been so moderate was the 1958-1962 period of relative stagnation, I went on to say that there was "a real danger of accelerated price rise if the present rate of monetary expansion continues, and the figures . . . show some signs that such a tendency is already under way."

Since the rate of monetary expansion has actually been accelerated rather than simply continued, even greater pressure has been put on prices. Wholesale prices rose at the annual rate of 2.5 per cent from August, 1964, to August, 1965, at the annual rate of 3.7 per cent from May, 1965, to April, 1966. Consumer prices have been showing a similar pattern.

In the prior memorandum, I concluded that indefinite continuation of the then rate of monetary expansion would mean an ultimate rate of price rise in the neighborhood of 2 to 4 per cent per year, but that this ultimate rate would be reached only after prices had increased at a still higher rate for some time. Indefinite continuation of the rate of monetary expansion since August, 1965, would mean an ultimate rate of price rise of around 3.5 to 5.5 per cent a year. Again this rate would be reached only after a temporarily still higher rate.[3]

3. Interest Rates

In the earlier memorandum, I wrote "the continuation of the present rate of monetary growth will also make for higher interest rates, as changed price expectations overcome the liquidity effects of rapid monetary growth," though, I went on to say, "because of the many other factors affecting interest rates, one can have less confidence for interest rates than for prices that this effect will dominate."

[3] It may be of interest to report here more recent figures extending those given in my earlier memorandum on the rise in nominal income and prices to be expected from the observed rates of monetary rise. The following table compares the actual rates of change in nominal income and prices with the rates estimated from a single simple regression fitted to annual data for the ninety-four years from 1870-1963. In each of the three regressions used, the independent variable is the year-to-year rate of change in the money stock (defined as M_2):

In fact the accelerated rise in the money stock has been accompanied by the consequences suggested—a more rapid rise in interest rates. I realize that this assertion goes against the common belief that a rapid expansion in money produces a decline rather than a rise in interest rates. This common belief is correct in the very short run, as the next paragraph will illustrate, but it is precisely the reverse of the truth for periods of any length, as I shall illustrate more fully in section 7, below.

In addition to the more rapid rise from August, 1965, to April, 1966, as a whole, there was a bulge in interest rates in February and March, 1966, that in my opinion reflects, with a slight lag, the liquidity effects of the bulge in the money stock in December and January.

The extraordinarily rapid rate of increase in available reserves of banks in December led them to seek out investments, make advance commitments, and the like, which reduced pressure on medium- and long-term interest rates in early January. But these commitments became embarrassing when the Fed reversed course and drained banks of liquidity in January. The result was that banks had to unload investments to meet commitments, which depressed security prices, pushed up interest rates, and produced many of the symptoms of financial crisis in late February. The reversal of Fed policy at the end of January and the rapid rate

Rate of Change (Percentage per Year, continuously compounded)

Year	Nominal Income		Implicit Price Index		Wholesale Prices	
	Computed from regression	Actual	Computed	Actual	Computed	Actual
1962	5.9	6.9	1.57	1.09	1.55	0.30
1963	6.4	5.0	1.90	1.28	2.07	−0.30
1964	6.4	6.7	1.80	1.67	1.92	0.20
1965	7.6	7.5	2.35	1.79	2.76	1.97
1966 *	7.9	8.4	2.52	2.40	3.02	3.78

* Computed by assuming rate of change from first quarter 1965 to first quarter 1966 will continue throughout 1966.

It will be noted that the excellent agreement for nominal income has continued. More important, however, the actual price changes have been catching up with the computed ones, as the earlier memorandum argued was likely.

of rise in the money stock in March eased the money market and overcame the crisis. Interest rates on governments then declined from their February peaks. Since early April, they have again resumed their gradual upward movement in response, I believe, to the cumulative effects of the accelerated monetary growth. The recent reduction in the quantity of money may, however, produce another temporary stringency and another bulge in rates like that of February and March.[4]

Had monetary growth been precisely what it was in the past eight months, but had it proceeded steadily instead of erratically, interest rates would also have behaved more steadily. They would probably be now roughly at their present level, but they would not first have risen above that level, then declined, then risen.

4. Balance of Payments

In the earlier memorandum, I wrote "if (and this is a very big if) prices abroad were to be stable, then the U.S. could not for long continue the present rate of monetary expansion and also maintain the present levels of exchange rates. On the other hand, if prices abroad were to rise more rapidly than in the U.S., the present rate of monetary expansion could continue along with an improvement in the balance of payments." The acceleration of monetary expansion has put still further pressure on the balance of payments. The result has been that despite the introduction of informal yet fairly effective exchange controls, and despite continuation of rising prices abroad, the U.S. balance of payments has shown no appreciable improvement. Indeed, on current account, it has deteriorated.

5. Desirable Current Monetary Policy

The conclusion of the earlier memorandum was "that applying the lessons of the past to the present situation calls for a

[4 Such a bulge did in fact occur, culminating in the so-called credit "crunch" in the fall of 1966.]

moderate reduction in the rate of monetary growth. In principle, the best procedure would be to make the reduction by steps to the rate around which it is desired to hold it at least for some time. However, we are probably sufficiently close to the desired rate that it would be adequate to make the reduction in one step. A partial compromise would be to choose as the new target a rate close to the top of the desirable range of 4 to 6 per cent for M_2."

Actual policy has moved in precisely the opposite direction. And the results, as we have seen, have been precisely those to be expected: increased inflationary pressure, higher interest rates, continued or intensified balance of payments pressure.

If it was desirable last September to reduce the rate of growth of the money stock, it is surely even more essential to do so now. However, there is this difference. We have now moved even farther away from the desirable range of 4 to 6 per cent for M_2, and while I still am inclined to recommend that we move to the top of the range in one step, I am no longer as confident that this is the proper policy as I was last September. A case could be made for making the decline in two or more steps. My main reason for believing that the case is not strong is that monetary expansion has been so erratic in the past eight months that a one-step movement would be a smaller shock than the markets have several times experienced.

Whether in one or several steps, however, a reduction in the monetary growth rate seems to me essential if prices are to be kept reasonably stable and the present exchange rates are to be maintained.

Let me repeat, however, the warning in my earlier memorandum: "A moderate reduction in the rate of monetary growth was desirable a year or more ago and is desirable today. *The reduction should not, as has so often occurred in the past, be overdone*" (italics added).[5]

6. Consequences of Reducing Rate of Monetary Growth

Policy actions should not be undertaken without recognition of their adverse as well as favorable consequences. If the recom-

[5 Unfortunately, as stressed in the next item, the reduction was overdone.]

mended measures are taken, they are almost certain to produce, after some delay, an economic recession evidenced in a growth in unemployment and a decline in the rate of growth of output. That recession will be accompanied, as in 1957-58, by rising prices.

Given our past mistakes, I see no way of avoiding such a result and at the same time stemming inflationary pressure. In principle, there may exist a delicate tapering off of monetary growth that might enable us to approach asymptotically a stable price path without intervening recession. But even if such a strategy exists, which is by no means certain, I believe we do not know enough to achieve it.

As I argued in the earlier memorandum, if we continue the present monetary growth rate, price rises will accelerate, the rate of growth of output will decline, and a recession will occur. The only way to avoid such an outcome is to increase still more the rate of monetary growth. That would postpone a recession but only at the cost of further price rises. As these are incorporated in the public's price anticipations, a still more severe recession would then be required to change anticipations.

In my opinion, there is no perpetual trade off between inflation and unemployment. The trade off is between *acceleration* of inflation and unemployment, which means that the real trade off is between unemployment now and unemployment later. The high level of unemployment from 1958 to 1962, though undesirable and unnecessary, nonetheless had the side effect of creating a climate of anticipations favorable to the rapid growth and falling unemployment since. Unfortunately, we have dissipated this favorable effect by somewhat too high a rate of monetary growth since. As noted in the earlier memorandum, the change to a more expansionary monetary policy was highly desirable, but went too far. The result, as I have been emphasizing, has been an accumulation of inflationary pressures and a change in price anticipations that will return to plague us in the future and that will make higher unemployment at that time unavoidable.

The dilemma is that if the policy recommended in the preceding section is followed, and if it produces or is followed by a recession, there will be great pressure to reverse course and undertake rapid monetary expansion.[6] The result would be to start another round of inflationary pressure. Japan is an excellent example. It is now in the third such episode, each with a higher rate of price rise during successive expansions and also during successive recessions.

The correct policy, in my opinion, is to move to a sustainable rate of monetary growth and hold it there. As price anticipations are adjusted, recovery will set in without increased inflationary pressure. No other policy seems to me viable for more than a few years. Yet it will take both economic sophistication and real political courage to initiate this policy and even more to stick to it. The easy and tempting primrose path will be to postpone unpleasant adjustments to the future.

7. Why Has Monetary Expansion Accelerated?

In making these recommendations, I find myself extremely frustrated—as if I am not leaning against the wind, but spitting into it. There is and has been strong pressure toward inflation; monetary policy has been extremely expansive; there is therefore a clear case for restraint. Yet the opposite has happened. In the past eight months the quantity of money has been expanded at an even higher rate than earlier, though the earlier rate was already above that which is sustainable without inflation. Why? I intend this question to be serious, not merely rhetorical. I am frankly baffled. The Board can render great service to us as scholars and improve our capacity to offer sound counsel in the future, by helping us to understand the answer. The comments that follow are designed to stimulate such a response.

If I were to ask the members of the Board, or of the Open Market Committee, "Did you plan it that way? Did you intend

[6 Which is precisely what occurred. The too sharp reduction of monetary growth from April, 1966, to December, 1966, was followed by a slow-down in the economy, from roughly December, 1966, to mid-1967. This was met by unduly rapid monetary expansion, which terminated the slow-down, but at the cost of accelerating inflation. The Fed again reacted by slowing down, from about November, 1967, on, the rate of monetary expansion. As of this writing (April, 1968), it has this time not overdone the reduction. The next test will come if this deceleration of monetary growth produces a slowing down in the economy.]

currency plus demand deposits to grow at a rate of 7.6 per cent per year since last August? Or this total plus commercial bank time deposits to grow at a rate of 9.5 per cent?" I suspect the answer would be "no." If I asked, "Would you have preferred a slower rate of growth?," the answer would presumably be "yes." If I asked, "Could the System have made the rate lower than it was?," the answer would have to be "yes."

To the final question, "Why then did you not restrain the growth?," I can see only two plausible answers. One is, "We intended to and tried to, but were inefficient in achieving our objective." The other, and I suspect the one that would in fact be given, is "Restraining the growth in the money supply would have had other consequences that would have been seriously adverse. We had several targets or objectives in mind and, as it worked out, the best we could do on the money supply side, while not deviating too far from other objectives, was a 7.6 per cent rate of growth in M_1."

It is this answer which baffles me. What are the other consequences of, say, a 4 per cent instead of a 7.6 per cent growth rate in M_1 or a 6 per cent instead of a 9.5 per cent growth rate in M_2 that would have been seriously adverse? A financial panic? Inconceivable if the growth in the money supply had proceeded smoothly; entirely conceivable whatever the average rate of growth, if it had been highly erratic. Heavy unemployment? Hardly, in light of the inflationary pressure. Balance of payments problems? On the contrary, slower monetary growth would have eased the pressure.

The only consequence I can imagine that might be cited seriously is an undesired effect on interest rates. A lowered monetary growth rate, it might be argued, would have produced an even more rapid rise in interest rates, and the rise that occurred was as rapid as could be absorbed.

I wish to dwell somewhat more on this consequence because there seems to me such widespread misunderstanding about the relation between changes in the quantity of money and in interest rates. I do not myself see any harm in a still more rapid rise in interest rates, if that had been the outcome, but I shall do no more than mention that point. My main question is whether in fact a lower rate of monetary growth would have led to higher interest rates.

In discussing the bulge in interest rates in February-March, I have already noted that there is a short run tendency for acceleration in monetary growth to lower interest rates and retardation in monetary growth to raise them. This effect, which I shall call the liquidity effect, operates with a fairly brief lag and over a short period. Most contemporary discussion both recognizes this effect and takes it for granted that it is the only effect. That is a serious mistake. There are two other effects which run in the opposite direction, are longer lasting and, after a brief interval, dominate the liquidity effect. As a result, *the general tendency over longer periods is for acceleration of monetary growth to raise interest rates and for retardation to lower them*—precisely the opposite of the relation typically taken for granted.

The attached figure illustrates the positive relation between bank credit expansion and interest rates that is typical as an empirical matter. This figure plots for the post-accord period quarterly data on the rate of change of bank loans, and the Treasury bill rate. There is clearly a high positive correlation: high rates of loan expansion go along with high interest rates; low rates of loan expansion with low interest rates. The only substantial period that shows the negative relation most contemporary discussion takes for granted is mid-1955 to mid-1957, or two out of fifteen years. These movements in credit are themselves delayed reactions to changes in the rate of growth of the money stock: the credit changes lagging behind the monetary changes by about a year on the average. If we allow for this characteristic difference in timing, the changes in the quantity of money are also positively related to interest rates. These relations hold for other periods of U.S. history, for other countries, and for comparisons among countries. They are not a historical fluke.

What are the other effects that produce this positive relation? (1) The first is an income effect. An increased rate of monetary expansion produces an increased rate of rise in nominal income which increases the demand for loanable funds and also for money to hold, both of which offset the initial liquidity effect.

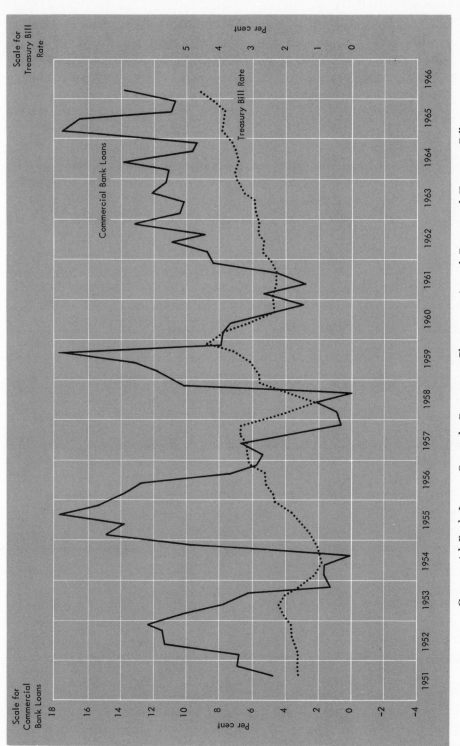

Commercial Bank Loans, Quarterly Percentage Changes at Annual Rates, and Treasury Bill Rate, Quarterly Averages, 1951 III–1966 I.

(2) The second is a price and price anticipations effect. Increased monetary growth raises prices, which reduces the *real* stock of money for any given nominal stock. More important, it affects anticipations of future rates of price rise. The higher the anticipated rates of price rise, the higher the nominal interest rate that borrowers are willing to pay and that lenders demand.[7]

As a practical matter, there is nothing wrong with looking at interest rates as an indicator of monetary ease or tightness, *provided* high interest rates are interpreted as a sign that money has been easy, and low interest rates are interpreted as a sign that money has been tight.

In terms of recent experience, if the growth rate since August, 1965, had been 4 per cent for M_1 instead of 7.6 per cent and 6 per cent for M_2 instead of 9.5 per cent, interest rates might have been somewhat higher than they were in September and October, 1965, but they would never have reached the levels they did in February and March, 1966, and they would now be lower than they are. Or, to put it in terms of the future, the surest way to prolong the rise in interest rates is to accelerate still further the rate of monetary expansion; the surest way to reverse the trend of interest rates is to reduce the rate of monetary expansion.

To return to the main question posed in this section, perhaps I have missed the point altogether and there is some other explanation than those I have given for the recent rapid rate of monetary expansion. I should certainly welcome any enlightenment on this issue.

[7] These are, of course, extremely dogmatic and oversimplified statements of these effects.

CURRENT MONETARY POLICY

Reprinted from *Newsweek*, Jan. 9, 1967.

I have been watching with increasing apprehension, concern and incredulity the behavior of the quantity of money over the past eight months. The Federal Reserve System clearly does not intend to produce a *serious* recession in 1967. Yet continuation of their present policy will make such an outcome all but inevitable.

The accompanying chart shows the reason for concern. It plots two monetary magnitudes: M_1, the total usually designated "the money supply" by the Fed; and M_2, a broader total that includes also time deposits at commercial banks. The striking feature of the chart is the sharp reversal in both totals in April 1966. Before then, both totals were growing rapidly. Since April, M_1 has actually declined—something it has rarely done except before and during severe recessions—and M_2 has grown at a sharply reduced rate. Since September, both totals have been declining.

This is the sharpest turnaround since the end of the war. Slower monetary growth was badly needed in order to stem inflation—but a good thing was carried too far.

Do Changes in the Quantity of Money Matter?

There is massive historical evidence that they do. *Every economic recession but one in the U.S. in the past century has been preceded by a decline in the rate of growth of the quantity of money.* And the sharper the decline, the more serious the subsequent recession—though this tendency is far from uniform.

Changes in monetary growth affect the economy only slowly— it may be six or twelve or eighteen months or even more before their effects are manifest. That is a major reason why the connection is easily overlooked.

Recent experience conforms to the historical record. Acceleration of monetary growth in 1962 was followed by economic expansion. The monetary growth rate was too high—but it took until 1965 for its cumulative effects to produce rising prices. The price rise started the Fed *talking* about the need for tighter money, but it *acted* in the opposite direction: monetary growth accelerated still more, intensifying inflationary pressure and producing the rapid price rises of recent months. The sharp braking of monetary growth in April 1966 has in turn only recently been showing up in spreading signs of pending recession.

Why Has the Fed Permitted the Quantity of Money to Behave So Erratically?

Primarily, I believe, because it has used misleading criteria of policy—it is inconceivable that the quantity of money as measured by M_1 could decline for eight months if the Fed had been determined to have it grow. It is as if a space vehicle took a fix on the wrong star. No matter how sensitive and sophisticated its guiding apparatus, it would go astray. Similarly, the men who guide the Fed have been going astray because they have been looking at interest rates and other measures of credit conditions rather than at the quantity of money.

Interest rates began rising in 1965 because of the sharp rise in

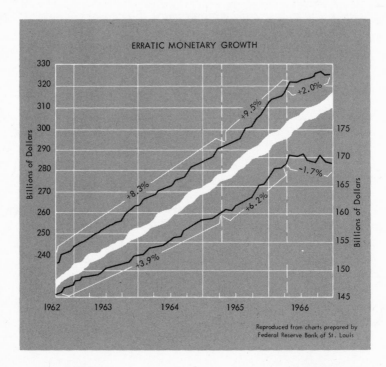

the demand for credit that accompanied the onset of inflation. The Fed slowed the rise by accelerating monetary growth—but the rates continued rising, and the Fed interpreted this as a sign that it had tightened, whereas in fact it had eased.

Similarly, interest rates are currently showing some weakness—because the demand for credit has been declining in response to monetary restriction since April 1966. Yet the Fed interprets the weakness as a sign that it has eased—whereas only the Fed's continued tightness prevents interest rates from falling more rapidly.

The Fed's erratic policy reflects also its failure to allow for the delay between its actions and their effects on the economy. Said Governor Robertson of the board in a recent speech: "Monetary policy will be formulated by the Federal Reserve, day by day, in the light of economic conditions *as they emerge*." This is a formula guaranteed to produce bad policy. If it is followed, the Fed will continue to step too hard on the brake until the recessionary effects are clear and unmistakable, and then will step too hard on the accelerator. Like a good duck hunter, the Fed should lead its target, not shoot where it now is.

What Policy Should the Fed Now Adopt?

It is almost surely too late to prevent a recession—that damage has already been done. It is not too late to prevent the recession from turning into a severe downturn. To that end, the Fed should at once act to increase the quantity of money at a rate of about 5 per cent per year for M_2. If the Fed adopted and persisted in such a policy, it could moderate the coming recession without paving the way for a new burst of inflation.

CURRENT MONETARY POLICY
Reprinted from *Newsweek*, Oct. 30, 1967.

Last January (NEWSWEEK, Jan. 9), I criticized the Federal Reserve Board for producing the sharpest turnaround in monetary growth since the end of the war—the sharp deceleration in growth beginning in April 1966 that is recorded in the accompanying chart. "Slower monetary growth was badly needed in order to stem inflation," I wrote, "but a good thing was carried too far."

The same month, the Fed reversed its policy. A decline in M_1, the total usually designated "the money supply" by the Fed, was succeeded by an even more rapid rate of growth than in 1965. Slow growth in M_2, a broader total including time deposits at commercial banks, was succeeded by one of the fastest rates of growth on record. The turnaround in January was even sharper than in the prior April, setting a new postwar record.

In my earlier column I wrote, "It is almost surely too late to prevent a recession—that damage has already been done. It is not too late to prevent the recession from turning into a severe downturn. To that end, the Fed should at once act to increase the quantity of money at a rate of about 5 per cent per year for M_2. If the Fed adopted and persisted in such a policy, it could moderate the coming recession without paving the way for a new burst of inflation."

There is much dispute about whether we have in fact experienced the recession that I saw looming, but the dispute is wholly semantic. Total output, which had been rising vigorously, showed no gain at all in the first quarter of 1967 and only a mild gain in the second quarter; industrial production fell absolutely; and so did civilian employment (from January 1967 to May 1967). The percentage of the labor force reported as unemployed rose slightly, despite an almost unprecedented recorded exodus from the labor force. A slowdown in economic activity clearly occurred. But many economic analysts regard it as too mild and too brief to justify calling it a full-fledged recession.

The Fed Reverses Too Much . . .

The slowdown was mild and brief because the Fed did turn around. Unfortunately, the Fed once again carried a good thing too far. Instead of increasing M_2 at 5 per cent per year, it increased it at two-and-a-half times that rate. The result was to moderate the recession (or slowdown, if you prefer), but also to pave the way for a new burst of inflation.

This monetary expansion, not the state of the Federal budget, deplorable as that is on other grounds, has produced the widening signs of inflationary pressure. Just as it took some time—from April 1966 to December 1966—for monetary tightness to slow down the economy, so also it took some time—from January 1967 to June or July 1967—for monetary ease to stimulate the economy. That is why we are only now seeing the effects, and still only the early effects, of the Fed's overreaction in January.

. . . But Passes the Buck

The Fed is naturally reluctant to accept responsibility for inflation. Consequently it blames Federal spending and says that only higher taxes will stop inflation. But that is simply passing the buck.

If the Fed lets the quantity of money continue to increase at the pace of recent months—8 per cent per year for M_1 and 12½ per cent for M_2—further acceleration of inflation is a near certainty, whether taxes are increased or not and whether Federal spending is reduced or not.

What happens to taxes is important. It may affect the level of government spending. It may affect the rate of interest that accompanies whatever monetary policy is followed. But it is not decisive for the course of prices.

The Fed's behavior in this episode is part of a general pattern. Throughout the postwar period—and for much of its life as well—the Fed has tended first to delay action and then, when it did act, to go too far. Too late and too much has been the general rule. The reasons for this pattern are complex—partly the economic analysis ac-

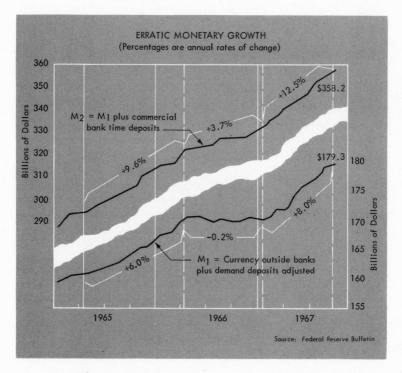

ERRATIC MONETARY GROWTH
(Percentages are annual rates of change)

cepted by the Fed, partly its administrative convenience, partly the political environment in which it operates. But the results are simple. Instead of offsetting other forces making for economic instability, the Fed has itself been a major source of instability.

It is almost surely too late to prevent an appreciable price rise— that damage has already been done. It is not too late to prevent the price rise from turning into a severe inflation. To that end, the Fed should at once act to limit the increase in the quantity of money to a rate of about 5 per cent per year for M_2. If the Fed adopted and persisted in such a policy, it could moderate the coming inflation without paving the way for a new recession.[1]

Any resemblance between this prescription and the one in my January column is not purely coincidental.

MONETARY POLICY

Reprinted from *Newsweek*, June 3, 1968

In two earlier columns on monetary policy, I was highly critical of the Federal Reserve System for acting too late and then, when it did act, for overreacting. This time, I come to praise, not to criticize. Since November 1967, the Fed has moved not only in the right direction but also by about the right amount.

The recent record is summarized in the accompanying table, which gives the annual rate of growth for two monetary totals, for in-

Rate of Change (per cent per year)

Period for Money	Money * M_1	M_2	Industrial Production	Consumer Prices	Period for Production and Prices
Apr. '65 to Apr. '66	6.0	9.6	9.9	3.7	Oct. '65 to Oct. '66
Apr. '66 to Jan. '67	—0.2	3.7	—2.3	2.3	Oct. '66 to July '67
Jan. '67 to Nov. '67	7.7	11.9	5.2	4.0	July '67 to Apr. '68
Nov. '67 to Apr. '68	4.7	5.3		Estimate	

* M_1 = Currency plus adjusted demand deposits. $M_2 = M_1$ plus time deposits in commercial banks.

[1 Shortly after this column appeared, the Fed did slow down the rate of monetary growth. From November, 1967 to March, 1968, the rate of growth of M_2 has been only a trifle over 5 per cent.]

dustrial production, which is a sensitive index of changes in economic activity, and for consumer prices. Because it takes time for monetary changes to exert their influence, the rates of growth of production and prices are given for periods that begin six months later than the corresponding periods for money.

As an aid in interpreting these numbers, let me note that a long-term rate of growth in M_2 of about 5 per cent per year would be consistent with roughly stable prices. The 5 per cent would match the growth in output and leave a little over to satisfy the desire of people to hold somewhat more money relative to their income as they become richer.

From April 1965 to April 1966, the Fed permitted the money supply to grow rapidly, despite signs that inflation was accelerating. At long last, in April 1966, it stepped on the brake—abruptly and, as the table shows, too hard. The result was the so-called "money crunch" in the fall of 1966, the slowdown in the economy recorded in the decline in industrial production, and a cut in price inflation from a rate of 3.7 per cent per year to a rate of 2.3 per cent per year.

The sharper response of production than of prices is typical. An inflationary process, once under way, develops an inertia of its own. It takes an economic slowdown to stop the acceleration of prices and, even then, it takes a long time to restore price stability. That is why it is so important to prevent inflation from gaining momentum.

Concerned by the signs of emerging slack in the economy, the Fed reversed policy in January 1967. This time, to its credit, it acted more promptly than usual. But, as usual, it reacted too sharply, not only restoring, but exceeding the earlier excessive rate of monetary growth.

As a result, I wrote last October, "it is almost surely too late to prevent an appreciable price rise—that damage has already been done. It is not too late to prevent the price rise from turning into a severe inflation. To that end, the Fed should at once act to limit the increase in the quantity of money to a rate of about 5 per cent per year for M_2. If the Fed adopted and persisted in such a policy, it could moderate the coming inflation without paving the way for a new recession."

It *was* too late to prevent an appreciable price rise. Prices have recently been rising at 4 per cent per year. But in November 1967, the Fed did reverse its policy, and M_2 has been growing since at only slightly more than 5 per cent per year.

There has not yet been time for this moderate policy to have much effect—as is reflected in the absence of any entries for production and prices in our table matching the final period for money. But if the Fed persists in its present policy, the exuberant expansion in the economy will taper off later this year and so will the rate of price rise—whether or not there is a tax increase. There may also be some rise in unemployment before the price inflation is brought under control, though any rise is likely to be small.

But will the Fed persist? Will it keep its cool? Or will continuing inflation lead it, as in April 1966, to step still harder on the brake in the hope of getting quicker results? Alternatively, will the first signs of reduced expansion and increased unemployment lead it, as in January 1967, to start the printing presses whirring again and set off a new burst of inflation?

The Fed's steadiness in the past six months—despite the gold crisis, high and rising interest rates and the controversy over government expenditures and taxes—is a hopeful augury.

Should There Be

an Independent

Monetary Authority?[1]

CHAPTER SIX The text for this paper, to paraphrase
the famous remark attributed to Poincaré, is, "Money
is too important to be left to the central bankers."
The problem that suggests this text is what kind of
arrangements should a free society set up for the control of monetary policy. The believer in a free society—a "liberal" in the original meaning of the word,
but unfortunately not in the meaning that is now
current in this country—is fundamentally fearful of
concentrated power. His objective is to preserve the
maximum degree of freedom for each individual separately that is compatible with one man's freedom
not interfering with other men's freedom. He believes that this objective requires that power be dispersed, that it be prevented from accumulating in
any one person or group of people.

[1 Reprinted from Leland B. Yeager (ed.), *In Search of a
Monetary Constitution* (Cambridge, Mass.: Harvard University
Press, 1962).]

The need for dispersal of power raises an especially difficult problem in the field of money. There is widespread agreement that government must have some responsibility for monetary matters. There is also widespread recognition that control over money can be a potent tool for controlling and shaping the economy. Its potency is dramatized in Lenin's famous dictum that the most effective way to destroy a society is to destroy its money. It is exemplified in more pedestrian fashion by the extent to which control over money has always been a potent means of exacting taxes from the populace at large, very often without the explicit agreement of the legislature. This has been true from early times, when monarchs clipped coins and adopted similar expedients, to the present, with our more subtle and sophisticated modern techniques for turning the printing press or simply altering book entries.

The problem is to establish institutional arrangements that will enable government to exercise responsibility for money, yet will at the same time limit the power thereby given to government and prevent the power from being used in ways that will tend to weaken rather than strengthen a free society. Three kinds of solutions have developed or have been suggested. One is an automatic commodity standard, a monetary standard which in principle requires no governmental control. A second is the control of monetary policies by an "independent" central bank. A third is the control of monetary policies by rules that are legislated in advance by the legislature, are binding upon the monetary authority, and greatly limit its initiative. This paper discusses these three alternatives with rather more attention to the solution through a central bank.

A Commodity Standard

Historically, the device that has evolved most frequently in many different places and over the course of centuries is a commodity standard, that is, the use as money of some physical commodity such as gold, silver, brass, or tin, or cigarettes, cognac, or various other commodities. If money consisted wholly of a physical commodity of this type, in principle there would be no need for control by the government at all. The amount of money in society would depend on the cost of producing the monetary commodity. Changes in the amount of money would depend on changes in the technical conditions of producing the monetary commodity and on changes in the demand for money.

This is an ideal that animates many believers in an automatic gold standard. In point of fact, however, as the system developed it deviated very far from this simple pattern, which required no governmental intervention. Historically, a commodity standard—such as a gold standard or a silver standard—was accompanied by the development of alternative forms of money as well, of fiduciary money of one kind or another, ostensibly convertible into the monetary commodity on fixed terms. There was a very good reason for this development. The fundamental defect of a commodity standard, from the point of view of the society as a whole, is that it requires the use of real resources to add to the stock of money. People must work hard to dig something out of the ground in one place—to dig gold out of the ground in South Africa—in order to rebury it in Fort Knox, or some similar place. The necessity of using real resources for the operation of a commodity standard establishes a strong incentive for people to find ways to achieve the same result without employing these resources. If people will accept as money pieces of paper on which is printed "I promise to pay so much of the standard commodity," these pieces of paper can perform the same functions as the physical pieces of gold or silver, and they require very much less in resources to produce. This point, which I have discussed at somewhat greater length elsewhere,[2] seems to me the fundamental difficulty of a commodity standard.

If an automatic commodity standard were feasible, it would provide an excellent solution to the liberal dilemma of how to get a stable monetary framework without the danger of irresponsible exercise of monetary powers. A full commodity standard, for example, an honest-to-goodness gold standard in which 100 per

[2] *A Program for Monetary Stability* (New York: Fordham University Press, 1959), pp. 4-8.

cent of the money consisted literally of gold, widely supported by a public imbued with the mythology of a gold standard and the belief that it is immoral and improper for government to interfere with its operation, would provide an effective control against governmental tinkering with the currency and against irresponsible monetary action. Under such a standard, any monetary powers of government would be very minor in scope.

But such an automatic system has historically never proved feasible. It has always tended to develop in the direction of a mixed system containing fiduciary elements such as bank notes, bank deposits, or government notes in addition to the monetary commodity. And once fiduciary elements have been introduced, it has proved difficult to avoid government control over them, even when they were initially issued by private individuals. The reason is basically the difficulty of preventing counterfeiting or its economic equivalent. Fiduciary money consists of a contract to pay standard money. It so happens that there tends to be a long interval between the making of such a contract and its realization, which enhances the difficulty of enforcing the contract to pay the standard money and hence also the temptation to issue fraudulent contracts. In addition, once fiduciary elements have been introduced, the temptation for government itself to issue fiduciary money is almost irresistible. As a result of these forces, commodity standards have tended in practice to become mixed standards involving extensive intervention by the state, which leaves the problem of how intervention is to be controlled.

Despite the great amount of talk by many people in favor of the gold standard, almost no one today literally desires to see an honest-to-goodness full gold standard in operation. People who say they want a gold standard are almost invariably talking about the present kind of standard, or the kind of standard that was maintained in the 1930's, in which there is a small amount of gold in existence, held by the central monetary authority as "backing"—to use that very misleading term—for fiduciary money, and with the same authority, a central bank or other government bureau, managing the gold standard. Even during the so-called "great days" of the gold standard of the nineteenth century, when the Bank of England was supposedly running the gold standard skillfully, the monetary system was far from a fully automatic gold standard. It was even then a highly managed standard. And certainly the situation is now more extreme. Country after country has adopted the view that government has responsibility for internal stability. This development, plus the invention by Schacht of the widespread direct control of foreign exchange transactions, has meant that few if any countries are willing today to let the gold standard operate even as quasi-automatically as it did in the nineteenth century.

Most countries in the world currently behave asymmetrically with respect to the gold standard. They are willing to allow gold to flow in and even to inflate somewhat in response, but almost none is willing either to let gold flow out to any large extent or to adjust to the outflow by allowing or forcing internal prices to decline. Instead, they are very likely to take measures such as exchange controls, import restrictions, and the like.

My conclusion is that an automatic commodity standard is neither a desirable nor a feasible solution to the problem of establishing monetary arrangements for a free society. It is not desirable because it would involve a large cost in the form of resources used to produce the monetary commodity. It is not feasible because the mythology and beliefs required to make it effective do not exist.

An Independent Central Bank

A second device that has evolved and for which there is considerable support is a so-called "independent" monetary authority—a central bank—to control monetary policy and to keep it from being the football of political manipulation. The widespread belief in an independent central bank clearly rests on the acceptance—in some cases the highly reluctant acceptance—of the view I have just been expressing about a commodity standard, namely, that a fully automatic commodity standard is not a feasible way to achieve the objective of a monetary structure that is both stable and free from irresponsible governmental tinkering.

The device of an independent central bank embodies the

very appealing idea that it is essential to prevent monetary policy from being a day-to-day plaything at the mercy of every whim of the current political authorities. The device is rationalized by assimilating it to a species of constitutionalism. The argument that is implicit in the views of proponents of an independent central bank—so far as I know, these views have never been fully spelled out—is that control over money is an essential function of a government, comparable to the exercise of legislative or judicial or administrative powers. In all of these, it is important to distinguish between the basic structure and day-to-day operation within that structure. In our form of government, this distinction is made between the constitutional rules which set down a series of basic prescriptions and proscriptions for the legislative, judicial, and executive authorities and the detailed operation of the several authorities under these general rules. Similarly, the argument implicit in the defense of an independent central bank is that the monetary structure needs a kind of a monetary constitution, which takes the form of rules establishing and limiting the central bank as to the powers that it is given, its reserve requirements, and so on. Beyond this, the argument goes, it is desirable to let the central bank have authority largely coordinate with that of the legislature, the executive, and the judiciary to carry out the general constitutional mandate on a day-to-day basis.

In recent times, the threat of extension of government control into widening areas of economic activity has often come through proposals involving monetary expansion. Central bankers have generally been "sound money men," at least verbally, which is to say, they have tended to attach great importance to stability of the exchange rate, maintenance of convertibility of the nation's currency into other currencies and into gold, and prevention of inflation. They have therefore tended to oppose many of the proposals for extending the scope of government. This coincidence of their views in these respects with those of people like myself, who regard narrowly limited government as a requisite for a free society, is the source of much of the sympathy on the part of this group of "liberals," in the original sense, for the notion of an independent central bank. As a practical matter, the central bankers seem more likely to impose restrictions on irresponsible monetary power than the legislative authority itself.

A first step in discussing this notion critically is to examine the meaning of the "independence" of a central bank. There is a trivial meaning that cannot be the source of dispute about the desirability of independence. In any kind of a bureaucracy, it is desirable to delegate particular functions to particular agencies. The Bureau of Internal Revenue can be described as an independent bureau within the Treasury Department. Outside the regular government departments, there are separate administrative organizations, such as the Bureau of the Budget. This kind of independence of monetary policy would exist if, within the central administrative hierarchy, there were a separate organization charged with monetary policy which was subordinate to the chief executive or officer, though it might be more or less independent in routine decisions. For our purposes, this seems to me a trivial meaning of independence, and not the meaning fundamentally involved in the argument for or against an independent central bank. This is simply a question of expediency and of the best way to organize an administrative hierarchy.

A more basic meaning is the one suggested above—that a central bank should be an independent branch of government coordinate with the legislative, executive, and judicial branches, and with its actions subject to interpretation by the judiciary. Perhaps the most extreme form of this kind of independence in practice, and the form that comes closest to the ideal type envisaged by proponents of an independent central bank, has been achieved in those historical instances where an organization that was initially entirely private and not formally part of the government at all has served as a central bank. The leading example, of course, is the Bank of England, which developed out of a strictly private bank and was not owned by or formally a part of the government until after World War II. If such a private organization strictly outside the regular political channels could not function as a central monetary authority, this form of independence would call for the establishment of a central bank through a constitutional provision which would be subject to

179

change only by constitutional amendment. The bank would accordingly not be subject to direct control by the legislature. This is the meaning I shall assign to independence in discussing further whether an independent central bank is a desirable resolution of the problem of achieving responsible control over monetary policy.

It seems to me highly dubious that the United States, or for that matter any other country, has in practice ever had an independent central bank in this fullest sense of the term. Even when central banks have supposedly been fully independent, they have exercised their independence only so long as there has been no real conflict between them and the rest of the government. Whenever there has been a serious conflict, as in time of war, between the interests of the fiscal authorities in raising funds and of the monetary authorities in maintaining convertibility into specie, the bank has almost invariably given way, rather than the fiscal authority. To judge by experience, even those central banks that have been nominally independent in the fullest sense of the term have in fact been closely linked to the executive authority.

But of course this does not dispose of the matter. The ideal is seldom fully realized. Suppose we could have an independent central bank in the sense of a coordinate constitutionally established, separate organization. Would it be desirable to do so? I think not, for both political and economic reasons.

The political objections are perhaps more obvious than the economic ones. Is it really tolerable in a democracy to have so much power concentrated in a body free from any kind of direct, effective political control? A "liberal" often characterizes his position as involving belief in the rule of law rather than of men. It is hard to reconcile such a view with the approval of an independent central bank in any meaningful way. True, it is impossible to dispense fully with the rule of men. No law can be specified so precisely as to avoid problems of interpretation or to cover explicitly every possible case. But the kind of limited discretion left by even the best of laws in the hands of those administering them is a far cry indeed from the kind of far-reaching powers that the laws establishing central banks generally place in the hands of a small number of men.

I was myself most fully persuaded that it would be politically intolerable to have an "independent" central bank by the memoirs of Emile Moreau, the governor of the Bank of France during the period from about 1926 to 1928, the period when France established a new parity for the franc and returned to gold. Moreau was appointed governor of the Bank of France in 1926, not long before Poincaré became premier after violent fluctuations in the exchange value of the franc and serious accompanying internal disturbances and governmental financial difficulties. Moreau's memoirs were edited and brought out in book form some years ago by Jacques Rueff, who was the leading figure in the recent [1958] French monetary reform.[3]

The book is fascinating on many counts. The particular respect that is most relevant for our present purpose is the picture that Moreau paints of Montagu Norman, governor of the Bank of England, on the one hand, and of Hjalmar Schacht, at that time governor of the Bank of Germany, on the other; they were unquestionably two of the three outstanding central bankers of the modern era, Benjamin Strong of the United States being the third. Moreau describes the views that these two European central bankers had of their functions and their roles, and implies their attitude toward other groups. The impression left with me— though it is by no means clear that Moreau drew the same conclusions from what he wrote, and it is certain that he would have expressed himself more temperately—is that Norman and Schacht were contemptuous both of the masses—of "vulgar" democracy— and of the classes—of the, to them, equally vulgar plutocracy. They viewed themselves as exercising control in the interests of both groups but free from the pressures of either. In Norman's view, if the major central bankers of the world would only co-operate with one another—and he had in mind not only himself and Schacht but also Moreau and Benjamin Strong—they could jointly wield enough power to control the basic economic destinies of the Western world in accordance with rational ends and objectives rather than with the irrational processes of either parliamentary democracy or laissez-faire capitalism. Though of

[3] Emile Moreau, *Souvenirs d'un gouverneur de la Banque de France* (Paris: Génin, [1954]).

course stated in obviously benevolent terms of doing the "right thing" and avoiding distrust and uncertainty, the implicit doctrine is clearly thoroughly dictatorial and totalitarian.[4]

It is not hard to see how Schacht could later be one of the major creators of the kind of far-reaching economic planning and control that developed in Germany. Schacht's creation of extensive direct control of foreign exchange transactions is one of the few really new economic inventions of modern times. In the older literature, when people spoke of a currency as being inconvertible, they meant that it was not convertible into gold or silver or some other money at a fixed rate. To the best of my knowledge, it is only after 1934 that inconvertibility came to mean what we currently take it to mean: that it is illegal for one man to convert paper money of one country into paper money of another country at any terms he can arrange with another person.[5]

I turn now to the economic or technical aspects of an independent central bank. Clearly there are political objections to giving the group in charge of a central bank so much power

[4 I have been fascinated (and horrified) at hearing the same phrases and arguments repeated over and over in the course of the lengthy discussions about "international monetary reform" that have been taking place at a rising tempo these past few years.]

5 Another feature of Moreau's book that is most fascinating but rather off the main track of the present discussion is the story it tells of the changing relations between the French and British central banks. At the beginning, with France in desperate straits seeking to stabilize its currency, Norman was contemptuous of France and regarded it as very much of a junior partner. Through the accident that the French currency was revalued at a level that stimulated gold imports, France started to accumulate gold reserves and sterling reserves and gradually came into the position where at any time Moreau could have forced the British off gold by withdrawing the funds he had on deposit at the Bank of England. The result was that Norman changed from being a proud boss and very much the senior partner to being almost a suppliant at the mercy of Moreau. Aside from the human drama, it emphasizes how important it is whether the rate of exchange is fixed 5 per cent too low or 5 per cent too high. Britain went back on gold in 1925 at a price of gold in terms of the pound that was probably something like 5 or 10 per cent too low, and France went back de facto at the end of 1926 and de jure in mid-1928 at a price of gold in terms of francs that was 5 or 10 per cent too high. This difference meant the difference between the French being at the mercy of the British and the British being at the mercy of the French. [Precisely this same pattern has been repeated from 1958 to 1968 with the same actors. France in 1958 devalued to a level that stimulated gold imports, just as it had at the end of 1926. And Britain was forced to devalue in November, 1967, just as it was in September, 1931.]

independent of direct political controls, but, it has been argued, there are economic or technical grounds why it is nevertheless essential to do so. In judging this statement, much depends on the amount of leeway that the general rule governing the central bank gives to it. I have been describing an independent central bank as if it could or would be given a good deal of separate power, as clearly is currently the case. Of course, the whole notion of independence could be rendered merely a matter of words if in fact the constitutional provision setting up the bank established the limits of its authority very narrowly and controlled very closely the policies that it could follow.

In the nineteenth century, when wide support for independent central banks developed, the governing objective of the central bank was the maintenance of exchange stability. Central banks tended to develop in countries that professed to have commodity currencies, which is to say had a fixed price for the commodity serving as the monetary standard in terms of the nominal money of the country. For two countries on the same standard, this meant a fixed rate of exchange between the corresponding national currencies. In consequence, the maintenance of such fixed rates had to be the proximate aim of the central bank if it was to achieve its major aim of keeping its currency convertible into standard money. The Bank of England, for example, was narrowly limited in what it could do by the necessity of keeping England on gold.

In the same way, in the United States when the Federal Reserve System was established in 1913, it never entered into the minds of the people who were establishing it that the System would really have much effective control internally in ordinary times. The Reserve System was established when the gold standard ruled supreme, and when it was taken for granted that the major factor determining the policy of the System, and hence the behavior of the stock of money in this country, would be the necessity of maintaining external equilibrium with the currencies of other countries. So long as the maintenance of a fixed exchange rate between one country's currency and the currencies of other countries was the overriding objective of policy, the amount of leeway available to the central bank was narrowly limited. It had some leeway with respect to minor movements of a short-term character, but it ultimately had to respond to the balance of payments.

The situation has changed drastically in this respect in the course of the past few decades. In the United States, which is of most immediate concern to us, the Reserve System had hardly started operations before the fundamental conditions taken for granted when it was established had changed radically. During World War I, most of the countries of the world went off gold. The United States technically remained on gold, but the gold standard on which it remained was very different from the one that had prevailed earlier. After the end of World War I, although other countries of the world gradually re-established something they called the gold standard, the gold standard never again played the role which it had before. Prior to World War I, the United States was effectively a minor factor in the total world economy, and the necessity of maintaining external stability dominated our behavior. After the war, we had become a major factor to which other countries had to adjust. We held a very large fraction of the world's gold. Many countries never went back on gold, and those that did went back in a much diluted form. So never again has there been anything like the close domination of day-to-day policy by the gold standard that prevailed prior to 1914. Under these circumstances, "independence" of the central bank has become something meaningful, and not merely a technicality.

One defect of an independent central bank in such a situation is that it almost inevitably involves dispersal of responsibility. If we examine the monetary system in terms not of nominal institutional organization but of the economic functions performed, we find that the central bank is hardly ever the only authority in the government that has essential monetary powers. Before the Federal Reserve System was established, the Treasury exercised essential monetary powers. It operated like a central bank, and at times a very effective central bank. More recently, from 1933 to 1941, the Federal Reserve System was almost entirely passive. Such monetary actions as were taken were taken predominantly by the Treasury. The Treasury engaged in open-market operations in its debt-management operations of buying and selling securities. It created and destroyed money in its gold and silver purchases and sales. The Exchange Stabilization Fund was established and gave the Treasury yet another device for engaging in open-market operations. When the Treasury sterilized and desterilized gold, it was engaging in monetary actions. In practice, therefore, even if something called an independent central bank is established and given exclusive power over a limited range of monetary matters, in particular over the printing of pieces of paper or the making of book entries called money (Federal Reserve notes and Federal Reserve deposits), there remain other governmental authorities, particularly the fiscal authority collecting taxes and dispersing funds and managing the debt, which also have a good deal of monetary power.

If one wanted to have the substance and not merely the form of an independent monetary authority, it would be necessary to concentrate all debt-management powers as well as all powers to create and destroy governmentally issued money in the central bank. As a matter of technical efficiency, this might well be desirable. Our present division of responsibility for debt management between the Federal Reserve and the Treasury is very inefficient. It would be much more efficient if the Federal Reserve did all of the borrowing and all of the managing of the debt, and the Treasury, when it had a deficit, financed it by getting money from the Federal Reserve System, and when it had a surplus, handed the excess over to the Federal Reserve System. But while such an arrangement might be tolerable if the Federal Reserve System were part of the same administrative hierarchy as the Treasury, it is almost inconceivable that it would be if the central bank were thoroughly independent. Certainly no government to date has been willing to put that much power in the hands of a central bank even when the bank has been only partly independent. But so long as these powers are separated, there is dispersal of responsibility, with each group separately regarding the other group as responsible for what is happening and with no one willing to accept responsibility.

In the past few years, I have read through the annual reports of the Federal Reserve System from 1913 to date, seriatim.

One of the few amusing dividends from that ordeal was seeing the cyclical pattern that shows up in the potency that the authorities attribute to monetary policy. In years when things are going well, the reports emphasize that monetary policy is an exceedingly potent weapon and that the favorable course of events is largely a result of the skillful handling of this delicate instrument by the monetary authority. In years of depression, on the other hand, the reports emphasize that monetary policy is but one of many tools of economic policy, that its power is highly limited, and that it was only the skillful handling of such limited powers as were available that averted disaster. This is an example of the effect of the dispersal of responsibility among different authorities, with the likely result that no one assumes or is assigned the final responsibility.

Another defect of the conduct of monetary policy through an independent central bank that has a good deal of leeway and power is the extent to which policy is thereby made highly dependent on personalities. In studying the history of American monetary policy, I have been struck by the extraordinary importance of accidents of personality.

At the end of World War I, the governor of the Federal Reserve System was W. P. G. Harding. Governor Harding was, I am sure, a thoroughly reputable and competent citizen, but he had a very limited understanding of monetary affairs, and even less backbone. Almost every student of the period is agreed that the great mistake of the Reserve System in postwar monetary policy was to permit the money stock to expand very rapidly in 1919 and then to step very hard on the brakes in 1920. This policy was almost surely responsible for both the sharp postwar rise in prices and the sharp subsequent decline. It is amusing to read Harding's answer in his memoirs to criticism that was later made of the policies followed. He does not question that alternative policies might well have been preferable for the economy as a whole, but emphasizes the Treasury's desire to float securities at a reasonable rate of interest, and calls attention to a then-existing law under which the Treasury could replace the head of the Reserve System. Essentially he was saying the same thing that I heard another member of the Reserve Board say shortly after World

War II when the bond-support program was in question. In response to the view expressed by some of my colleagues and myself that the bond-support program should be dropped, he largely agreed but said, "Do you want us to lose our jobs?"

The importance of personality is strikingly revealed by the contrast between Harding's behavior and that of Emile Moreau in France under much more difficult circumstances. Moreau formally had no independence whatsoever from the central government. He was named by the premier, and could be discharged at any time by the premier. But when he was asked by the premier to provide the Treasury with funds in a manner that he considered inappropriate and undesirable, he flatly refused to do so. Of course, what happened was that Moreau was not discharged, that he did not do what the premier had asked him to, and that stabilization was rather more successful. I cite this contrast neither to praise Moreau nor to blame Harding, but simply to illustrate my main point, namely, the extent to which a system of this kind is really a system of rule by men and not by law and is extraordinarily dependent on the particular personalities involved.

Another occasion in United States history which strikingly illustrates this point is our experience from 1929 to 1933. Without doubt, the most serious mistake in the history of the Reserve System was its mismanagement of monetary matters during those years. And this mismanagement, like that after World War I, can very largely be attributed to accidents of personality. Benjamin Strong, governor of the Federal Reserve Bank of New York from its inception, was the dominant figure in the Reserve System until his death at a rather early age in 1928. His death was followed by a shift of power in the system from New York to Washington. The people in Washington at the time happened to be fairly mediocre. Moreover, they had always played a secondary role, were not in intimate touch with the financial world, and had no background of long experience in meeting day-to-day emergencies. Further, the chairmanship changed hands just prior to the shift of power and again in mid-1931. Consequently, in the emergencies that came in 1929, 1930, and 1931, particularly in the fall of 1930, when the Bank of United States failed in

New York as part of a dramatic series of bank failures, the Federal Reserve System acted timorously and passively. There is little doubt that Strong would have acted very differently. If he had still been governor, the result would almost surely have been to nip the wave of bank failures in the bud and to prevent the drastic monetary deflation that followed.

A similar situation prevails today. The actions of the Reserve System depend on whether there are a few persons in the System who exert intellectual leadership, and on who these people are; its actions depend not only on the people who are nominally the heads of the System but also on such matters as the fate of particular economic advisers.

So far, I have listed two main technical defects of an independent central bank from an economic point of view: first, dispersal of responsibility, which promotes shirking responsibility in times of uncertainty and difficulty, and second, an extraordinary dependence on personalities, which fosters instability arising from accidental shifts in the particular people and the character of the people who are in charge of the system.

A third technical defect is that an independent central bank will almost inevitably give undue emphasis to the point of view of bankers. It is exceedingly important to distinguish two quite different problems that tend to be confused: the problem of credit policy and the problem of monetary policy. In our kind of monetary or banking system, money tends to be created as an incident in the extension of credit, yet conceptually the creation of money and the extension of credit are quite distinct. A monetary system could be utterly unrelated to any credit instruments whatsoever; for example, this would be true of a completely automatic commodity standard, using only the monetary commodity itself or warehouse receipts for the commodity as money. Historically, the connection between money and credit has varied widely from time to time and from place to place. It is therefore essential to distinguish policy issues connected with interest rates and conditions on the credit market from policy issues connected with changes in the aggregate stock of money, while recognizing, of course, that measures taken to affect the one set of variables may also affect the other, and that monetary measures may have credit effects as well as monetary effects proper.

It so happens that central-bank action is but one of many forces affecting the credit market. As we and other countries have seen time and again, a central bank may be able to determine the rate of interest on a narrow range of securities, such as the rate of interest on a particular category of government bonds, though even that only within limits and only at the expense of completely giving up control over the total stock of money. A central bank has never been able to determine, at all closely, rates of interest in any broader or more fundamental sense. Postwar experience in country after country that has embarked on a cheap-money policy has strikingly demonstrated that the forces which determine rates of interest broadly conceived—rates of return on equities, on real property, on corporate securities—are far too strong and widespread for the central bank to dominate. It must sooner or later yield to them, and generally rather soon.

The central bank is in a very different position in determining the quantity of money. Under systems such as that in the United States today, the central bank can make the amount of money anything it wishes. It may, of course, choose to accept some other objectives and give up its power over the money supply in order to try to keep "the" or "a" rate of interest fixed, to keep "free reserves" at a particular level, or to achieve some other objective. But if it wishes, it can exercise complete control over the stock of money.

This difference between the position of the central bank in the credit markets and in determining the money supply tends to be obfuscated by the close connection between the central bank and the banking community. In the United States, for example, the Reserve banks technically are owned by their member banks. One result is that the general views of the banking community exercise a strong influence on the central bank and, since the banking community is concerned primarily with the credit market, central banks are led to put altogether too much emphasis on the credit effects of their policies and too little emphasis on the monetary effects of their policies.

In recent times, this emphasis has been attributed to the effects of the Keynesian Revolution and its treatment of changes in the stock of money as operating primarily through the liquidity preference function on the interest rate. But this is only a particular form of a more general and ancient tendency. The real-bills doctrine, which dates back a century and more, exemplifies the same kind of confusion between the credit and the monetary effects of monetary policy. The banking and currency controversy in Britain in the early nineteenth century is a related example. The central bank emphasized its concern with conditions in the credit market. It denied that the quantity of money it was creating was in any way an important consideration in determining price levels or the like, or that it had any discretion about how much money to create. Much the same arguments are heard today.

The three defects I have outlined constitute a strong technical argument against an independent central bank. Combined with the political argument, the case against a fully independent central bank is strong indeed.

Legislative Rules

If this conclusion is valid, if we cannot achieve our objectives by giving wide discretion to independent experts, how else can we establish a monetary system that is stable, free from irresponsible governmental tinkering, and incapable of being used as a source of power to threaten economic and political freedom? A third possibility is to try to achieve a government of law instead of men literally by legislating rules for the conduct of monetary policy. The enactment of such rules would enable the public to exercise control over monetary policy through its political authorities, while at the same time preventing monetary policy from being subject to the day-to-day whim of political authorities.

The argument for legislating rules for monetary policy has much in common with a topic that seems at first altogether different, namely, the Bill of Rights to the Constitution. Whenever anyone suggests the desirability of a legislative rule for control over money, the stereotyped answer is that it makes little sense to tie the monetary authority's hands in this way because the authority, if it wants to, can always do of its own volition what the rule would require it to do, and, in addition, has other alternatives; hence "surely," it is said, it can do better than the rule. An alternative version of the same argument applies to the legislature. If the legislature is willing to adopt the rule, it is said, surely it will also be willing to legislate the "right" policy in each specific case. How then, it is said, does the adoption of the rule provide any protection against irresponsible political action?

The same argument could apply with only minor verbal changes to the first amendment to the Constitution and, equally, to the entire Bill of Rights. Is it not absurd, one might say, to have a general proscription of interference with free speech? Why not take up each case separately and treat it on its own merits? Is this not the counterpart to the usual argument in monetary policy that it is undesirable to tie the hands of the monetary authority in advance; that it should be left free to treat each case on its merits as it comes up? Why is not the argument equally valid for speech? One man wants to stand up on a street corner and advocate birth control; another, communism; a third, vegetarianism; and so on, ad infinitum. Why not enact a law affirming or denying each the right to spread his particular views? Or, alternatively, why not give the power to decide the issue to an administrative agency? It is immediately clear that if we were to take up each case separately, a majority would almost surely vote to deny free speech in most cases and perhaps even in every case. A vote on whether Mr. X should spread birth control propaganda would almost surely yield a majority saying "no"; and so would one on communism. The vegetarian might perhaps get by, although even that is by no means a foregone conclusion.

But now suppose all these cases were grouped together in one bundle, and the populace at large was asked to vote for them as a whole: to vote whether free speech should be denied in all cases or permitted in all alike. It is perfectly conceivable, if not highly probable, that an overwhelming majority would vote for free speech; that, acting on the bundle as a whole, the people would vote exactly the opposite to the way they would have voted on each case separately. Why? One reason is that each person feels much more strongly about being deprived of his right to free speech when he is in a minority than he feels about depriving somebody else of the right to free speech when he is in the majority. In consequence, when he votes on the bundle as a whole, he gives much more weight to the infrequent denial of free speech to himself when he is in the minority than to the frequent denial of free speech to others. Another reason, and one that is more directly relevant to monetary policy, is that if the bundle is viewed as a whole, it becomes clear that the policy followed has cumulative effects that tend neither to be recognized nor taken into account when each case is voted on separately. When a vote is taken on whether Mr. Jones may speak on the corner, it is not clearly affected by favorable effects of an announced general policy of free speech, and an affirmative vote will not produce these effects. In voting on the specific case, it is only peripherally relevant that a society in which people are not free to speak on the corner without special legislation is a society in which the development of new ideas, experimentation, change, and the like are all hampered in a great variety of ways. That these ways are obvious to all is due to our good fortune of having lived in a society that did adopt the self-denying ordinance of not considering each case of speech separately.

Exactly the same considerations apply in the monetary area. If each case is considered on its merits, the wrong decision is likely to be made in a large fraction of cases because the decision-makers are examining only a limited area and are not taking into account the cumulative consequences of the policy as a whole. On the other hand, if a general rule is adopted for a group of cases as a bundle, the existence of that rule has favorable effects on people's attitudes and beliefs and expectations that would not follow even from the discretionary adoption of precisely the same policy on a series of separate occasions.

Of course, the general rule need not be explicitly written down or legislated. Unwritten constitutional limitations supported unthinkingly by the bulk of the people may be as effective in determining decisions in individual cases as a written constitution. The analogy in monetary affairs is the mythology of gold, referred to earlier as a necessary ingredient of a gold standard if it is to serve as an effective bulwark against discretionary authority.

If a rule is to be legislated, what rule should it be? The rule that has most frequently been suggested by people of a generally "liberal" persuasion is a price-level rule; namely, a legislative direction to the monetary authorities that they maintain a stable price level. I think this is the wrong kind of rule. It is the wrong kind of rule because the objectives it specifies are ones that the monetary authorities do not have the clear and direct power to achieve by their own actions. It consequently raises the earlier problem of dispersing responsibilities and leaving the authorities too much leeway. There is unquestionably a close connection between monetary actions and the price level. But the connection is not so close, so invariable, or so direct that the objective of achieving a stable price level is an appropriate guide to the day-to-day activities of the authorities.

The issue of what rule to adopt is one that I have considered at some length elsewhere.[6] Accordingly, I will limit myself here to stating my conclusion. In the present state of our knowledge, it seems to me desirable to state the rule in terms of the behavior of the stock of money. My choice at the moment would be a legislated rule instructing the monetary authority to achieve a specified rate of growth in the stock of money. For this purpose, I would define the stock of money as including currency outside commercial banks plus all deposits of commercial banks. I would specify that the Reserve System should see to it that the total stock of money so defined rises month by month, and indeed, so far as possible, day by day, at an annual rate of X per cent, where X is some number between 3 and 5. The precise definition of money adopted and the precise rate of growth chosen make far less difference than the definite choice of a particular definition and a particular rate of growth.

I should like to emphasize that I do not regard this proposal as a be-all and end-all of monetary management, as a rule which is somehow to be written in tablets of gold and enshrined for all

[6] *A Program for Monetary Stability*, pp. 77-99.

future time. It seems to me to be the rule that offers the greatest promise of achieving a reasonable degree of monetary stability in the light of our present knowledge. I would hope that as we operated with it, as we learned more about monetary matters, we might be able to devise still better rules which would achieve still better results. However, the main point of this paper is not so much to discuss the content of these or alternative rules as to suggest that the device of legislating a rule about the stock of money can effectively achieve what an independent central bank is designed to achieve but cannot. Such a rule seems to me the only feasible device currently available for converting monetary policy into a pillar of a free society rather than a threat to its foundations.

The Demand for Money [1]

CHAPTER SEVEN   The term "money" is ordinarily used in two quite different senses. We speak of a man having "money" in his pocket, and we also speak of him as "making money," even when he is not a counterfeiter. I shall use the term solely in the first sense, since the term "income" is available for the second.

The economic function of "money" in this sense is to permit exchange without barter, to enable an individual to exchange the goods or services he owns for other goods or services he wishes to consume or to hold without having to match up each transaction. Instead he can sell at one time to one set of individuals for generalized purchasing power and buy at a different time from other individuals by drawing on his stock of generalized purchasing power. Money in

[1 This paper was read before the American Philosophical Society meetings in Philadelphia on November 10, 1960 and printed in the *Proceedings of the American Philosophical Society*, Vol. 105, No. 3, June, 1961.]

this sense consists of anything that serves the function of providing a temporary abode for general purchasing power.

Money has at times consisted of wampum, stones, cigarettes, cognac, and, of course, such precious metals as gold and silver. Today it consists mostly of less tangible stuff, of promises to pay in the form of the pieces of paper we carry in our pockets and the entries on the books of banks that are misleadingly labeled deposits. It is somewhat arbitrary and a matter of considerable dispute just where it is best to draw the line between the promises to pay that are termed "money" and other very similar promises to pay that are termed "near-moneys" or "liquid assets." For the purposes of this paper, I shall designate as money the non-banking public's holdings of currency and all deposits, demand and time, in commercial banks.[2]

Each of us separately can make the amount of money in his possession anything he wishes subject to the limits imposed by his total wealth and borrowing capacity. If at any moment of time, he wishes to hold more cash, he can sell other assets, or borrow; if he wishes to hold less, he can buy other assets, or repay debts. Over time, of course, he can also add to his cash balances by spending less than his receipts, and subtract from his cash balances by spending more than his receipts.

All of us together, however, are in a very different position. Broadly speaking, the total amount of money available to be held by all together is determined by the monetary structure, or the monetary authorities—currently in this country, the Federal Reserve System—largely independently of the actions of the holders of money. Under these circumstances, one man can add to his cash balances only because somebody else reduces his. If all of us together were to try to reduce or add to our cash balances, we could not do so; somebody or other would have to hold the amount of money and no more than the amount of money that there is available to hold. We would all of us, as it were, simply be playing a game of musical chairs.

For example, an attempt by all of us to reduce our cash balances would mean that we were all of us trying to spend on

<hr />

[2] In more technical terminology, currency outside banks plus demand deposits adjusted plus time deposits in commercial banks.

assets (such as houses and bonds) and on current consumption more than we were simultaneously receiving from the sale of assets and current services. But this is clearly impossible since one man's expenditures are another man's receipts and double entry books must balance. However, the attempt would have important effects. It would produce spirited bidding for assets and other goods which would raise their prices. At higher prices, the same number of dollars would correspond to a smaller total of goods and services. There would be some price level at which the community would no longer wish to reduce its cash balances. Although frustrated in the attempt to change the number of dollars of money held, the community would have succeeded in reducing the amount of cash balances expressed in terms of goods and services, its "real" balances, as they are generally termed.

Conversely, an attempt by all of us to add to our cash balances would mean an attempt to spend less than we were receiving which would tend to mean a decline in total expenditures and in prices. Nominal balances would remain the same but real balances would rise.

In short, the public cannot determine the nominal amount of money, but it can make the real amount anything it wishes to by bidding prices up or down, in the process raising or lowering money income. This essential difference between the situation as it appears to the individual, who can determine his own cash balances but must take prices and money income as beyond his control, and the situation as it is to all individuals together, whose total cash balances are outside their control but who can determine prices and money income, is perhaps the most important proposition in monetary theory and certainly the source of greatest confusion to the layman. It is also what gives such importance to the subject matter of the present paper, namely, the factors that determine the amount of cash balances the public wishes to hold.

This topic is an ancient one, of course, and abstract analyses date back several centuries. Quantitative analyses have been much rarer, for the usual reason that satisfactory data covering a sufficiently long period have been lacking. In the past few years, two sets of data have become available from studies of the

197

National Bureau of Economic Research which permit a far more searching empirical analysis than has heretofore been possible of the factors determining the amount of its wealth that the public wishes to hold in the form of money. One, directly relevant to monetary analysis, is a series of comprehensive estimates of the stock of money in the United States covering nearly the past century, constructed by Anna J. Schwartz and myself. The other, relevant to a much wider range of studies, is a series of estimates of national income covering nearly the same period, constructed by Simon Kuznets.

The income estimates are important for a study of the demand for money because the amount of money demanded clearly depends in the first instance on how much exchange there is for money to mediate, which is to say, on the volume of goods and services to be exchanged and the prices at which they exchange. Total national income is one index and perhaps the best single index, of the amount of exchange to be effected. Consequently, we can allow for the size of the economy by expressing the stock of money as a ratio to the flow of income, measuring money stocks in terms of the number of months of income to which they are equivalent (or, as is perhaps more usual, using the reciprocal of this ratio, the income velocity of circulation).

When the money stock is expressed in these terms, the most striking feature of its behavior over the past century is its fairly steady and persistent rise (chart 1). Around 1880 the public at large, including individuals, all business enterprises other than banks, and all governmental units other than the Federal Treasury, held a stock of money equal in value to about two-and-one-half months' income. Today, the public's stock of money corresponds to more than seven months' income, or nearly three times as much.

The most plausible explanation of this rise in the stock of money is that it reflects the associated quintupling of per capita real income, which is to say, of the average level of living. With a rise in the level of real income, people may want to increase their stock of money more or less than proportionately, just as a rise in level of living means a less than proportionate increase in expenditures on bread but a more than proportionate increase in

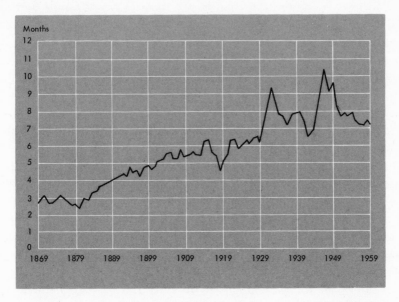

Chart 1. Months of Income Held as Money Actual, 1869-1959.

the stock of durable consumer goods. Judged by the long-period evidence, money is in this respect a "luxury" like durable consumer goods, rather than a "necessity" like bread. A one per cent increase in real per capita income has on the average been associated with an increase in real per capital money holdings of about one and two-thirds per cent.

The general covariation of money, expressed as a ratio to income, and of per capita real income over the past nine decades in the United States is not by itself very strong evidence that changes in the one are a consequence of changes in the other. The covariation might be coincidence, or it might be attributable to common third factors. And, indeed, some recent work has attributed the rise in the money-income ratio to a decline in interest rates rather than to a rise in real per capita income.[3] This explanation, too, is plausible on abstract grounds. The lower the

[3] See Latane, Henry A., Income velocity and interest rates—a pragmatic approach, *Hearings on Employment, Growth and Price Levels* before Joint Economic Committee, Congress of the United States, Part 10: 3435-3443, Washington, D.C., 1960.

interest rate, the less income is sacrificed by holding wealth in the form of money rather than in the form (say) of bonds, hence the larger the fraction of their wealth that people would tend to hold in that form. However, a number of pieces of empirical evidence indicate rather strongly that the rise in per capita real income is far more important a factor explaining the rise in the money-income ratio than is any change in interest rates. First, the covariation of the money-income ratio with real per capita income has obtained for a much longer period of time than the covariation with interest rates. Both the monetary ratio and real per capita income have risen pretty regularly over the past nine decades, whereas interest rates have been constant or rising over long stretches of that period. Second, for a number of foreign countries for which data are available, the covariation between the money-income ratio and real per capita income has been in the same direction and of roughly the same magnitude as in the United States, though changes in income have not always borne the same relation to changes in interest rates as in the United States. Third, data on deposits per capita and income per capita are available for different states in the United States. These cross-section data display roughly the same relation as the time-series data.

One reason why uncertainty attaches to the meaning of the longer-period relation is because a very different relation prevails for the shorter periods corresponding to business cycles. The money-income ratio generally falls during cyclical expansion when real per capita income is rising and generally rises during cyclical contraction when income is falling. Over cycles, therefore, the money-income ratio and real per capita income move in opposite directions whereas over long periods they move in the same direction.

The explanation for this apparent contradiction that currently seems to me most plausible exemplifies the tendency so often noted in science for results obtained in one connection to have applications in other wholly unexpected connections, for the same kind of formal problem to arise in very different substantive contexts. In work that I did some time ago on consumer spending and saving, I developed a hypothesis (partly to explain apparent contradictions in that field between time-series studies and cross-section studies) which had as its central feature a distinction between income as recorded by statisticians, which I called measured income, and a longer term concept of income to which consumers adjust their spending, which I called permanent income.[4] It turns out that this same distinction, applied to prices as well as to income, can reconcile the apparent contradiction between the cyclical and secular behavior of the money-income ratio.

Let us suppose that holders of money, whether individuals or business enterprises, adjust their holdings not to their current receipts or current prices but to the receipts and prices they expect to prevail over a somewhat longer future period. This difference will be of little significance for long-period data; over decades, the expected or permanent magnitudes will move in the same direction as the measured magnitudes. But the difference will be important over cycles. In a cyclical expansion, measured income will presumably rise decidedly more than permanent income. The stock of money might therefore rise more than in proportion to permanent income, which is what it does over longer periods, yet less than in proportion to measured income, which is what it does over cycles. The distinction between the two concepts of income in this way can provide a reconciliation of the cyclical and secular results.

A statistical analysis based on this distinction, initially computed for the period 1873-1954, gave extremely good results. These computations used not only the general ideas just outlined that were derived from the consumption study but also the supplementary notion, which, interestingly enough, had as one of its origins a study of hyperinflations,[5] that expected income could be estimated as a weighted average of past measured incomes, the weights declining exponentially. Moreover, the numerical values of the weights derived in the consumption study were carried over to the money computations. For the rest, the computations were based entirely on averages for whole business cycles, that is, for the period running from the trough of one cycle to the

[4] Friedman, Milton, A theory of the consumption function, Princeton, National Bureau of Economic Research, 1957.
[5] Cagan, Phillip, The monetary dynamics of hyperinflation, in Studies in the quantity theory of money, edited by Milton Friedman, 37-39, Chicago, 1956.

trough of the next, or from the peak of one cycle to the peak of the next. From such cycle averages we estimated an equation connecting the actual stock of money held per capita, adjusted for changes in expected prices, with expected real income per capita. We then used this equation, plus the yearly values of prices and income, to compute the hypothetical amounts of money that would have been demanded if the public had reacted precisely in accordance with our estimated equation. The resulting hypothetical money-income ratio is shown in Chart 2 along

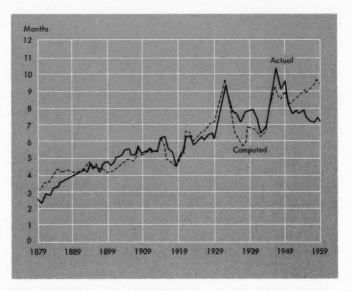

Chart 2. Months of Income Held as Money, Actual and Computed, 1879-1959.

with the actual. The most striking feature of the results is not the general concordance but rather the agreement between the cyclical movements of the two series despite the fact that no use was made of intracyclical movements in deriving the statistical relation.[6]

[6] For a full exposition, see Friedman, Milton, The demand for money: some theoretical and empirical results, *Occasional Paper No. 68*, National Bureau of Economic Research, 1959, reprinted from *Journal of Political Economy*, August, 1959.

That a fairly simple relation of this kind approximates actual experience over a century and from year to year as well as decade to decade is striking testimony to the fundamental persistence of essentially unchanged behavior patterns with respect to money holdings, behavior patterns that have determined the public's response to the great changes occurring in the economy's monetary circumstances.

Despite the generally good fit of the statistical relation, there are a number of sizable discrepancies. One is for the early years of our period, from about 1879 to 1890. The money and income data are least accurate for this period and there is external evidence that this may well explain the discrepancy. A much more disturbing discrepancy is for the period after World War II, when the money-income ratio fell decidedly relative to the level that would have been expected on the basis of our statistical relation. This discrepancy was already notable when the analysis just described was completed and published. It became even wider in the next few years as additional data became available.

One striking feature about the discrepancy is that it is present only in the major postwar movements in the money-income ratio, not in its cyclical movements. Our statistical relation continues to reproduce with a high degree of fidelity the cyclical movements in the money-income ratio. The discrepancy does not therefore raise any doubts about the importance of the distinction between measured and permanent magnitudes.

The phenomenon underlying the discrepancy is that over the postwar period money balances have fallen relative to income (velocity has risen), whereas, as we have seen, from the Civil War to World War II, money balances tended to rise relative to income. This phenomenon has attracted much attention and numerous explanations have been suggested. The most plausible attribute the postwar decline in the money-income ratio to the postwar rise in interest rates, or to expectations of inflation, or to the growth of savings and loan shares and other substitutes for money, or to some combination of all three factors. It may be that these factors account for some part of the postwar decline in the money-income ratio. However, I am myself persuaded, on the basis of a more intensive examination of the evidence than time permits detailing here, that even all together they can account at most for only a minor part of the discrepancy.

A more promising explanation that I am currently investigating is that the discrepancy reflects a very different factor, namely, the public's expectations about the likely degree of economic stability. This explanation has great appeal both on analytical grounds and in terms of its qualitative concordance with the experience of the past four decades. Given that money is held as a temporary abode for generalized purchasing power, the amount people will desire to hold must surely depend on their expectations about future contingencies. If they anticipate a highly stable world, with minor fluctuations in income, employment, interest rates, and prices, they will feel much less of a need to retain relatively large amounts of their wealth in the form of money than if they anticipate considerable instability, involving wide fluctuations in income, employment, interest rates, and prices.

The explanation accords qualitatively with the behavior of the money-income ratio over the past four decades. The 'twenties with its widespread belief that a "new era" had dawned was a period when, on this interpretation, people might have been expected to hold relatively low cash balances and, in fact, the money-income ratio is low during this period relative to its long period trend. The enormous increase in uncertainty after the 1929 crash was promptly accompanied by a sharp increase in money balances relative to income. While nominal money balances declined sharply as a result of the unfortunate policies followed by the monetary authorities, income fell still more sharply as a result of the reaction of the public, so that money balances rose sharply relative to income. Money balances remained high relative to income throughout the uncertain 'thirties, and fell only as the approach and then outbreak of war in Europe quieted fears of continued economic depression. After the United States entered the war, and even more as the end of the war approached, expectations again shifted. The experience of the 'thirties combined with the recollection of the collapse of prices after World War I to instill widespread uncertainty about postwar experience. Money balances rose to an unprecedentedly high level relative to income. Finally, and here we come to the period that has attracted most attention, after the end of the war, as one recession after another turned out to be mild, fears of a great depression receded, confidence grew in the continuation of a high and relatively stable level of economic activity, and cash balances fell substantially relative to income. This postwar change in expectations must be about over. Hence, if this interpretation is correct, the factors accounting for the postwar decline in the money-income ratio have spent their force, and the ratio may be expected to resume its long-period upward trend. Whether it does so will be a critical test of the interpretation.[7]

This qualitative account suggests that changes in the public's expectations about economic instability were in the right direction to account for the major deviations of the money-income ratio from its historical relation to expected income. It leaves open, however, the question whether such changes in expectation could account for the magnitude of the observed deviations. In order to get some evidence on this point, I have been trying to supplement the qualitative analysis by a quantitative analysis. The results of my initial experiments are mixed. On the one hand, the introduction of a measure of expected instability analogous to the measure of expected income accounts, in a statistical sense, for a large part of the deviations since the early 1930's. On the other hand, the measure in its present form makes the fit of our relation to experience decidedly worse for the period prior to 1920. Clearly, much further work is needed before we can tell whether this promising lead will turn out to be a dead end or to open up new vistas.[8]

It should be emphasized that I have been reporting on research in progress and that the findings reported are still tentative. This is especially so with respect to the role assigned to expectations about economic stability, and even more, the particular device adopted to get an empirical measure of such ex-

[7 Since 1960, the money-income ratio does appear to have resumed its upward trend. It has risen most years since and by 1967 was more than 6% higher than in 1960.]

[8 We have still (1968) not been able to get a satisfactory quantitative translation for this qualitative analysis, even though subsequent experience has remained consistent with the qualitative analysis.]

pectations. This variable and this device have not heretofore been used, so far as I know, in this or any other comparable connection. Hence, even if they should turn out to give good results for the United States, we must await further applications to data for other countries and to other problems of a similar character before we can have substantial confidence that favorable results in the present instance are more than a happy accident.

Another respect in which our work is tentative is that we have so far not been able to isolate the effect in the United States of a set of variables that occupy a central place in the theoretical analysis of the demand for money, namely, variables determining the cost of holding money in the form of cash rather than of other assets. Interest rates measure this cost if the alternative is a bond or loan; the rate of change of prices measures this cost if the alternative is physical commodities. Under circumstances where these costs have varied widely, as for example in hyperinflation, their effect is clear and manifest, so experience supports theoretical expectations. In the United States, on the other hand, these costs have apparently varied over a sufficiently narrow range that their effects are hard to disentangle from the effect of the myriad other factors that influence desired cash balances and that we label "chance." Perhaps, once we have determined fairly accurately the effects of what seem to be the much more important variables of expected real income and expected stability of income, we shall be able to isolate more satisfactorily the effects of interest rates and rates of change of prices.

The stakes in these investigations are high. If the factors governing money-holding propensities are known, and if these effects are highly stable, we shall be armed with a powerful apparatus for the amelioration of what has been for centuries a basic problem of economic life: the fluctuating value of the monetary unit.

The Balance of Payments

PART THREE   Memories are short. Mention the balance of payments in the U.S. today, and the immediate association is with balance of payments deficits, with the problem of how to reduce the number of dollars that U.S. residents or the U.S. government want to spend, lend, or give away abroad and how to increase the number of dollars that foreigners want to acquire to spend, lend, or give away in the U.S. Yet in the first decade after the war, the problem appeared to be precisely the opposite. The U.S. was then tending to run a huge balance of payments surplus. Foreigners were complaining not about the excess dollars they were acquiring but about the shortage of dollars. Just as now there is much talk about the basic "structural" sources of the U.S. deficit, and the major changes in U.S. policy and extensive international co-operation that will be required to "solve" the U.S. deficit, then also there was much talk about a permanent dollar shortage, about why it was so intractable, and about the major changes in the policies of European countries and of international agencies that would be required to "solve" the U.S. surplus.

It puts the present situation in much better perspective if we recognize that it is part of a slow movement of a pendulum, first from one extreme, then to the other. One country's deficit must be some other countries' surpluses. If the U.S. has large deficits, as now, then other countries must have surpluses. If, after the war, we had large surpluses, then other countries must have had deficits.

Both the dollar shortage after the war and the dollar excess today are manifestations of the same basic factor—the attempt by the countries of the world to maintain a system of fixed exchange rates without unifying their currencies. Let government fix any price—be it of silver or of gold, of wheat or of housing space—at a level that does not clear the market and a shortage or an excess is bound to develop. If the price is fixed too low, sellers will want to sell less than buyers will want to buy and there will be a shortage—as of housing space during the war and in New York City today, as of silver in the few years before the Treasury let its price go free in 1967, or as of gold in the few years before the central bankers let its price go free in 1968. If the price is fixed too high, sellers will want to sell more than buyers will want to buy and there will be an excess—as of wheat in most of the postwar period, and of silver and gold from 1934 to the 1950's.

The exchange rates that were fixed in the early postwar period made the dollar too cheap in terms of foreign currencies. Hence there was a shortage of dollars. The exchange rates today make the dollar too expensive. Hence there is an excess of dollars.

The first item in this section was written during the first swing of the pendulum and hence applies these basic principles to the postwar dollar shortage. The conclusion—that the best solution would be to set the dollar free and let its price be determined in the market—is just as applicable to the present situation, as is clear from the next two items in this section—my presentation in a "rational debate" conducted by the American Enterprise Institute and a series of five columns from *Newsweek* dealing with the recurrent crises of 1967 and 1968.

As these items make clear, I have for many years been in favor of setting free the prices of both gold and the dollar and letting them be determined by private trading in open markets. Time and again when I have made these proposals, I have been told that, however much sense they might make on economic grounds, they were not politically feasible. I have been, in effect, advised to stop wasting my time on idle dreams of a fundamental solution and instead devote my attention to exploring more superficial expedients that had some chance of being politically feasible. The most recent occasion on which I was reproached in this vein was in the course of taping a program for educational TV in which another economist and I discussed the balance of payments problem. Less than three weeks after taping this program, the political unfeasibility came to pass: the price of gold was set free.

I am tempted to draw two conclusions. (1) Economists are poor judges of political feasibility and had better stick to their own knitting. (2) Basic economic forces are stronger than professions by political officials, however exalted their positions.

The items discussed so far were all concerned with rather current events and immediate policy issues. The last two items in this section discuss the same basic questions but on a more fundamental level. The first is concerned with showing the economic difference between a unified currency, one in which different countries use essentially a single currency, though they may give it different names, and a collection of national currencies linked by fixed exchange rates. A real gold standard, such as prevailed in most of the Western world from 1879 to 1914, was an example of a unified currency. The pseudo gold standard that has prevailed since 1934 is an example of the second. Enormous damage has been done by the widespread failure to recognize this difference, by the tendency to look at the name rather than the substance.

The final item elaborates on some of these points, especially on the political implications of adopting a system of linking national currencies by fixed (pegged) exchange rates. Experience since 1965, when this paper was written, has dramatically underscored some of the dangers I saw in the attempt to peg exchange rates. Great Britain has been forced to devalue and even to let her domestic policy be largely dictated by central bankers in other countries. The U.S. has been in the humiliating position of being lectured to—and more than lectured to—by DeGaulle, of having to call emergency meetings of foreign central bankers to bail us out of our own ill-chosen policies. And withal, we are being told we must adjust our domestic policies not to our domestic needs but to what foreign central bankers say is good for us.

This may be political feasibility. It is both political and economic foolishness.

Why the Dollar Shortage? [1]

CHAPTER EIGHT The so-called "dollar shortage" that has plagued the world since the end of World War II is a striking example of the far-ranging consequences that can flow from the neglect of simple economic truths. The "dollar shortage" is said to result from "fundamental structural maladjustments" and to require extensive American aid to foreign countries. It has led to the proliferation of complicated systems of direct controls over transactions involving foreign exchange in one country after another; yet these controls have been powerless to prevent the frequent recurrence of the difficulties that led to their imposition. So far, 1953 is the first odd postwar year that Great Britain, the one-time international banker of the world, has not experienced a dramatic foreign exchange crisis. International conference has fol-

[1] This article is reprinted from *The Freeman*, Vol. 4, No. 6, December 14, 1953.

lowed international conference, and yet the "dollar" problem persists.

This certainly appears a complicated and intractable problem. Yet its fundamental cause and cure are alike simple: the dollar shortage is a result of governmentally controlled and rigid exchange rates; if exchange rates were freed from control and allowed to find their own levels in a free market, as the Canadian dollar now does,[2] the dollar shortage would evaporate overnight. The need to conserve dollars would no longer serve as an excuse for exchange controls, import and export quotas, and the rest of that complicated paraphernalia of modern mercantilism. On the other hand, so long as exchange rates continue to be determined by governmental fiat, and to be held rigid except for occasional devaluations or appreciations, there is almost no hope for the successful elimination of direct controls over international trade. Future attempts at liberalization of trade, however numerous and high-sounding the international agreements which they produce, will be doomed to the resounding failure that has marked the noble experiments of recent years.

But surely, you will say, the situation cannot be as simple as that. If it were, the able men who help determine national and international policy would long since have recognized the cause and put the cure into effect. And so they would have, if they did not regard the cure as worse than the disease. The real puzzle is not the cause and cure of the dollar shortage *per se*, but the stubborn and widespread reluctance to accept this particular cure. In part, this is simply another version of the general puzzle why there has been such a loss of faith in the price system in the modern era. But it also has rather special features of its own, since some of the most stubborn opposition has come from people who are firm believers in the price system in other connections.

An exchange rate is a price like any other price. At the present [1953] official rate of exchange, it costs $2.80 to buy one pound sterling; or, stated the other way, .357 of a pound (7

[2 The exchange rate of the Canadian dollar was determined in a free market from October, 1950 to May, 1962, when it was pegged at 92.5 U.S. cents to the Canadian dollar.]

shillings, 1⅚ pence) to buy one dollar.[3] It is clear that the lower
the price of an ordinary commodity, say, shoes, the larger will
be the number of pairs consumers want to buy and the smaller
will be the number that suppliers want to sell. In the same way,
the lower the price of a dollar in terms of the pound sterling, the
larger will be the number of dollars that Britons and others want
to buy, and the smaller will be the number of dollars that Americans (and others) want to sell. A dollar shortage in Britain
means that, *at the existing price of the dollar in shillings and
pence,* the number of dollars people want to buy is larger than
the number others want to sell.

At the official rate of exchange between the pound sterling
and the dollar, the dollar has been artificially cheap during most
of the postwar period. In consequence there has been a dollar
shortage. Unwilling to see this dollar shortage eliminated by a
change in the price of the pound (except when driven to periodical devaluations by unbearable pressure), or by other devices
we shall consider below, the British government has employed
direct controls over imports, exports, and other exchange transactions to eliminate the gap between the number of dollars demanded at the official price and the number supplied. And we
have of course aided them to eliminate the gap by making dollars
available through Marshall and other aid. Had the price of the
pound been free to fluctuate, the gap would have been eliminated
automatically by the operation of the free market—but then so
also would the apparent necessity for dollar aid and for direct
controls, which suggests one set of reasons why this cure has not
been regarded with favor.

It may seem like belaboring the obvious to emphasize at
such length that "dollar shortage" is a strictly meaningless phrase
unless the price of the dollar in terms of foreign currencies is
prevented by some means from responding to market forces;
that there cannot be a "shortage" except at some fixed price. Yet
the neglect of this elementary economic truism is a major source
of the floods of nonsense that have been written about the dollar
shortage.

[3 In November, 1967, the official rate of exchange was devalued from $2.80
a pound to $2.40 a pound, i.e., the price of one dollar was raised to 8 shillings, 4
pence.]

Even so eminent and sophisticated a journal as the London *Economist,* in a special supplement on "Living with the Dollar" published in November, 1952, discusses in detail the causes of the "dollar gap" in the past and its prospects for the future without even mentioning the exchange rate assumed in making the calculations, much less giving it any role at all as a cause of the dollar gap.

If I am right that the dollar shortage is a manifestation of fixed rates of exchange between different currencies, why has it appeared in such virulent form only in recent years? For decades prior to World War I and for some of the time between the two World Wars, many exchange rates, in particular the rate between the pound sterling and the dollar, were rigidly fixed under the then prevailing gold standard. Yet no dollar shortage in the modern sense emerged.

Real *vs.* Nominal Prices

The answer to this apparent paradox is to be found in a closer examination of the market for foreign exchange. Generally, people want to buy pounds with dollars in order to buy British goods and services. How many pounds they want to buy depends not only on the number of dollars they have to pay for a pound but also on the price of British goods in terms of pounds. To the purchaser of a British motor car, for example, a 10 per cent decline in the dollar price of the pound, with no change in the British price of the car, is identical to a 10 per cent decline in the British price of the car with no change in the dollar price of the pound. In either case, he can buy the British car with 10 per cent fewer dollars and so is more likely to do so than he otherwise would. The "real" price of foreign exchange can therefore alter even though its nominal price does not.

And this is precisely what tended to happen under the gold standard. If at any time Britain was tending to buy more from the United States than it was selling—that is, was tending to run a deficit—it would pay for some of the deficit by shipping gold. Since gold was the basis for the domestic supply of money, this would tend to produce deflationary conditions at home, which the Bank of England would frequently reinforce by other measures. Prices and incomes within Britain would therefore tend to fall. Conversely, the gold receipts of the United States would increase the money stock and produce rising prices. Together, these changes in internal prices produced a decline in the real price of the pound in terms of dollars.

Under an operating gold standard, then, it is only the nominal price of foreign exchange that is rigid. The real price varies with the internal prices in the various countries. And internal prices themselves are determined by external conditions: they must be whatever prices are required to equate the demand and supply of foreign exchange at the nominally rigid rate. Whether a country is inflating or deflating depends on the state of its balance of payments, and cannot at the same time be determined by domestic considerations.

The domination of internal monetary policy by external forces in this way is good insofar as it inhibits irresponsible governmental tinkering with money, but bad insofar as it makes one nation suffer from the irresponsible tinkerings of others. But whether good or bad in the abstract, it is clear that few nations are now willing to allow their internal monetary policies to be dominated by external forces. The emergence of full employment as a predominant goal of domestic policy spelled the end to a system in which the changes in the real price of foreign exchange required to equate demand and supply were brought about by automatic changes in internal prices. With rigid nominal exchange rates, foreign exchange shortages were inevitable—though only the particular rates chosen and the particular internal price levels explain why it was a dollar shortage rather than a pound shortage.

It is little wonder that direct controls over foreign trade have burgeoned in the postwar period despite strong pressures and the sincere desire, at least in some quarters, to eliminate them by international agreement. The price system has not been permitted to operate in the foreign exchange market. As in other markets, the only alternative is direct control of transactions by the state.

If the countries of the world would follow Canada's example,[4] they could remove at one blow all import restrictions and export subsidies, all restrictions on capital flows, all discriminatory measures, without fear that a dollar shortage would arise. Freedom of foreign trade from restrictions would promote greater freedom of internal trade as well, and the one would reinforce the other in increasing the efficiency and productivity of the world as a whole and each nation separately. Experiments in this direction promise dividends every bit as rich and remarkable as have been produced in various countries—notably Germany—by experiments in freeing domestic economies.

Flexible exchange rates have been opposed in part because of simple misunderstanding; particularly, the belief that they necessarily imply unstable exchange rates. This by no means need be so. If, indeed, flexible exchange rates were unstable, it would be because of underlying instability in the economic conditions affecting international trade, and, in particular, in the internal monetary policy of the various countries. Pegging the exchange rate does nothing in itself to reduce this instability; it simply diverts its expression into other channels—exchange crises, direct controls, and the like. The ultimate ideal is a world in which exchange rates, while free to vary, are in fact highly stable because of real stability in the internal policies of the various countries. This result is far more likely to be achieved if each country bears the major burden of its own monetary instability—as it does under a system of flexible rates—than if monetary instability in any one country is transmitted directly to its trading partners—as it is under rigid exchange rates.

A Left-Right Coalition

The strength of the opposition to flexible exchange rates is in larger measure, however, to be explained by the remarkable

[4 Unfortunately, as noted above, Canada returned to a fixed rate, not because the floating rate did not work well but because the government tried to manipulate it to offset bad monetary policy and in the process set off a speculative movement. When it started the manipulation, it had no intention of fixing the rate but it finally did so, largely in desperation, to stop the speculative movement it had itself unleashed.]

coalition that has opposed it; a coalition of the central planners and the central bankers of the world—the extreme left and the extreme right of the political spectrum. The central planners of the world have no faith in a free price system; they prefer to rely on the control of economic activity by state officials. They therefore favor direct controls over imports and exports for their own sake and would do so regardless of the method of fixing exchange rates. Fixed exchange rates have, however, the enormous political virtue, from their point of view, that they make such controls seem like an inescapable necessity enforced by balance of payments difficulties. Many people are for this reason led to favor direct controls, or at least tolerate them, who would otherwise oppose them vigorously. And once direct controls are accepted over international transactions, they strongly foster and facilitate the imposition of internal controls as well.

The central bankers of the world and numerous other proponents of a fully operative gold standard are fervent defenders of the price system in most other manifestations. Yet they oppose its application to exchange rates because they cling to the shadow of rigid rates in the hope of getting the substance of external restraints on domestic monetary policy. The result has been support for a system which makes the worst of both worlds. The postwar system of exchange rates, temporarily rigid but subject to change from time to time by governmental action, can provide neither the certainty about exchange rates and the freedom from irresponsible governmental action of a fully operative gold standard, nor the independence of each country from the monetary vagaries of other countries, nor the freedom of each country to pursue internal monetary stability in its own way that are provided by truly flexible exchange rates. This postwar system sacrifices the simultaneous achievement of the two major objectives of vigorous multilateral trade and independence of internal monetary policy on the altar of the essentially minor objective of a rigid exchange rate. Belief in economic internationalism has in this way been a major factor contributing to the tragic growth of economic nationalism in the postwar era.

Free Exchange Rates [1]

CHAPTER NINE Economists may not know much. But we do know one thing very well: how to produce shortages and surpluses. Do you want to produce a shortage of any product? Simply have government fix and enforce a legal *maximum* price on the product which is less than the price that would otherwise prevail. That is how the great housing "shortage" of postwar years was produced—by legal fixing of maximum rents. That is why New York City which is the only city in the country that still has legal rent control is also the only city that still has a housing shortage of the wartime type.

Do you want to produce a surplus of any product? Simply have government fix and enforce a legal *minimum* price above the price that would

[1 Reprinted from Milton Friedman and Robert V. Roosa, *The Balance of Payments: Free vs. Fixed Exchange Rates* (Rational Debate Seminars, American Enterprise Institute for Public Policy Research, Washington, D.C., 1967).]

otherwise prevail, either by making it illegal to pay less or by offering to buy all that is offered at that price. That is why there is a surplus of unskilled youths seeking jobs—because the government makes it illegal for enterprises to pay less than the legal minimum wage. That is why we were plagued for so many years by agricultural surpluses—because the government pegged farm prices at levels above those that would have cleared the market.

The same fixed price may at one time produce a surplus and at another a shortage. An excellent example is the price of silver. When, at the end of 1933, the U.S. government first offered to buy all newly produced domestic silver at 64-64/99 cents an ounce, this price was well above the price that would clear the market—at the end of 1932, silver had been selling on the open market for as low as 25 cents an ounce. The result of this action plus the subsequent Silver Purchase Act of 1934 which authorized purchases abroad as well, plus subsequent rises in the fixed price, was a veritable flood of silver. We drained China, Mexico, and the rest of the world, more than tripling our stocks of silver. Since 1955, however, the price has been below the price that would clear the market—thanks to price inflation at home and abroad and despite further rises in the pegged price to $1.29. As a result, there is now a shortage instead of a surplus. We are keeping the price down only by rapidly depleting our reserves. We shall be forced to let it rise sometime in the next few years.[2]

Wheat may be or may become another example. For many years, the great problem was the surplus generated by our pegged price. We were forced to build mammoth storage facilities, to impose extensive restrictions and controls on farmers to keep down their output, to tolerate a different price at home and abroad, controlling foreign trade in wheat in order to do so. Now, as world population and food needs are booming and inflation proceeds on its merry way, the pegged wheat price may be or may become too low. If so, our stocks will be rapidly drained.

As these examples suggest, the technique of fixing prices is an extremely powerful tool. The result will often appear far out of proportion to the cause. Fix the price only a little too high and

[2] As occurred not long after the lecture was delivered.

ll appear to be a tremendous surplus because the price
ultaneously discourage buyers and encourage sellers. In
, it will cause the disappointed sellers to make multiple
hich will make the supply look larger than it is. Every
attempt to curtail supply by government regulation will be met
by the ingenuity of the myriad of private suppliers trying to find
some way around the regulations, so that there will be a continual
tug-of-war, with the regulations piling ever higher. Fix the price
only a little too low and there will appear to be a tremendous
shortage, because the price will simultaneously encourage buyers
and discourage sellers. In addition, disappointed buyers will
stand, or have stand-ins, in more than one queue.

The situation is reminiscent of Micawber's law, as reported
by Charles Dickens, "Annual income twenty pounds, annual
expenditure nineteen six, result happiness. Annual income twenty
pounds, annual expenditure twenty pounds ought and six, result misery."

The apparent disproportion between cause and effect is the
major hindrance—as I have discovered again and again—to public
understanding of the phenomenon. How can it be, the ordinary
man is likely to say, that prohibiting landlords from raising the
rent—surely no more than a simple act of justice—can have such
far-reaching effects as long lists of people seeking apartments
relative to apartments available, widespread complaints of a
shortage of housing space—even though the number of dwelling
units per person may be at its all-time maximum—the development of black markets, the deterioration of rental housing, and
so on and on? Can it be, the same intelligent layman is likely to
say, that the entire complicated farm surplus problem, with its
panoply of regulations, elections among farmers, plowing under
of hogs, taking land out of cultivation—that this whole problem
simply reflects government's attempt to assure parity prices for
farmers? Surely something more basic and fundamental must be
involved.

Yet the truth is, nothing more is involved. Fix prices—and
the problems will multiply; let prices find their own level in free
markets—and the problems will disappear. The abolition of rent
control everywhere in the United States except New York City

shortly after the war is one dramatic example. The "shortages" disappeared almost overnight. The real problems of high cost of building and of urban blight of course remained—but the false problems disappeared. And in this case, New York City remained as a control to illuminate the source of the problems. The abolition of price control in Germany by Ludwig Erhard one Sunday afternoon in 1948 is another and even more dramatic example. That was all it took to release Germany from the chains that were producing stagnation at a level of output half the prewar level and to permit the German miracle to occur.

All of this may seem far afield from my announced topic but it is not. The problem of the balance of payments is simply another example of the far-reaching effects of government price fixing, complicated only by two facts: first, that two sets of prices are involved—the price of gold in terms of various national currencies, and the price of national currencies in terms of one another; second, that more than one country is involved.

The existence of two sets of prices is a relic of an earlier day, when there was a real gold standard, and "dollar," "pound," and "franc" were simply names for different amounts of gold. Under such a gold standard, government's role is primarily simply as a mint, to certify the weight and fineness of the gold, coin it on demand, issue warehouse certificates for gold, and redeem the certificates—though in practice governments also issued promises to pay gold not fully backed by gold. Under such a system, exchange rates were kept in narrow bounds—within the "gold points"—not by government price fixing but by the private shipment of gold whenever the market price varied by enough to make it worthwhile to acquire a foreign currency by shipping gold rather than by an exchange transaction. Exchange rates stayed within narrow limits for the same reason and in the same way that the price of sugar in New York never deviates much from the price of sugar in Chicago—because if it did deviate, it would pay private traders to ship sugar.

The movements of gold that kept exchange rates in line also served to produce adjustments that made the gold flows self-limiting. The country shipping gold experienced a decline in the quantity of money; the country receiving gold, a rise.

The monetary changes in turn affected incomes and prices, and therewith the demand for foreign exchange, lowering the demand in the country shipping gold, and raising it in the country receiving gold. The key feature of this process was that it was completely automatic and gradual. There was no way the gold movements could be prevented from affecting the money stock. A small discrepancy called forth a small adjustment. There was a unified currency system, not a collection of national currencies linked by fixed rates. Such a unified currency does not exist today on a worldwide scale though it still exists among the different states of the U.S., between Britain and some of its colonial territories, like Hong Kong, and in many similar cases.

The situation today is clearly very different. Gold is a commodity whose price is supported by the government—like wheat or butter. The major difference is that we support the price only for foreigners, not for U.S. citizens, since it is illegal for U.S. citizens to hold gold except for numismatic or industrial purposes. In addition, gold has the special property that at the moment there is a highly elastic foreign demand for it, so we can always sell it to acquire foreign exchange. Clearly, we could peg the price of gold even though exchange rates were not fixed. For example, Canada's having a floating exchange rate, as it did from 1950 to 1962, did not prevent us from continuing to peg the price of gold even though Canada is a large producer of gold. There would have been a conflict only if Canada had also tried to peg the price in terms of Canadian currency.

The levels at which exchange rates are now fixed are calculated from the official price of gold each nation lists with the International Monetary Fund. But it is clear that exchange rates are not kept within narrow bounds by the movement of gold. Most countries that have fixed exchange rates with one another do not freely buy and sell gold. The U.S. does indirectly on the London gold market with the cooperation of the Bank of England, but it does so in order to peg the gold price, just as we sell silver to peg the silver price, not as the primary means of fixing exchange rates. We could abandon the pegging of the price of gold and yet continue to peg exchange rates, just as the pegging of exchange rates does not require the pegging of the price of lead, or copper, or steel. Gold is now at most window dressing, not the kingpin of the monetary system that determines the quantity of money. Hence, I propose in this paper to concentrate on exchange rates, leaving mostly to one side, as a subsidiary issue, the price of gold.

The second complication is that more than one government is involved. Consider, for specificity, the case of Britain and the United States. The official price of the pound sterling in terms of the dollar is $2.80,[3] but our agreement with the IMF permits the price to fluctuate a bit on each side of that, roughly between $2.82 and $2.78. The U.S. is committed to keeping the price from rising above $2.82—since that would constitute a depreciation of the U.S. currency; the British are committed to keeping the price from falling below $2.78—since that would constitute a depreciation of the British currency. Of course, there is nothing to prevent either country from engaging in transactions that help the other keep its commitment, but that is the formal division of responsibility.

The U.S. can keep the price from rising above $2.82 only by offering to sell all the pounds demanded at that price—i.e., to buy all the dollars offered; the British can keep the price from falling below $2.78 only by offering to buy all the pounds offered at that price—i.e., to sell all the dollars demanded at that price. How can the two countries succeed?

Suppose, that, at a price of $2.82 per pound, the number of dollars that people or governments wish to use to buy pounds in order to spend, lend, or give away is greater than the number of dollars that other people or governments wish to acquire with pounds. Suppose, that is, that the U.S. has a potential balance-of-payments deficit. How can the U.S. keep the price at $2.82? Clearly, there are basically only two ways: by providing the additional pounds, either out of its own reserves of foreign exchange or by borrowing them from someone else; or by inducing or forcing people to change the number of pounds they seek to buy. And the converse statements hold for the British in the contrary case.

To use the language that has become common, there are

[3 Since the British devaluation in November, 1967, $2.40.]

two problems: the liquidity problem—having enough reserves to be able to meet demands; the adjustment problem—keeping demand in line with supply. This is the precise counterpart of the problem for wheat: the liquidity problem—accumulating or decumulating wheat stocks; the adjustment problem—keeping down the production of wheat or stimulating its consumption.

Superficially, it looks as if the liquidity problem could be easily solved simply by reversing the tasks assigned the United States and Britain. Let Britain keep the price of the pound sterling from rising above $2.82 by offering to sell an unlimited number of pounds at that price and let the United States keep the price of the pound from falling below $2.78 by offering to buy an unlimited number of pounds at that price. Each can always do so. Britain manufactures pounds and the United States manufactures dollars, so each can always meet its commitments. However, in doing so, each is in effect giving the other country a blank check on its own goods and services. If the price of the pound were tending to rise, Britain would be accumulating dollars. The counterpart would be a flow of goods from Britain to the United States. Britain would in effect be giving the United States an unintended loan at a zero interest rate. This is precisely what happened to Germany for many years: it accepted a large inflow of dollars, which meant that it was selling a larger dollar volume of goods than it was buying; it was implicitly exporting goods on credit. Clearly no country will be willing to do this indefinitely.

Yet this approach is worth mentioning, because it is the lure that underlies all the talk of an international agreement to create "paper gold," new international reserves. At bottom, what is involved is an agreement by countries to make automatic loans to one another. Every country will be in favor of such an agreement, in principle. But each will want a different agreement—one that enables it to borrow much and commits it to lending little. Thus I predict, without fear of successful contradiction, that despite all the appearance of agreement in principle, no effective agreement will in fact be reached.[4]

[4 A tentative agreement in principle to create "paper gold" in the form of S.D.R.'s (Special Drawing Rights) has been reached among the major countries

To return to the United States' liquidity problem. The alternative to Britain's providing an unlimited line of credit at zero interest is for the United States to build up reserves in advance from which it can meet excess demands for pounds—this is indeed the important role played by our gold stocks—or to arrange to borrow as the occasion demands.

Clearly, potential deficits cannot be met indefinitely out of reserves. Reserves are necessarily limited. Clearly, also, to meet the deficits indefinitely by governmental borrowing abroad would be costly and undesirable. And, on the other side, no country will be willing to accumulate another country's currency indefinitely. *Reserves alone cannot do the job.* There must be some adjustment mechanism.

What possible adjustment mechanisms are there? One is the standard gold-standard mechanism—changes in the quantity of money, income, and prices internally. After all, the only reason a problem arises is because the existence of central banks interferes with this mechanism. With central banks, a payment deficit need not mean a reduction in the quantity of money, because the central bank can offset it, and a surplus need not mean an increase. Indeed, central banks are a necessary—and today almost a sufficient—condition for a balance-of-payments problem.

A central bank could do deliberately what the real gold standard did automatically. To correct the United States balance-of-payments deficit, it could reduce the quantity of money (or reduce the rate of growth), lowering incomes and prices—or letting them rise less rapidly than in other countries. This would reduce the demand for foreign exchange and increase its supply.

The United States has done this to some extent. It is clear that monetary policy was tighter than it otherwise would have been from 1956-61 because of the balance-of-payments problem. But it is also clear that it is both unlikely that the United States would put major reliance on this adjustment mechanism and

but (1) France has already refused to participate; (2) the details have not yet been settled; (3) the date of proposed issuance of S.D.R.'s is some years away; (4) even the amounts now talked about are small by comparison with either existing reserves or total world trade. Hence, I remain sceptical that any plan, involving more than token amounts, will ever become effective.]

undesirable that it should do so. It is unlikely because of the government's commitment to full employment. It is almost inconceivable that any administration, of either party, would be willing to force a significant domestic recession or depression to resolve a balance-of-payments problem. It is undesirable that the United States put major reliance on this adjustment mechanism partly because foreign trade is so small a part of our economy—it is absurd to force 95 per cent of the economy to adjust to 5 per cent rather than the other way around. More basically, it is undesirable because many of the adjustments forced on us are likely to be the product not of changes in the real forces of demand or supply but of monetary manipulations of other countries.

This adjustment mechanism is the one which the proponents of fixed rates regard as the "discipline" imposed by the fixed-rate system. But it is a peculiar discipline. The discipline of fixed rates forced inflation on Germany in the past decade at least as effectively as it forced deflation on us. The only discipline is to keep in step with the rest of the world, not to march in the right direction. In any event, it is clearly a discipline that we are not willing to accept.

The only other adjustment mechanism—while pegging exchange rates—is to control by direct or indirect means the amount of foreign exchange people try to buy—the counterpart to restrictions on the production of wheat. Britain and other countries have, of course, extensive exchange control. A resident of Britain may not exchange pounds for dollars without the explicit permission of a government official. This has involved extraordinarily detailed control of the day-to-day life of the British citizen—where he may go on a vacation, what books he may read, and so on, ad infinitum.

We have so far avoided explicit exchange control, but we have interfered in many ways with private trade—some serious, some niggling, some demeaning. Oil import quotas, meat quotas, and quotas and tariffs on many other products have been justified as means of "saving" foreign exchange. The niggling reduction of the duty-free tourist's allowance has the same origin. So has the demeaning spectacle of our negotiating "voluntary" quotas on exports from Hong Kong and Singapore and Japan. Our high officials have gone hat-in-hand to France and Germany and other countries to plead for earlier repayments of loans and special purchases of American goods. We have required recipients of foreign aid to buy American goods—giving with one hand and taking away with the other. We have preached free trade and practiced restriction. And most recently, we have gone in for "voluntary" controls on foreign lending by banks and foreign investment by enterprises. And the end is not yet.[5]

With all this we have not succeeded. The experience of countless price-fixing schemes has been repeated. Let the fixed price differ from the price that would clear the market, and it will take herculean efforts to hold it.

Consequently, we have also been driven to the final adjustment mechanism—changes in the exchange rate. We profess to have kept the exchange rate rigid. Yet we have in effect devalued it selectively. That is what the interest equalization tax amounts to. For purposes of buying foreign securities, the dollar has been devalued by 15 per cent, and a further devaluation is proposed. That is also what our program of reducing the foreign exchange component of military expenditures amounts to. Our military authorities are instructed to compare the cost in dollars at the official exchange rate of purchasing an item abroad with the cost in dollars of buying it in the United States. If the cost in the United States exceeds the foreign cost by less than x per cent, they are instructed to buy it at home—paradoxically to save dollars. I do not know what x is but I understand that it is sizable, something over 50 per cent. The tying of foreign aid is another example.

We sneer at South American countries that adopt multiple exchange rate systems. Yet that is what we have adopted—only in concealed form.

There is one and only one satisfactory solution: abolish governmental price fixing. Let exchange rates become free market prices determined primarily by private dealings. Let the government simply stay out of the picture.

[5 In January, 1968, the President made these restrictions compulsory, a form of explicit exchange control, and asked Congress to enact barriers to tourism.]

Suppose, under such a system, that, at a price of $2.80 to the pound, the number of dollars that people want to use to buy pounds to spend, lend, or give away is greater than the number of dollars holders of pounds want to acquire. The eager buyers will offer to pay more. The price of the pound will be bid up. As it rises, buyers of pounds will be discouraged—because a higher price of the pound means a higher price in dollars for goods and services bought abroad—and the sellers of pounds will be encouraged—because a higher price of the pound means that they can buy more United States goods and services with a given number of pounds. At some price, say $3.08, the number of dollars offered will be equal to the number of dollars demanded.

This rise in the price of the pound by 10 per cent will have had precisely the same effect on the relative costs to Americans and Britons of American and British goods as a decline of 10 per cent in United States prices with no change in British prices, or a rise of 10 per cent in British prices with no change in United States prices. But how much easier it is to have the exchange rate change by 10 per cent than to get a *general* decline in all United States prices by 10 per cent. Why not have one price—and that a potentially highly flexible one—do the adjusting rather than require the myriads of domestic prices to vary, with all their stickiness and all the side effects? Why not have the dog wag the tail, instead of the tail wag the dog?

As this example suggests, a system of floating exchange rates completely eliminates the balance-of-payments problem—just as in a free market there cannot be a surplus or a shortage in the sense of eager sellers unable to find buyers or eager buyers unable to find sellers. The price may fluctuate but there cannot be a deficit or a surplus threatening an exchange crisis. Floating exchange rates would put an end to the grave problems requiring repeated meetings of secretaries of the Treasury and governors of central banks to try to draw up sweeping reforms. It would put an end to the occasional crisis producing frantic scurrying of high governmental officials from capital to capital, midnight phone calls among the great central banks lining up emergency loans to support one or another currency.

Indeed this is, I believe, one of the major sources of the opposition to floating exchange rates. The people engaged in these activities are important people and they are all persuaded that they are engaged in important activities. It cannot be, they say to themselves, that these important activities arise simply from pegging exchange rates. They must have more basic roots. Hence, they say, it is simpleminded to believe that freeing exchange rates would eliminate the problem. That is what the allied advisers engaged in price control, rationing, and the like told Erhard that summer in 1948. That is why he removed price controls on a Sunday, when they were not in their offices to countermand his edicts.

Under a system of floating exchange rates, the liquidity problem disappears. There is no need for official foreign exchange reserves. Private individuals will provide the reserves needed—just as they do in commodities that trade in a free market. If a given movement in exchange rates seems temporary, it will be in the self-interest of private holders of exchange to dampen the move by speculation and they can be counted on to do so.

With floating rates, we could therefore terminate at once the frustrating and ineffective negotiations for a new international liquidity arrangement—negotiations that are in any event bound to fail. More important, we could abolish at once the interest-equalization tax and informal exchange controls.

Most important of all, floating rates would enable us to separate issues and determine our national policies on the right grounds. Monetary and fiscal policy could be directed toward pursuing internal stability without being hamstrung by the balance of payments. We could decide how much foreign aid to give in terms of our resources and our values, not by the irrelevant consideration of the currency in which it is expressed. We could instruct the military to buy in the cheapest market and keep the real costs to a minimum—not turn them into a foreign exchange authority. We could conduct foreign policy in terms of our true national interests—not in terms of the effect on gold flows. We could behave in foreign trade like a great nation, not like a mendicant, by unilaterally moving toward freer trade without having to be concerned about balance-of-payments problems.

This last point perhaps deserves a slight digression. Not the least of the advantages of floating rates, in my opinion, is that it makes it so much easier for the layman to understand the merits of free trade. With rigid rates, the first effect of a reduction in tariffs is an increase in imports without any immediate effect on exports. It looks as if imports have simply displaced domestic products and so produced unemployment. It takes a subtle chain of reasoning to show that this is only part of the story, that the increase in imports will have indirect effects that will ultimately lead to an expansion of exports so that the final result is an increase in foreign trade not an increase in unemployment. And, indeed, with our present nearly paralyzed adjustment mechanism, the indirect effects may be long delayed and highly unreliable.

With floating rates, a reduction in tariffs will also produce an attempted increase in imports. But how can this be realized? Only if the importers can get some foreign exchange. To do so they will bid up its price which immediately makes exports more attractive to foreigners. The first effect of a reduction in tariffs is thus a rise in the price of foreign exchange and a simultaneous increase in imports and exports. There is not even a temporary importation of unemployment.

The floating rate provides the protection to the balance of payments that is essential if we are to move significantly to ease barriers to trade. In the absence of such protection, it appears as if we can afford to reduce barriers only in return for a reciprocal reduction of barriers by others. The result is the kind of drawn-out and ineffective negotiations that are currently nearing their appointed end in connection with the Kennedy round.

What objections have been raised against floating rates?

One is the allegation that we cannot move to floating rates on our own, that just as two governments are now involved in pegging each rate, so it will take two to unpeg. This is in one sense correct, yet it is irrelevant. The United States can announce that it will no longer try to keep the dollar from depreciating— i.e., in the case of the pound, no longer try to prevent the price of the pound from rising above $2.82. If Britain wants to take on the task of keeping the price of the pound from rising, fine.

It can do so only by either being willing to accumulate dollars indefinitely—which is to say, by extending us an unlimited line of credit—or by adapting its internal policy to ours, so that the free market rate stays below $2.82. In either case, we can only gain, not lose. Similarly, if it chooses to continue to keep the price of the pound from falling, that again is no cause for concern on our part. It can only do so by using dollar reserves, which we must be ready to permit, or again by aligning its internal policy with ours.

I think it highly likely that if we announced that our government will no longer intervene in the exchange market, a fair number of other countries would peg their currencies to ours. I see no harm in that and much good. Perhaps we could begin to build up a truly unified currency area—not a collection of national currencies linked by pegged rates. A system of floating exchange rates has basically much more in common with a real gold standard—in that both leave private individuals free to buy and sell currencies as they wish and both are free of government intervention—than either has with our present system.

A second objection that is raised is that floating exchange rates would be highly unstable and that unstable rates would add to the uncertainty and difficulty of conducting foreign trade. However, floating rates need not be highly unstable. Canada had floating rates from 1950 to 1962 and they were highly stable. If floating rates are highly unstable, it will be because the internal monetary policies of the countries or some other aspects of their economy are highly unstable. But in that case, the uncertainty is there and the only question is what form it takes. Under a real gold standard, the uncertainty would be about internal price levels, because they would reflect the instability. Under pegged exchange rates, the uncertainty would be about whether exchange would be available, that is, what the exchange controls would be like. If anything, the uncertainty about the price of foreign exchange under a floating rate system is the easiest for a trader to protect himself against by hedging in a futures market.

A related argument is that the uncertainty under floating rates would be greater than under other systems because floating rates would give rise to destabilizing speculation. When I first began writing on this subject nearly two decades ago, I took this objection seriously. I no longer do. In the interim, there have been a considerable number of careful empirical studies of speculation under floating rates. None has produced a clear example of destabilizing speculation on any significant scale. And the bulk of the evidence strongly supports the view that speculation has generally been clearly stabilizing. I think it is time therefore that this bug-a-boo is given a decent burial—at least until somebody can come up with some real evidence that it is more than a bug-a-boo.

Another objection to floating rates is that it reduces the attractiveness of a country as a financial center. This can be correct. It may well be that Britain was at one time well advised on this score to maintain rigid rates with other countries or that Switzerland is now. But this seems to me not a relevant objection for the United States. First, our international financial activity is not a major industry. Second, its development is interfered with at least as much by the measures—like the interest equalization tax and "voluntary" controls on foreign lending—that we take to peg the rates as it would be by floating rates. Third, the formation of a "dollar" bloc, suggested as a possibility above, might be a favorable development. Fourth, without the interest equalization tax, informal exchange controls, and extensive trade barriers, the dollar would very likely be used even more extensively than it is as an international currency. Paradoxical though it seems, letting rates float, and removing controls, may be the most effective way to strengthen New York's role as a financial center.

The major objection raised against floating rates is one already mentioned—that it would remove the "discipline" which fixed rates are said to impose on domestic economic policy, that it would open the door to irresponsible inflationary monetary policy. This objection has merit if the alternative were a real gold standard. It has some merit for countries like Italy and Japan that have been susceptible to highly inflationary policies, that have been willing to submit to the discipline of the balance of payments, and for which foreign trade is a substantial part of total trade. It has negligible merit for the United States. Foreign trade is so small a part of total trade, and our reserves are so large, that we can neglect the balance of payments for long stretches of time, letting small disturbances build up into big ones. And even then, we are not willing to submit to the discipline. Instead, we resort to import quotas, tariffs, multiple exchange rates, and informal exchange controls. The same discipline which produced these, incidentally also produced inflationary pressure from 1945 to 1956 when we were accumulating gold and foreign exchange. The discipline is asymmetrical: we yield to it when it imposes inflation on us; we resist it when it calls for deflation. That is a kind of discipline that I think we can do without.

These are the objections to floating rates. But they are not the reasons why we do not—and very likely shall not—adopt floating rates.

The most important reason we stick to pegged rates is the tyranny of the status quo. The United States has taken the public position that the dollar will be defended. The President and other high officials have committed themselves over and over again to the proposition that the dollar will not be devalued, that the present system of pegged rates is one of the great postwar achievements, which the United States will support with might and main. Once such a position is taken, it takes a major crisis to produce a change.[6]

A second reason is the confusion between a real gold standard and the pseudo gold standard we now have. The public at large and in particular the financial community hankers after the freedom from government intervention of a real gold standard. It confuses the pegged rates of our present system with the rigid rates of a real gold standard.

A third reason is the confusion between devaluation and a system of floating rates. A particular exchange problem can be met by changing the level at which the exchange rate is pegged. Such a system, under which the level at which the exchange rate is pegged is changed at substantial intervals of time, is the worst of both worlds. An adjustable peg provides neither the cer-

[6 Just as it took a major gold crisis to produce a change, in March, 1968, in our policy of pegging the world price of gold.]

tainty of a truly fixed rate nor the flexibility of a floating rate. It is certain to be subject to destabilizing speculation. Such a system must be sharply distinguished from a system of floating rates. Devaluation of the dollar to a new pegged level would, in my opinion, be most unwise; whereas establishment of a system of floating rates is eminently to be desired.

A final reason is what may be called the Arizona effect. As you may know, the death rate from tuberculosis is higher in Arizona than in any other state in the country. Clearly, Arizona must be a most unhealthy place to live. Similarly, floating exchange rates have often been adopted as a last resort by countries experiencing grave financial crises when all other devices have failed. That is a major reason why they have such a bad reputation.

Gold and the Dollar,

May, 1967 — March, 1968

CHAPTER TEN This chapter is a running commentary on an eventful year in the annals of international finance. At its outset, the U.S. Treasury was pegging the price of silver at $1.29 an ounce, and of gold at $35 an ounce.

In June, the price of silver was freed. In November, sterling was devalued, and there was a run on gold. I predicted that the price of gold too would not be held, and promised a later column on the dollar. Early in January, 1968, President Johnson proposed a drastic program of controls which provided a striking point of departure for the promised column.

As our gold stock continued to decline, the President proposed—and I discussed—repeal of the gold requirement for Federal Reserve Notes.

Repeal was hastened by the great gold rush in the first two weeks of March, 1968, which ended with the freeing of the market price of gold—and also produced the reams of newspaper stories at which I poked fun in the final column.

235

The story is not yet over. A dollar crisis is still to come, and hopefully, like the gold crisis, will turn out to be a blessing by forcing us to free the dollar.

A DOLLAR IS A DOLLAR

Reprinted from *Newsweek*, May 15, 1967.

A dollar is a dollar is a dollar. But why should it also be exactly 7 English shillings, 1 penny, and 3 farthings; [1] 4 French francs and 94 centimes, and 4 German marks?

The explanation is very different today than it was in an earlier era. In 1913, for example, anyone could take $20.67 to the U.S. Treasury and exchange it for one fine ounce of gold. He could take the ounce of gold to London, go to the Bank of England, and exchange it for 4 pounds, 4 shillings, 11 pence, and 1 farthing; or he could take it to Paris, go to the Bank of France, and exchange it for 107 francs and 10 centimes. As a result, the price of the pound could not vary much from its then official parity of $4.8665, or the franc from its then official parity of $0.1930.

A Real Gold Standard

If the pound became appreciably more expensive than $4.8665, alert U.S. financiers would get pounds, not by buying them on the market, but by exchanging dollars at the U.S. Treasury for gold, shipping the gold to London, and converting it into pounds at the Bank of England. If the pound became appreciably cheaper than $4.8665 (i.e., the dollar became more expensive) alert British financiers would get dollars by reversing the process. In this way, the cost of shipping gold set narrow limits—termed the "gold points"—on the price of the pound sterling.

That was a real gold standard. Gold circulated in the form of coin and gold certificates. Britain and the U.S. in effect had a common currency differing only in the names attached to an ounce of gold. Individuals were free to buy or sell dollars for pounds or pounds for

[1 Since British devaluation in November, 1967, 8 English shillings, 4 pence.]

dollars at any price. The price of the one currency in terms of the other stayed within narrow limits for the same reason and in the same way that the price of sugar in New York never deviates much from the price of sugar in Chicago—because if it did deviate, it would pay private traders to ship sugar.

The situation today is very different. The dollar and the pound are no longer names for different amounts of gold. They are names for separate national currencies. There still are official prices of gold. But these official prices serve primarily as a means to calculate the official price of the pound in terms of dollars ($2.80).[2] Holders of paper money cannot automatically exchange it for gold at the official prices—indeed, since 1934, when the official U.S. price was raised to $35 an ounce, it has been illegal for U.S. residents to hold gold, except for numismatic or industrial purposes. Gold is now [1967] a commodity whose price is supported by governmental action—like butter. Gold no longer determines the quantity of money.

Pegged Exchange Rates

The price of the pound sterling is kept at $2.80, not by market forces, but by the British and U.S. governments who peg it at that level by buying and selling dollars and pounds at the official price. They can succeed only by controlling the amount people offer to buy and sell. In Britain, it is illegal for residents to trade pounds for dollars except with the permission of a government official. The U.S. still does not have explicit exchange control, but we have extensive informal controls—ask the businessman who seeks to invest abroad or the banker who seeks to lend abroad.

The pegging of exchange rates is the basic reason for our balance-of-payments problem—just as the pegging of rents is the basic reason for the housing "shortage" in New York City; the pegging of the price of silver for the rapid depletion of our silver reserves; the pegging of the price of butter for the accumulation of stocks of butter.

We should set the dollar free and let its price in terms of other currencies be determined by private dealings. Such a system of floating exchange rates would eliminate the balance-of-payments problem, thereby enabling us to abolish the income-equalization tax and informal exchange controls, and to move unilaterally toward freer trade.

[2 Now, $2.40.]

Paradoxically, most leaders of the financial community are against this free-market solution. They confuse the present use of gold as window dressing with a real gold standard. Staunch opponents of government price-fixing in other areas, they support it in this one. They need to examine their clichés.

THE PRICE OF GOLD

Reprinted from *Newsweek*, January 1, 1968.

The gold rush of 1967 has subsided. But the lull is temporary. The hard fact is that the price of gold will not be held at $35 an ounce for many more years. The price of gold will be raised or permitted to rise.[1] The only questions are when and how.

A higher dollar price of gold need not mean a change in exchange rates. If the price of gold in terms of other currencies rose by the same percentage, all exchange rates would remain the same. What will or should happen to the dollar price of gold is a different question from what will or should happen to the price of the dollar in terms of other currencies. This column deals with the first question; a later column will deal with the second.

Gold Is Cheap

The price of gold was last changed on Jan. 31, 1934, when President Roosevelt set it at $35 an ounce. At the time, that was a very high price, and it attracted a flood of gold to the United States. However, other prices have nearly tripled since then. The same price is therefore now low, and our gold stocks are melting away.

At the present price, private purchase of gold exceeds world production.[2] The price is held down to $35 an ounce only by supplementing current production from existing monetary stocks of gold, notably, of course, the U.S. stock. The situation is precisely what it was for silver before June 1967. The U.S. Treasury was then pegging the price

[1 The price of gold in private dealings was set free and permitted to rise in February, 1968.]

[2 For details, see Herbert Woolley, "New Patterns, New Outlook for World Gold," *Engineering and Mining Journal*, October 1967.]

of silver at $1.29 an ounce. Declining silver stocks forced the Treasury to free the price. It is now around $2 an ounce.

Only two things could prevent a similar outcome for gold: (1) a fall in other prices in the U.S.; (2) a fall in the world demand for gold.

The price of gold was constant at $20.67 an ounce from 1879 to 1933 because the U.S. was then willing to let other prices adjust to the fixed price of gold. We no longer are. We have let other prices get far out of line. No Administration and no Federal Reserve Board will tolerate a major deflation to bring other prices back in line with the price of gold. And they need not do so. We no longer have a real gold standard in which the amount of gold determines the amount of money. Gold has been demoted to a commodity whose price is pegged.

In 1933, Congress made it illegal for U.S. citizens to hold gold. This misguided measure reduced domestic demand. If we could do the same thing internationally, and enforce it, the price of gold might well fall rather than rise. But Congress's writ does not run abroad. A further reduction in the demand for gold requires that either private people or central banks be induced to hold less gold.

Only long years of experience with stable money will wean private individuals from the attachment to gold produced by centuries of experience with monetary instability.

Central banks have in recent years held some paper dollars instead of real gold—but only under great pressure from us. That is why our government is striving to get them to accept a new international money—paper gold instead of real gold. But this effort will not succeed. Despite the widely publicized agreement in principle at Rio, conflicts of interest between countries on details will, in my opinion, prevent the creation of more than a token amount of paper gold.

The likely outcome is that we shall experience a series of successive crises like the 1967 gold rush. If we wish, we can surmount one or several more. But sooner or later, we shall have to throw in the sponge.

Free the Price of Gold

When that occurs, we could raise the price of gold to a new level, say, $50 an ounce, and try to hold it there. That would be a serious mistake. It would be far better simply to stop buying and selling gold at a fixed price, as we did with silver.

But why wait? We should at once stop pegging the price of gold.

We should today—as we should have yesterday and a year ago and ten years ago and in 1934—announce that the U.S. will no longer buy or sell gold at any fixed price (except perhaps for a final sale to meet commitments to foreign central banks). We should simultaneously remove all legal restrictions on transactions by U.S. citizens in gold. We should let the price of gold be a free market price, not a pegged price. That would have no adverse economic effects—domestically or internationally. And it would take back the loaded guns we have handed to foreign holders of dollars—notably to General de Gaulle.

THE PRICE OF THE DOLLAR

Reprinted from *Newsweek*, January 29, 1968.

How low we have fallen! The United States, the land of the free, prohibits its businessmen from investing abroad and requests its citizens not to show their faces or open their pocketbooks in foreign ports. The United States, the wealthiest nation in the world, announces that its foreign policy will no longer be determined by its national interest and its international commitments but by the need to reduce government spending abroad by $500 million.

And for what? Are we so poor that we must forgo profitable opportunities to invest capital abroad? The same President who imposes curbs on foreign investment boasts that our income is at an all-time high. Foreign investment in 1967 was less than 5 per cent of total investment and less than 1 per cent of total income.

Are we wasting so much of our substance on foreign travel that we must be cajoled by our betters to stay home? Total spending on foreign travel in 1967 was less than 1 per cent of total consumer spending.

Are government coffers so empty that reducing expenditures abroad by $500 million justifies shaping our whole foreign policy to that end? The President has not hesitated to recommend total Federal expenditures approaching $200 billion.

An Oft-Told Tale

Why then have we imposed such far-reaching restrictions on our citizenry? To put it bluntly, because a small number of public officials

—in the U.S. and abroad—cannot as yet bring themselves to admit their impotence to fix the price of the dollar in terms of other currencies. Like modern King Canutes, they have been commanding the tide not to rise—and apparently are determined to continue until we are engulfed by it.

This is an old story. Let the government seek to peg a price—be it of wheat or housing or silver or gold or pounds sterling—and it will be driven, as if by an invisible hand, to impose restrictions on producers and consumers in order to contain a surplus or to ration a shortage. It can do so for a time, but only for a time. The tide is too strong.

"In the meantime," as I testified to Congress nearly five years ago, "we adopt one expedient after another, borrowing here, making swap arrangements there, changing the form of loans to make the figures look good. Entirely aside from the ineffectiveness of most of these measures, they are politically degrading and demeaning. We are a great and wealthy nation. We should be directing our own course, setting an example to the world, living up to our destiny. Instead, we send our officials hat in hand to make the rounds of foreign governments and central banks; we put foreign central banks in a position . . . to exert great influence on our policies; we are driven to niggling negotiations with Hong Kong and with Japan and for all I know, Monaco, to get them to limit voluntarily their exports. Is this posture suitable for the leader of the free world?"

Set the Dollar Free

We should instead say to the people of the world: a dollar is a dollar. You may borrow dollars in the U.S. or abroad from anyone who is willing to lend. You may lend dollars in the U.S. or abroad to anyone who is willing to borrow. You may buy dollars from or sell dollars to anyone you wish at any price that is mutually agreeable. The U.S. Government will not interfere in any way. On the contrary, it will dismantle immediately its present restrictions: repeal the interest-equalization tax; dissolve the cartel agreement among banks to restrict foreign lending; remove quotas, "voluntary" or otherwise, on imports; stop resorting to World War I emergency legislation to threaten with prison terms businessmen who invest abroad; refrain from interfering with the right of its citizens to travel when and where they will.

If a foreign country wishes to peg the price of its currency in terms of the dollar, we should not interfere. It can succeed only by voluntarily holding dollars, or adjusting its internal monetary policy to ours or engaging in exchange control. In no case can it force us to impose restrictions on the use of dollars.

If we set the dollar free, and at the same time followed responsible fiscal and monetary policies, many another country would be well advised to link its currency with ours. That would promote not only our domestic objectives but also a healthy development of international trade. That is the right way to make the dollar a truly international currency—not behaving like a banana republic.

THE GOLD REQUIREMENT

Reprinted from *Newsweek*, February 19, 1968.

Present law limits the dollar amount of Federal Reserve Notes that may be outstanding to four times the value of the gold in the Treasury. A bill to repeal this requirement, requested by President Johnson, has been favorably reported by committees in both the House and the Senate and will no doubt be enacted soon.[1]

President Johnson gave two reasons for repeal: first, that making the entire gold stock available to meet foreign demands would enhance our ability to keep the price of gold at $35 an ounce and, second, that, by increasing confidence in the dollar, it would also contribute to reducing the balance-of-payments deficit.

These are bad reasons for a good measure.

Removing the gold requirement will not enable us to keep the price of gold at $35 an ounce. At most, it will encourage us to prolong the misery and to sell a larger fraction of our gold stock at a low price before we give up the futile attempt.[2]

Removing the gold requirement will not contribute to reducing the balance-of-payments deficit. At most, it will encourage us to meet a larger fraction of the deficit by shipping gold and to delay effective measures.

Repealing the gold requirement is desirable for a very different reason: to make the law correspond to present reality.

[1 It has since been enacted.]
[2 As we did shortly after this column appeared.]

An Anachronistic Survival

The gold requirement is an anachronistic survival of an earlier era. From 1879 to 1933, gold circulated as coin, and paper money was redeemable in gold. This made for a close link between money and gold. During those 54 years, the amount of money was never more than twelve times that of gold, never less than five times.

Withdrawal of gold from circulation and prohibition of the private ownership of gold in 1933 combined with developments in the rest of the world to convert gold from the kingpin of the monetary system into a commodity whose price is pegged. After President Roosevelt raised the official price of gold from $20.67 to $35 an ounce in 1934, our gold stocks grew explosively until the amount of money equaled only two and a half times the amount of gold. Then, as other prices rose, $35 an ounce became cheap and our gold stocks declined. However, the quantity of money continued to rise until it is now 30 times the amount of gold.

The link between gold and the quantity of money has become a rubber band. A real gold standard has become a pseudo gold standard.

Whether desirable or not, it is impossible to restore now the close link that prevailed before 1933. The legal requirement for a gold cover is therefore a snare and a delusion. It professes to restrain the monetary authority. It does not do so. It serves rather to conceal the true situation.

Removal of the gold requirement will make it crystal clear that there is no effective restraint on the powers of the men in charge of our monetary system. These men are and have been able and disinterested public servants. Yet it is undesirable in a democracy that they should have enormous power, with only the vaguest mandate about how to use that power, and with no effective legislative control over the exercise of the power.

An Effective Restraint

Removal of the gold requirement offers an occasion for Congress to impose an effective restraint to replace the present ineffective gold cover. Congress could best do so by instructing the Fed to produce a steady rate of growth in a specified monetary total—say, between 3 and 5 per cent a year in a total defined as currency plus all adjusted deposits of commercial banks, time and demand.

If the present gold crisis leads Congress to enact such a rule, it will have proved a blessing in disguise. Monetary policy is not a panacea for all our ills. But steady and moderate monetary growth would make a major contribution to economic stability and to the avoidance of both inflation and deflation. It would provide a monetary climate favorable to the effective operation of those basic forces of enterprise, ingenuity, invention, hard work and thrift that are the true springs of economic growth.

A legislated rule would also restore power to Congress where it belongs. It would eliminate the present grant of large, unspecified, uncontrollable power to men not responsible to the electorate. However able, however public-interested are the men who hold such power, their possession of it is abhorrent to the fundamental values of a democratic society whose ideal is rule by law, not by men.

GOLDEN CLICHÉS

Reprinted from *Newsweek*, April 1, 1968.

Like the rest of you, I have been reading reams of newspaper stories on gold. Unlike most of you, I specialize professionally in money and I have been impressed—and depressed—by the appeal to ritual incantations to conceal the emptiness of thought. Let me cite some examples.

1. *"Why does the U.S. keep losing gold?"* The U.S. hasn't lost gold. Extremely careful track is kept of the gold at Fort Knox and in the sub-basement of the New York Federal Reserve Bank. I doubt that a single ounce of gold has been lost. Stolen, perhaps. But lost, no. What the U.S. did was to sell gold. We have sold a lot of it. We may have sold it at too low a price but that means giving part of it away, not losing it.

2. *"The $35 price of gold is the keystone of international finance."* Now just what does that mean? That international finance would come tumbling down if the price were $50 or $20.67 (as it was for 54 years from 1879 to 1933)? The $35 price lasted only 34 years. International finance has been around for thousands of years. This is the kind of

phrase which enables those who have nothing to say to say nothing—impressively.

3. *"The gold-buying spree threatens the very existence of the international money system."* What would a world look like in which no international money system existed? Would all international trade be barter? The American tourist swapping bourbon he toted from home for a ticket to the Folies-Bergère? The only thing that was ever threatened by the gold-buying spree was a loss of face by those governmental officials who proclaimed that they could keep the price of gold fixed while letting all other prices rise.

4. *Removal of the gold-cover requirement "freed the nation's entire gold stock of $11.4 billion to back the dollar overseas."* Nonsense. Removing the gold-cover requirements simply made it legal to sell more gold abroad in an attempt, that sooner or later had to prove vain, to keep the price of gold abroad pegged at $35 an ounce. For the purpose of "backing the dollar overseas," in the sense of enabling people who wish to dispose of dollars to do so, selling them copper or silver or the Congressional Record would do just as well.

5. *"The dollar is in danger."* Of what? My dollar is in danger of being spent before I know it. What about yours? Were the dollars owned by foreigners in some other kind of danger? The answer presumably is that they were in danger of not continuing to be able to command 1/35th of an ounce of gold. Why should that have been of great concern to us—except as we made rash promises that came home to roost? Why should it produce frantic moves by high government officials? International conferences of central bankers?

6. *"The dollar is weak."* A minor variant of the preceding, generally used when the reference is to the price of the dollar in terms of a foreign currency. Again, why is it vital to us whether the price of the dollar is 4 marks even or 3 marks and 90 pfennigs? As for gold, only because we have been so unwise as to commit ourselves to pegging exchange rates.

7. *But, says the pundit, "fixed exchange rates are the cornerstone of the postwar liberalization of multilateral trade on a nondiscriminatory basis."* Say that again. Our interest-equalization tax, oil-import quotas, voluntary credit restraint, restriction of foreign investment are signs of "liberalization"? On a "nondiscriminatory basis"? Congress is now considering tourist taxes, a tax on imports, and a subsidy to exports in order to shore up the fixed exchange-rate system—to promote liberalization of trade? I've heard that before. "It was necessary to destroy the city to save it."

245

The gold rush was a blessing. It forced us to do what we should have done of our own volition long since: let the price of gold be set in the free market. Hopefully, the continuation of an "official" market at $35 an ounce is a pure face-saving gesture that will involve few or no transactions. The plain fact is that few things are currently less important to the ordinary citizen of the U.S. than whether the price of gold is $20 an ounce, $35 an ounce or $70 an ounce.

But a free market in gold alone will not resolve our balance-of-payments problem. For that, it is necessary to free also the market for foreign exchange. The U.S. should renounce any commitment to peg exchange rates. We could then eliminate at once the growing restraints that are being imposed on what U.S. citizens can do with their dollars. Why should you be free to make any deal you want with a used-car salesman—but not with a Frenchman offering francs?

Real and Pseudo

Gold Standards [1,2]

CHAPTER ELEVEN International monetary arrangements have held a consistently important place
among the topics discussed at the meetings of our
Society. This is eminently fitting, since there is probably no other major facet of economic policy with
respect to which liberals (in the sense of our Society)
reach such divergent conclusions from the same underlying principles.

One group, of which Philip Cortney is a distinguished member, favors a continuation of the for-

[1] Paper written for the Mont Pelerin Society meetings in
September, 1961. [The Mont Pelerin Society is an international
society of persons committed to free private markets and limited
government as essential prerequisites for a free society. This is the
position originally termed "liberal" and the one to which that
term still refers in continental Europe. In the United States, "liberal" has come to have a very different meaning. In this paper, I
used it in its original meaning.]

[2 Reprinted from *The Journal of Law and Economics,* Vol.
IV, October, 1961. (University of Chicago Press); also published
in German translation in *Ordo,* 1962.]

mal linking of national currencies to gold, rigid exchange rates between different national currencies, a doubling or more than doubling of the official price of gold in terms of national currencies, and an abandonment of governmental measures designed to evade the discipline of gold. This group is apparently indifferent about whether gold circulates as coin; it is satisfied with a gold bullion standard.

A second group, represented by the Economists' National Committee on Monetary Policy, also favors a continuation of the formal linking of national currencies to gold together with rigid exchange rates between different national currencies. But it emphasizes the importance of gold coinage and of a widespread use of gold coin as money in national as well as international payments. Apparently, this group believes there is no need for a change in present official prices of gold, or, at least, in the United States price.

A third group, of which I count myself a member, favors a separation of gold policy from exchange-rate policy. It favors the abandonment of rigid exchange rates between national currencies and the substitution of a system of floating exchange rates determined from day to day by private transactions without government intervention. With respect to gold, there are some differences, but most of us would currently favor the abandonment of any commitment by governments to buy and sell gold at fixed prices and of any fixed gold reserve requirements for the issue of national currency as well as the repeal of any restrictions on private dealings in gold.

I have stated and defended my own policy views elsewhere at some length.[3] Hence, I would like to use this occasion instead to explore how it is that liberals can reach such radically different conclusions.

My thesis is that current proposals to link national currencies rigidly to gold whether at present or higher prices arise out of a confusion of two very different things: the use of gold as money, which I shall call a "real" gold standard; governmental fixing

---

[3] See, in particular, "The Case for Flexible Exchange Rates" and "Commodity-Reserve Currency," in my *Essays in Positive Economics,* pp. 157-203, 204-50 (1953), and *A Program for Monetary Stability,* pp. 77-84 (1959).

of the price of gold, whether national or international, which I shall call a "pseudo" gold standard. Though these have many surface features in common, they are at bottom fundamentally different—just as the near identity of prices charged by competitive sellers differs basically from the identity of prices charged by members of a price-ring or cartel. A real gold standard is thoroughly consistent with liberal principles and I, for one, am entirely in favor of measures promoting its development, as, I believe, are most other liberal proponents of floating exchange rates. A pseudo gold standard is in direct conflict with liberal principles as is suggested by the curious coalition of central bankers and central planners that has formed in support of it.

It is vitally important for the preservation and promotion of a free society that we recognize the difference between a real and pseudo gold standard. War aside, nothing that has occurred in the past half-century has, in my view, done more to weaken and undermine the public's faith in liberal principles than the pseudo gold standard that has intermittently prevailed and the actions that have been taken in its name. I believe that those of us who support it in the belief that it either is or will tend to be a real gold standard are mistakenly fostering trends the outcome of which they will be among the first to deplore.

This is a sweeping charge, so let me document it by a few examples which will incidentally illustrate the difference between a real and a pseudo gold standard before turning to an explicit discussion of the difference. My examples are mostly for the United States, the country whose monetary history I have studied in most detail.

A. Examples of Effects of a Pseudo Gold Standard

1. UNITED STATES MONETARY POLICY AFTER WORLD WAR I

Nearly half of the monetary expansion in the United States came after the end of the war, thanks to the acquiescence of the Federal Reserve System in the Treasury's desire to avoid a fall in the price of government securities. This expansion, with its accompanying price inflation led to an outflow of gold despite the great demand for United States goods from a war-ravaged world and despite the departure of most countries from any fixed parity between their currencies and either gold or the dollar. The outflow of gold finally overcame Treasury reluctance to see the price of government securities fall. Beginning in late 1919, then more sharply in January, 1920, and May, 1920, the Federal Reserve System took vigorous deflationary steps that produced first a slackening of the growth in the stock of money and then a sharp decline. These brought in their train a collapse in wholesale prices and a severe economic contraction. The near-halving of wholesale prices in a twelve-month period was by all odds the most rapid price decline ever experienced in the United States before or since. It was not of course confined to the United States but spread to all countries whose money was linked to the dollar either by having a fixed price in terms of gold or by central bank policies directed at maintaining rigid or nearly rigid exchange rates. Only those countries that were to experience hyperinflation escaped the price collapse.

Under a real gold standard, the large inflow of gold up to the entry of the United States into the war would have produced a price rise to the end of the war similar to that actually experienced. But neither the postwar rise nor the subsequent collapse would have occurred. Instead, there would have been an earlier and milder price decline as the belligerent nations returned to a peacetime economy. The postwar increase in the stock of money occurred only because the Reserve System had been given discretionary power to "manage" the stock of money, and the subsequent collapse occurred only because this power to manage the money had been accompanied by gold reserve requirements as one among several masters the System was instructed to serve.

Under a wholly fiduciary currency, with floating exchange rates, the initial postwar expansion might well have occurred much as it did, though the depreciating value of the dollar in terms of other currencies might have been a quicker and a more effective check than slowly declining gold reserves. But the subsequent collapse would almost surely not have occurred. And neither the initial price inflation nor the subsequent price collapse would have been communicated to the rest of the world.

The world-wide inflation and then collapse was at the time a severe blow to a belief in free trade at home and abroad, a blow whose severity we now underrate only because of the later catastrophe that overshadowed it. Either a real gold standard or a thoroughly fiduciary standard would have been preferable in its outcome to the pseudo gold standard.

2. UNITED STATES MONETARY POLICY IN THE 1920's AND BRITAIN'S RETURN TO GOLD

There is a widespread myth among gold standard advocates that the United States monetary policy during the 1920's paved the way for the Great Depression by being unduly inflationary. For example, Cortney writes, "the Federal Reserve Board succeeded in the 1920's in holding up the price level for a surprising length of time by an abnormal expansion of inflationary credit, but in so doing it helped produce the speculative boom." [4] Nothing could be farther from the truth. The United States monetary policy in the 1920's and especially in the late 1920's, judged in terms of either a real gold standard in the abstract or prior United States experience, was if anything unduly deflationary.

The sharp 1920-21 price decline had brought prices to a level much closer to the prewar level than to the postwar peak though they were still appreciably above the prewar level. Prices rose only moderately in the subsequent cyclical expansion which reached its peak in 1923. From then until 1929, wholesale prices actually fell, at a rate of roughly 1 per cent a year.

As to gold, credit, and money, the Federal Reserve System sterilized much of the gold inflow, preventing the gold from raising the stock of money anything like as much as it would have done under a real gold standard. Far from the Reserve System engaging in an "abnormal expansion of inflationary credit," Federal Reserve credit outstanding in June, 1929, was 33 per cent lower than it had been in June, 1921, and only 16 per cent higher than in June, 1923, although national income was nearly 25 per cent higher in 1929 than in 1923 (in both money and real terms).

[4] In Introduction to Charles Rist, *The Triumph of Gold*, p. 8 (1961).

From 1923 to 1929, to compare only peak years of business cycles and so avoid distortion from cyclical influence, the stock of money, defined to include currency, demand deposits, and commercial bank time deposits, rose at the annual rate of 4 per cent per year, which is roughly the rate required to match expansion of output. On a narrower definition, excluding time deposits, the stock of money rose at the rate of only 2½ per cent per year.[5]

The deflationary pressure was particularly strong during the great bull market in stocks, which happened to coincide with the first few years after Britain returned to gold. During the business cycle expansion from 1927 to 1929, wholesale prices actually fell a trifle: one must go back to 1891-93 to find another expansion during which prices fell, and there has been none since. The stock of money was lower at the cyclical peak in August, 1929, than it had been 16 months earlier. There is no other occasion from the time our monthly data began in 1907 to date when so long a period elapsed during a cyclical expansion without a rise in the stock of money. The only other periods of such length which show a decline have an end point in the course of severe contractions (1920-21, 1929-33, 1936-37).

So far as the United States alone was concerned, this monetary policy may have been admirable. I do not myself believe that the 1929-33 contraction was an inevitable result of the monetary policy of the 1920's or even owed much to it. What was wrong was the policy followed from 1929 to 1933, as I shall point out in a moment. But internationally, the policy was little short of catastrophic. Much has been made of Britain's mistake in returning to gold in 1925 at a parity that overvalued the pound. I do not doubt that this was a mistake—but only because the United States was maintaining a pseudo gold standard. Had the United States been maintaining a real gold standard, the stock of money would have risen more in the United States than it did, prices would have been stable or rising instead of declining, the United States would have gained less gold or lost some, and the pressure on the pound would have been enormously eased. As it was, by

[5] These statements are based on estimates of the stock of money from 1867 to date constructed by Anna J. Schwartz and me in connection with a study for the National Bureau of Economic Research. Hereafter, I will use the term "stock of money" as referring to the first of these two definitions.

sterilizing gold, the United States forced the whole burden of adapting to gold movements on other countries. When, in addition, France adopted a pseudo gold standard at a parity that undervalued the franc and proceeded also to follow a gold sterilization policy, the combined effect was to make Britain's position untenable. The adverse consequences for faith in liberal principles of the deflationary policies adopted in Britain from 1925 to 1931 in the vain effort to maintain the re-established parity are no less obvious than they were far-reaching.

3. UNITED STATES POLICY IN 1931 TO 1933

United States monetary behavior in 1931 to 1933 is in some ways a repetition of that from 1920 to 1921, but on a more catastrophic scale, in less fortunate circumstances, and with less justification. As we have seen, in 1919 the Reserve System deviated from the policy that would have been dictated by a real gold standard. In 1920, when it saw its gold reserves declining rapidly, it shifted rules, overreacted to the outflow, and brought on a drastic deflation. Similarly, from 1922 to 1929, the Reserve System sterilized gold and prevented it from exercising the influence on the money stock that it would have had under a real gold standard. And again in 1931, when Britain went off gold and the United States experienced an outflow of gold, the Reserve System shifted rules, overreacted to the outflow, and catastrophically intensified a deflation already two years old.

The circumstances were less fortunate in 1931 than in 1920 in two different respects, one domestic and the other foreign, and both in some measure the Reserve System's own creation.

The domestic difference was that the deflationary action of 1920 came at the end of a period of expansion which was widely regarded as temporary and exceptional, and served to intensify without necessarily prolonging a recession that would probably have occurred anyway. The deflationary action of 1931 came after two years of severe contraction which had been showing some signs of terminating; probably served to nip in the bud a revival; and both greatly intensified and substantially prolonged the contraction, turning it into the most severe for nearly a century.

This difference was largely the Reserve System's creation because of its inept handling of the banking difficulties that started in the fall of 1930. Until that date, the contraction, while rather severe, had shown no signs of a liquidity crisis. Widespread bank failures culminating in the failure of the Bank of United States in late 1930 changed the nature of the contraction. This episode turned out to be the first of a series of liquidity crises, each characterized by bank failures and runs on banks by depositors anxious to convert deposits into currency, and each producing strong downward pressure on the stock of money. The Reserve System had been set up with the primary aim of dealing with precisely such crises. It failed to do so effectively but not because it lacked the power or the knowledge. At all times, it had ample power to provide the liquidity that the public and the banks desperately sought and the provision of which would have cut short the vicious chain reaction of bank failures. The System failed because accidents of personality and shifts of power within the System left it with no dominant personality who could avoid the usual outcome of committee control: the evasion of responsibility by inaction, postponement, and drift. More fundamentally yet, the failure reflected the danger inherent in a monetary system that gave great power to a small number of men and therefore was vulnerable to such accidents of personality and shifts of power. Had the liquidity crisis been cut short at its onset in 1930 and the Bank of United States kept from failing (as very likely would have occurred before the Federal Reserve System), the economy would probably have been vigorously expanding by September, 1931, instead of being precariously balanced on the verge of another liquidity crisis.

The international difference in circumstances that was less fortunate in 1931 than in 1920 was the monetary situation in other countries. In many countries, monetary arrangements in 1920 were in a state of flux, so they could adapt with some rapidity. By 1931, a new pattern of international monetary arrangements had become established, in considerable measure under the patronage of the Federal Reserve Bank of New York, as well as the

Bank of England and the Bank of France. More serious and more directly to be laid at the Reserve System's door, its gold sterilization policy had, as we have seen, increased the problem of adjustment for many other countries and so left them more vulnerable to new difficulties. In the event, the monetary world split in two, one part following Britain to form the sterling area; the other, following the United States, in the gold bloc. The sterling area countries all reached bottom and began to expand in late 1931 or early 1932; most gold bloc countries experienced further deflation and did not reach bottom until 1933 or 1934.

The deflationary monetary actions had less justification in the fall of 1931 than in 1920 for two different reasons. First, in 1920, the Federal Reserve System was still in its infancy, untried and inexperienced. Set up under one set of conditions, it was operating under a drastically different set. It had no background of operation in peacetime, no experience on which to base judgments. By 1931, the System had more than a decade of experience and had developed a well-articulated body of doctrine, which underlay the gold sterilization policy and which called for its offsetting an outflow of gold rather than reinforcing its deflationary effect. Second, the gold situation was drastically different. By early 1920, the gold stock was declining rapidly and the Reserve System's gold reserve ratio was approaching its legal minimum. Prior to September, 1931, the System had been gaining gold, the monetary gold stock was at an all-time high, and the System's gold reserve ratio was far above its legal minimum—a reflection, of course, of its not having operated in accordance with a real gold standard. The System had ample reserves to meet the gold outflow without difficulty and without resort to deflationary measures. And both its own earlier policy and the classic gold standard rules as enshrined by Bagehot called for its doing so: the gold outflow was strictly speculative and motivated by fear that the United States would go off gold; the outflow had no basis in any trade imbalance; it would have exhausted itself promptly if all demands had been met.

As it was, of course, the System behaved very differently. It reacted vigorously to the external drain as it had not to the internal drain by raising discount rates within a brief period more sharply than ever before or since. The result was a major intensification of the internal drain, and an unprecedented liquidation of the commercial banking system. Whereas the stock of money had fallen 10 per cent from August, 1929, to August, 1931, it fell a further 28 per cent from August, 1931, to March, 1933. Commercial bank deposits had fallen 12 per cent from August, 1929, to August, 1931; they fell a further 35 per cent from August, 1931, to March, 1933. Never was there a more unnecessary monetary collapse or one which did more to undermine public acceptance of liberal principles.

Once again, either a real gold standard throughout the 1920's and '30's or a consistent adherence to a fiduciary standard would have been vastly preferable to the actual pseudo gold standard under which gold inflows and minor gold outflows were offset and substantial actual or threatened gold outflows were overreacted to. And this pattern is no outmoded historical curiosity: witness the United States reaction to gold inflows in the early years after World War II and its recent [1960] reaction to gold outflows; witness the more recent German sterilization of gold inflows. The pseudo gold standard is very much a living menace.

4. UNITED STATES NATIONALIZATION OF GOLD

After going off gold in March, 1933, the United States reestablished a fixed official price of gold in January, 1934, raising the price to $35 an ounce. Many current proponents of a rise in the official price of gold approve this action, regarding it as required to bring the value of the gold stock into line with an allegedly increased fiduciary circulation. Perhaps a rise in the price of gold was desirable in 1934 but it cannot be defended along these lines, at least for the United States itself. In 1933, the ratio of the value of the gold stock to the total stock of money was higher than it had been in 1913 or at any date between. If there be any valid argument for a rise in the price of gold along these lines, it is for 1929, not 1934.

Whatever may be the merits of the rise in the price of gold, there can be little doubt that the associated measures, which were taken in order that the rise in the price of gold should have the effect desired by the Roosevelt administration, represented a fundamental departure from liberal principles and established precedents that have returned to plague the free world. I refer, of course, to the nationalization of the gold stock, the prohibition of private possession of gold for monetary purposes, and the abrogation of gold clauses in public and private contracts.

In 1933 and early 1934, private holders of gold were required by law to turn over their gold to the federal government and were compensated at a price equal to the prior legal price, which was at the time very decidedly below the market price. To make this requirement effective, private ownership of gold within the United States was made illegal except for use in the arts. One can hardly imagine a measure more destructive of the principles of private property on which a free enterprise society rests. There is no difference in principle between this nationalization of gold at an artificially low price and Fidel Castro's nationalization of land and factories at an artificially low price. On what grounds of principle can the United States object to the one after having itself engaged in the other? Yet so great is the blindness of some supporters of free enterprise with respect to anything touching on gold that as recently as last year [1960] Henry Alexander, head of the Morgan Guaranty Trust Company, successor to J. P. Morgan and Co., proposed that the prohibition against the private ownership of gold by United States citizens be extended to cover gold held abroad! And his proposal was adopted by President Eisenhower with hardly a protest from the banking community.

Though rationalized in terms of "conserving" gold for monetary use, prohibition of private ownership of gold was not enacted for any such monetary purpose, whether itself good or bad. The circulation of gold and gold certificates had raised no monetary problems either in the 1920's or during the monetary collapse from 1930 to 1933. Except for the final weeks just preceding the banking panic, the internal drain had not been for gold but for currency of any kind in preference to deposits. And the final gold drain was the consequence of the rumors, which proved correct, that Roosevelt planned to devalue. The nationalization of gold was enacted to enable the government to reap the whole of the "paper" profit from the rise in the price of gold—or perhaps, to prevent private individuals benefiting from the rise.

The abrogation of the gold clauses had a similar purpose. And this too was a measure destructive of the basic principles of free enterprise. Contracts entered into in good faith and with full knowledge on the part of both parties to them were declared invalid for the benefit of one of the parties!

This collection of measures constituted a further step away from a real gold standard to a pseudo gold standard. Gold became even more clearly a commodity whose price was fixed by governmental purchase and sale and rationing rather than money or even a form of money.

5. INTERNATIONAL MONETARY FUND AND POSTWAR EXCHANGE POLICY

I agree fully with Professor Rist's criticisms of the International Monetary Fund and the arrangements it embodied.[6] These arrangements are precisely those of a pseudo gold standard: each country is required to specify a formal price of gold in terms of its own currency and hence, by implication, to specify official exchange rates between its currency and other currencies. It is forbidden to change these prices outside narrow limits except with permission. It commits itself to maintaining these exchange rates. But there is no requirement that gold serve as money; on the contrary, many of the IMF provisions are designed to prevent it from doing so.

The results have been anything but happy from a liberal viewpoint: widespread controls over exchange transactions, restrictions on international trade in the form of quotas and direct controls as well as tariffs; yet repeated exchange crises and numerous changes in official exchange rates have occurred. No doubt, conditions are now far better than shortly after the war, but clearly in spite of the IMF and not because of it. And the danger of foreign exchange crises and accompanying interferences with trade is hardly over. In the past year, the United

[6] See Charles Rist, *op. cit.* supra note 4, pp. 188-93.

States moved toward direct interferences with trade to cope with a balance of payments problem; Germany appreciated; and Britain is now in difficulties.

B. The Distinction between a Real and a Pseudo Gold Standard

Because of its succinctness and explicitness, Cortney's numbered list of prerequisites for the restoration of "monetary order by returning to an international gold standard" forms an excellent point of departure for exploring the difference between a real and a pseudo gold standard. His point number (6) concludes "the price of gold will have to be raised to at least $70 an ounce." His point number (7) is "Free markets for gold should be established in all the important countries, and trading in gold, its export and import should be absolutely free." [7] Here is the issue in a nutshell. Can one conceive of saying in one breath that worldwide free markets should be established in, say, tin, and in the next, that the price of tin should "be raised" to some specified figure? The essence of a free market is precisely that no one can "raise" or "fix" price. Price is at whatever level will clear the market and it varies from day to day as market conditions change. If we take Cortney's point (7) seriously, we cannot simultaneously take his point (6) seriously, and conversely.

Suppose we follow up the logic of his point (7) and suppose a free market prevails in gold. There might then develop, as there has in the past, a real gold standard. People might voluntarily choose to use gold as money, which is to say, to express prices in units of gold, and to hold gold as a temporary abode of purchasing power permitting them to divide an act of barter into a sale of goods or services for money and the purchase of goods or services with money. The gold used as money might be called different things in different languages: "or" in French, "gold" in English; it might be measured in different units: say, in grams in France and ounces in the United States; special terms such as "napoleon" or "eagle" might develop to designate con-

[7] *Ibid.*, p. 37.

venient amounts of gold for use in transactions, and these might differ in different countries. We might even have governments certifying to weight and fineness, as they now inspect scales in meat markets, or even coining "eagles," "double-eagles," and the like. Changes in nomenclature or in units of measure, say, the shift from ounces to grams, might be made by legislation, but these would clearly have no monetary or income or redistributive effects; they would be like changing the standard units for measuring gasoline from gallons to liters; not comparable to changing the price of gold from $35 an ounce to $70 an ounce.

If such a real gold standard developed, the price of commodities in terms of gold would of course vary from place to place according to transportation costs of both the commodities and of gold. Insofar as different countries used gold, and used different units, or coins of different size, the price of one kind of gold in terms of another would be free to vary in accordance with preferences by each country's citizens for the one kind or the other. The range of variation would of course be limited by the cost of converting one kind of gold into another, just as the relative price of commodities is similarly limited.

Under such a real gold standard, private persons or government might go into the business of offering storage facilities, and warehouse receipts might be found more convenient than the gold itself for transactions. Finally, private persons or governments might issue promises to pay gold either on demand or after a specific time interval which were not warehouse receipts but nonetheless were widely acceptable because of confidence that the promises would be redeemed. Such promises to pay would still not alter the basic character of the gold standard so long as the obligors were not retroactively relieved from fulfilling their promises, and this would be true even if such promises were not fulfilled from time to time, just as the default of dollar bond issues does not alter the monetary standard. But, of course, promises to pay that were in default or that were expected to be defaulted would not sell at face value, just as bonds in default trade at a discount. And this is what has happened when a system like that outlined has prevailed in practice (e.g., in much of the pre-Civil War period in the United States).

Such a system might, and I believe would, raise grave social problems and foster pressure for governmental prohibition of, or control over, the issue of promises to pay gold on demand.[8] But that is beside my present point, which is that it would be a real gold standard, that under it there might be different national names for the money but there would not be in any meaningful sense either national currencies or any possibility of a government legislating a change in the price of gold.

Side by side with such a standard, there could, of course, exist strictly national currencies. For example, in the United States from 1862-79, greenbacks were such a national currency which circulated side by side with gold. Since there was a free market in gold, the price of gold in terms of greenbacks varied from day to day, i.e., in modern terminology, there was a floating rate of exchange between the two currencies. Since gold was in use as money in Britain and some other countries, its main use in the United States was for foreign transactions. Most prices in the United States were quoted in greenbacks but could be paid in gold valued at the market rate. However, the situation was reversed in California, where most prices were quoted in gold but could be paid in greenbacks at the market rate. No doubt, in this historical episode, the expectation that greenbacks would some day be made promises to pay gold had an effect on their value by expanding the demand for them. But this was not essential to the simultaneous coexistence of the two currencies, so long as their relative price was freely determined in the market, just as silver and gold, or copper and silver, have often simultaneously circulated at floating rates of exchange.

If a government abjured a national currency, it might still borrow from the community in the form of securities expressed in gold (or bearing gold clauses), some of which might be demand obligations and might be non-interest bearing. But it would thereby surrender everything that we now call monetary policy. The resources it could acquire by borrowing would depend on the interest it was willing to pay on interest-bearing securities and on the amount of non-interest bearing demand securities the public was willing to acquire. It could not arbitrarily issue any

[8] See my A Program for Monetary Stability, pp. 4-9 (1959).

amount of non-interest bearing securities it wished without courting inability to meet its promises to pay gold and hence seeing its securities sink to a discount relative to gold. Of course, this limitation in governmental power is precisely what recommends a real gold standard to a liberal, but we must not make the mistake of supposing that we can get the substance by the mere adoption of the form of a nominal obeisance to gold.

The kind of gold standard we have just been describing is not the kind we have had since at least 1913 and certainly not since 1934. If the essence of a free market is that no one can "raise the price," the essence of a controlled market is that it involves restrictions of one kind or another on trade. When the government fixes the price of wheat at a level above the market price, it inevitably both accumulates stocks and is driven to control output—i.e., to ration output among producers eager to produce more than the public is willing to buy at the controlled price. When the government fixes the price of housing space at a level below the market price, it inevitably is driven to control occupancy—i.e., to ration space among purchasers eager to buy more than sellers are willing to make available at the controlled price. The controls on gold, like the related controls on foreign exchange, are a sure sign that the price is being pegged; that dollar, pound, etc., are not simply different names for different sized units of gold, but are national currencies. Insofar as the price of gold in these currencies and the price of one currency in terms of another are stable over considerable periods, it is not because of the ease of converting one quantity of gold into another and not because conditions of demand and supply make for stable prices, but because they are pegged prices in rigged markets.

The price of $35 an ounce at which gold was supported by the United States after January, 1934, was initially well above the market price—like the price at which wheat is currently being supported. The evidence in both cases is the same: a rapid expansion of output and the accumulation of enormous stockpiles. From 1933 to 1940, production in the United States rose from less than 2.6 million ounces to 6 million ounces; in the world, from 25 million ounces to 41 million ounces; the gold stock in the Treasury rose from 200 million ounces to 630 million, or by 1¾ times as much as the total of world output during the intervening period. Had this pace of increase in output and stock continued, the gold purchase program might well have been limited in scope; perhaps, as the United States silver purchase program finally was, to domestic output alone.

But the war intervened, which stopped the inflow of gold and brought a major rise in the stock of money. The resultant rise in other prices with no change in the price of gold has altered the character of the fixed United States price. It is now probably below the market price (given the present monetary use of gold), like rents under rent control. The evidence is again in both cases the same; a reduction in production, a decline in stocks, and a problem of rationing demanders. The United States gold output is now [1961] less than in 1933 though world output still exceeds the level of that year. The United States gold stock has declined to roughly 500 million ounces, well below its wartime peak but still 2½ times its level when the present price for gold was established.[9] The restriction on the ownership of gold abroad by United States citizens is a first, and feeble, step toward still tighter rationing of demanders. The gentlemen's agreement among central banks not to press for conversion of dollar balances into gold is a more far-reaching if still rather weak additional step. The history of every attempt at government price fixing suggests that if the pegged price is far below the market price for long, such attempts are doomed to fail.[10]

Doubling the price of gold would no doubt reverse the situation and raise the pegged price again above the market price. Gold production and United States gold stocks would no doubt rise. But to what avail? Gold would still be simply a commodity whose price is supported; countries would continue with their separate monetary policies; fixed exchange rates would freeze the only market mechanism available under such circumstances to adjust international payments; foreign exchange crises would continue to succeed one another; and direct controls of one kind

[9 As of March, 1968, the gold stock was roughly 300 million ounces.]
[10 As this one did, in March, 1968.]

or another would remain the last resort, and one often appealed to, for resolving them.

This kind of pseudo gold standard violates fundamental liberal principles in two major respects. First, it involves price fixing by government. It has always been a mystery to me how so many who oppose on principle government price fixing of all other commodities can yet approve it for this one. Second, and no less important, it involves granting discretionary authority to a small number of men over matters of the greatest importance; to the central bankers or Treasury officials who must manage the pseudo gold standard. This means the rule of men instead of law, violating one of our fundamental political tenets. Here again, I have been amazed how so many who oppose on principle the grant of wide discretionary authority to governmental officials are anxious to see such authority granted to central bankers. True, central bankers have on the whole been "sound money" men with great sympathy for private enterprise. But since when have we liberals tempered our fear of concentrated power by trust in the particular men who happen at a particular moment to exercise it? Surely our cry has been very different—that benevolent or not, tyranny is tyranny and the only sure defense of freedom is the dispersal of power.

C. Conclusion

Let me close by offering a proposal, not for reconciling our views, but at least for possible agreement among us on one part of the gold problem. Can we not all agree with Mr. Cortney's point (7): the establishment of a thoroughly free market in gold, with no restrictions on the ownership, purchase, sale, import, or export of gold by private individuals? This means in particular, no restrictions on the price at which gold can be bought or sold in terms of any other commodity or financial instrument, including national currencies. It means, therefore, an end to governmental price fixing of gold in terms of national currencies.

The major problem in achieving such a reform is, as for the United States wheat program, the transitional one of what to do with accumulated government stocks. In both cases, my own view is that the government should immediately restore a free market, and should ultimately dispose of all of its stocks. However, it would probably be desirable for the government to dispose of its stocks only gradually. For wheat, five years has always seemed to me a long enough period so I have favored the government committing itself to dispose of ⅕ of its stocks in each of five years. This period seems reasonably satisfactory for gold as well, and hence my own proposal for the United States, and also other countries, would be that the government should sell off its gold in the free market over the next five years. Perhaps the greater ratio of the accumulated stock to annual production for gold than for wheat makes a longer transitional period appropriate. This seems to me a matter of expediency not of principle.

A worldwide free market in gold might mean that the use of gold as money would become far more widespread than it is now. If so, governments might need to hold some gold as working cash balances. Beyond this, I see no reason why governments or international agencies should hold any gold. If individuals find warehouse certificates for gold more useful than literal gold, private enterprise can certainly provide the service of storing the gold. Why should gold storage and the issuance of warehouse certificates be a nationalized industry?

The Political Economy

of International Monetary

Arrangements [1]

CHAPTER TWELVE A major source of confusion in discussing international monetary arrangements is the
tendency to refer to "the" not "a" gold standard, as
if the term "gold standard" had a single unambiguous
meaning. Four years ago, in a paper entitled "Real
and Pseudo Gold Standards," [2] I stressed the am-
biguity of the term and, in particular, the importance of distinguishing between two broad classes
of monetary arrangements, both termed "gold standards," one class—real gold standards—entirely consistent with liberal principles but currently seriously
supported by very few and well outside the range
of alternatives that are politically feasible, the other
—pseudo gold standards—basically contradictory to

[1] A slightly revised version of a paper presented at the 15th
General Meeting of the Mont Pelerin Society, Stresa, Italy, September, 1965. Also published in French translation in *Les Funde-
ments Philosophique de Systèmes Économique*, Essays by Jacques
Rueff and in his honor, Paris, 1967, pp. 384-395.
  [2 Chapter Eleven.]

liberal principles yet supported by many liberals out of either confusion or a mistaken belief that the form will sooner or later prove a step toward the substance. The apparent support for "a" gold standard gives an illusory appearance of agreement because much of the agreement is on words and conceals very wide disagreement about the content to be given to the words.

In this paper, I shall first summarize in somewhat different terms the main point made in my earlier paper and then turn to a set of issues that are only referred to but not discussed in that paper, namely, the political implications of alternative international monetary arrangements.

1. Unified Currency vs. National Currencies Linked by Pegged Rates

The crucial distinction made in my earlier paper is between a unified currency and a collection of separate currencies linked to one another at pegged rates, whether through the mechanism of gold or not. The use of precisely the same currency in different areas—as of the U.S. dollar in different states of the United States or of the pound sterling in different parts of the United Kingdom —is the most obvious example of a unified currency. However, a situation in which different areas attach different names to the currency or use pieces of paper with different pictures or printed in different languages can, from an economic point of view, also represent a unified currency. It will do so if the different names are simply designations for a common medium into which all the local currencies are continuously convertible at specified and unchangeable terms, without question and without discretion on the part of any political authority. A "real" gold or silver standard is an obvious example. The currency is no less unified because the words "dollar" or "pound" or "franc" are used in different countries to refer to claims to specified physical amounts of gold. There are also many less obvious examples. The Hong Kong dollar is a unified currency with the British pound sterling; and so is the Singapore dollar—or, I should say, was, prior to the establishment of Malaysia.

Elements of a unified currency circulating in different places will have rates of exchange in terms of one another that are not rigidly fixed. For example, prior to par clearance by the Federal Reserve in the United States, there were active markets for internal exchange. A dollar payable in Chicago could sometimes be exchanged for more than a dollar payable in New York, sometimes for less. Under the gold standard from 1879 to 1914, which came very close to being a unified currency, the price of the U.S. dollar in terms of the pound sterling varied within the gold points. Currently, the price of a Hong Kong dollar in pounds sterling varies slightly from day to day. In all these examples, the narrowness of the variation arises from a market force, the low costs of transportation of the currencies, not from administrative price fixing. It is comparable to different local prices for sugar, for example, in areas among which sugar is freely traded without tariffs, export subsidies, or other forms of governmental or private price manipulation.

As these examples suggest, the decisive economic characteristic of a unified currency is precisely that transfers of currency take place automatically, requiring no administrative action to effect them, and not being interfered with by such administrative action. If a resident of Illinois makes a payment to a resident of New York, this transaction, taken by itself, necessarily reduces the money balances of Illinois residents and increases those of New York residents—as is most obvious when the payment takes the form of the literal transfer of currency. If residents of Illinois as a whole are paying more to residents of New York than they are receiving in return, then the amount of money held by residents of Illinois necessarily goes down on this account (i.e., neglecting payments to or receipts from other areas) and that held by residents of New York necessarily goes up.

Contrast this situation with one that seems superficially the same: two national currencies linked by governmentally pegged exchange rates. A resident of the United States can make a payment to a resident of France in one of two ways. He can acquire the francs at the official price from the Federal Reserve or Treasury (at one or more removes), and transfer the francs to the French resident. In that case, the amount of francs held by French residents in the first instance automatically goes up. Whether the amount of dollars held by U.S. residents goes down depends on what the Federal Reserve does with the dollars transferred to it. If it wishes to, it can prevent the transaction from reducing the amount of dollars in the U.S., letting it simply reduce its franc reserves. Alternatively, the U.S. resident can transfer a dollar balance to the Frenchman, who takes it to the Bank of France for exchange into francs. In that case, the amount of dollars held by U.S. residents in the first instance automatically goes down, but whether the amount of francs held by French residents goes up depends on where the Bank of France gets the francs it issues to him, whether by creating them or by acquiring them through open market operations. And, of course, the Bank of France or the Federal Reserve can, if it wishes, offset the increase in francs, in the first case, or decrease in dollars, in the second. If the residents of the U.S. as a whole are paying more to residents of France than they are receiving in return, then the amount of money held by residents of the United States goes down on this account (i.e., neglecting payments to and receipts from other areas) if and only if the Federal Reserve so wills, and the amount of money held by residents of France goes up if and only if the Bank of France so wills.

I am clearly grossly oversimplifying, and may seem to be belaboring the irrelevantly obvious. Yet the distinction I am stressing is critical. Balance of payments problems cannot arise under a unified currency. One area may have economic difficulties, or may experience declining prices; its residents may become poorer and some may go bankrupt; but as an area, it cannot have a balance of payments problem. There can never be any more of a problem about how to effect international or interregional payments than about how to effect domestic payments; indeed, it is not easy to distinguish the one problem from the other. Illinois has no balance of payments problem—it does not even have statistics from which it could tell whether it is experiencing a deficit or a surplus in its out-of-state payments. And Hong Kong is in precisely the same position.

Balance of payments problems are a consequence of a shift from a unified currency system to a system of national currencies linked by pegged rates, which is to say, they are a consequence of the intervention of an administrative agency, generally a national central bank, into the payment process. A central bank or its equivalent is a necessary condition for balance of payments problems. In modern conditions, one can go farther; with rare exceptions, it is both a necessary and a sufficient condition for occasional balance of payments problems. Malaysia will provide a nice test case. Prior to the establishment of Malaysia as an independent country, it had no central bank and no balance of payments problem; the local currency was "hard" and foreign reserves large. A few years back, it established a central bank. Within a few years, I predict, it will join the other "developing nations"—to use the most recent euphemism—by experiencing an exchange crisis.

The reason why a central bank is a necessary condition for balance of payments problems is obvious from the foregoing. The reason why it should so often be a sufficient condition is only slightly less obvious. With a unified currency, adjustments tend to be immediate and gradual. A small outflow of money produces a small internal effect and conversely, large maladjustments have little chance to develop. A central bank could act so as to achieve precisely the same results—indeed this was the aim of the British Bank Act of 1844, though unfortunately the Act applied only to currency and not to deposits. But a central bank need not act to achieve the same results as under a unified currency and it is exceedingly unlikely to do so. That would in effect render it a superfluity, a mere machine, the managers of which have no role except to look at the relevant dials. Central bankers are like the rest of us; they want to play a part, to exert an influence on the course of events. And in the present political climate, with the assignment to government and the assumption by government of explicit responsibility for economic conditions, any central bankers who did not exercise their powers would not have a long tenure in office.

Central bankers therefore, and properly so, exercise "judgment" about whether a particular outflow or inflow is temporary and should be offset and prevented from having an effect on the quantity of money; or "structural" and should be reinforced.

Needless to say, the temptation is to offset—certainly for outflows and only to a slightly less extent for inflows. Sometimes this action is a correct and desirable policy and prevents unnecessary, though minor, adjustments. At least occasionally, the judgment is wrong, in which case actions to offset the flow permit minor maladjustments to build up to major ones. Strong measures are then required at long last when weak ones would have sufficed initially. This result is inevitable and does not involve any criticism of central bankers. Given their assignment, they may perform it better or worse; the better the performance, the more infrequent will be severe maladjustments; but no matter how well they perform it, they will produce occasional balance of payments problems. And these problems will have all the consequences with which we have become familiar: financial crises, restrictions on international trade, exchange control in open or concealed form.

There is nothing new in all this. I have been covering ground that is familiar even if generally ignored. Equally familiar is the alternative arrangement that can reconcile the existence of central banks controlling the volume of national currencies with free international trade, equilibrium in foreign payments, and the absence of balance of payments problems, namely, a system of freely floating exchange rates among national currencies.[3]

The basic fact is that a unified currency and a system of freely floating exchange rates are members of the same species even though superficially they appear very different. Both are free market mechanisms for interregional or international payments. Both permit exchange rates to move freely. Both exclude any administrative or political intermediary in payments between residents of different areas. Either is consistent with free trade between areas, or with a lessening of trade restrictions.

On the other hand, national currencies linked by pegged

<hr>

[3] For my own prior discussions of these issues, see "The Case for Flexible Exchange Rates" in my *Essays in Positive Economics* (University of Chicago Press, 1953), pp. 157-203; *A Program for Monetary Stability* (Fordham University Press, 1959), pp. 77-84; and my testimony before the Joint Economic Committee of the U.S. Congress (November 14, 1963) in Joint Economic Committee, *Hearings on the United States Balance of Payments*, Part 3, 88th Cong., 1st Sess. (U.S. Printing Office, 1963), pp. 451-58, 500-25.

exchange rates, whether or not through the mechanism of gold, and a system of variable exchange rates, controlled and manipulated by governmental bodies, either through an adjustable peg or day-to-day market operations, are also members of the same species. Both are interventionist standards. Neither, in my opinion, is consistent with a permanent lessening of barriers to international trade, but only with oscillating barriers as nations shift from surplus to deficit.

2. Political Implications of Different Arrangements

The political implications of the alternative arrangements have received less attention than these economic issues. Yet these political implications are both vitally important and have been greatly illuminated by recent experience.

The key political issues are in their essentials the same as those that arise domestically about the desirability of an independent central bank: 1) Is it desirable to have a system in which a small number of individuals, not directly responsible to the electorate and, in principle, not even indirectly responsible by being under the authority of the political executive, have great power to influence the economic course of events by controlling the monetary system? To have a monetary power, coordinate with the executive, legislative, and judicial? 2) Whether desirable or not, is it possible? Can such a system long endure?

I have elsewhere stated at length why I have answered the first question in the negative for national central banks.[4] All the arguments there adduced apply if anything with even more force in the international sphere.

I was myself fully persuaded of this view by a remarkable book, edited by an eminent fellow-member of the Mont Pelerin Society, Jacques Rueff: Emile Moreau's *Souvenirs d'une Gouverneur de la Banque de France,* and I have been greatly strengthened in my convictions by recent experience.

Moreau was the head of the Bank of France in the later

[4] See "Should there be an Independent Monetary Authority?" Chapter Six.

'20s during the period when the franc was stabilized and re-pegged to gold. His memoirs give a fascinating account of his domestic experience, and, even more pertinent for our present purpose, of the relations among the great central bankers of the time. That period comes perhaps closer than any other to the ideal that seems currently to animate many who favor "strengthening of the arrangements for international monetary cooperation" through the exercise of "multilateral surveillance . . . through existing international consultative bodies," to use the euphemisms of the recent study by the Deputies of the Group of Ten.[5] It was a period when the acceptance of the idea of independent central banks was at its zenith, even the U.S. having finally come most of the way. It was the era of the great Central Bank Governors: Moreau in France, Schacht in Germany, Strong in the U.S., and above all, Norman in Britain, and of continuous interchange and cooperation among them. It was also, as Mr. Rueff has so tellingly stressed, the era of the gold-exchange standard, which, as I fully agree with him, made the system much more vulnerable to monetary mistakes than it had been. It was a period therefore from which we have much to learn about the implications of the kind of arrangements for international monetary cooperation we have had and that we seem in the process of strengthening.

Montagu Norman was perfectly clear about the political issue. To judge from Moreau's memoirs, as well as from Henry Clay's biography, Norman was contemptuous alike of the vulgar masses and the monied classes. He envisaged a group of enlightened central bankers running the economic world as it should be run, largely free from domestic political control and powerful enough to dominate the private monied group. Though he never expressed it that way, his aim was a benevolent dictatorship by a technically skilled and disinterested oligarchy of central bankers.

Today also no one expresses it in this way. Yet in fact the central political issue is how much power should be given to such an oligarchy. (Fortunately, also, there is today a subsidiary

[5] *Ministerial Statement of the Group of Ten and Annex Prepared by Deputies*, August 10, 1964, p. 9.

political issue which did not exist then, namely, which oligarchy —the central bankers, or the international civil servants of the I.M.F.) It is not the announced intention of our present arrangements, or of any of the various proposals for strengthening international monetary cooperation, to delegate significant political power over internal economic policy to foreign central bankers or officials of an international agency. But that is unquestionably their effect.

That this is a very real issue was illustrated dramatically by the recent experience of the British, just after the Labor government came into power. Personally, I disagree sharply with the particular policies that the newly elected Labor government apparently wishes to follow, and regard the policy changes imposed on Britain by the central bankers as the price of the rescue of sterling [in 1964] as very likely far better for Britain itself. Yet that does not alter the fact that British internal policy was shaped by officials who were not responsible to the British electorate and in directions that had not emerged through the regular political process. In this respect, I find myself in complete sympathy with those Labor supporters who regard it as nearly intolerable that the "gnomes in Zurich" should have a veto power over internal British economic policy.[6]

The changes in recent years in U.S. economic policy as a result of balance of payments pressures, and thereby indirectly, the influence of foreign central bankers and other monetary officials on U.S. domestic policy have been less dramatic and more gradual than the changes in British policy but not clearly less important.

An equally clear demonstration has been the international political power that has been reaped by Germany and, more recently, by France under de Gaulle as a result of their balance of payments surpluses. From defeated and prostrate countries dependent on the good will and mercy of the U.S. and, to a lesser extent, Britain, the tables have turned until their political power far exceeds their basic economic strength.

[6 The devaluation of sterling in November, 1967, provides another example. It was followed by a domestic austerity policy widely regarded as the price demanded by other central bankers for not matching the British devaluation and for assisting Britain in supporting the pound at its new parity.]

It is extraordinary with what fidelity this experience reproduces the pattern of the '20s, as revealed by Moreau's memoirs in more personal terms. To begin with, Norman was clearly the leading figure and his attitude toward Moreau and France was, at best, condescending, the attitude of the strong to the weak, of the virtuous to the errant, of the wise teacher to the willing but rather dull pupil. But then, thanks to the overvaluation of the pound and the undervaluation of the franc when they were respectively stabilized, France started gaining gold and accumulating sterling balances. Moreau was put in a position in which at any time he could have driven Britain off the gold standard simply by recalling his sterling balances. And the memoirs reveal a radical change in Norman's attitude toward Moreau. He becomes a mendicant instead of an alms-giver, a seeker after Moreau's advice instead of a self-righteous giver of advice, willing to do almost anything that will keep Moreau from withdrawing French sterling balances.

I agree very much with Jacques Rueff that the situation then and now was exacerbated by the gold-exchange standard, that if a system of national currencies linked by fixed rates is to exist, it is far better for all official reserves to be in gold than for some national currencies to be used as reserve currencies. However, I do not agree with him that it is currently desirable to move to such a situation by a substantial rise in the price of gold. The reason I disagree is that the situation would not be basically altered, only rendered somewhat less volatile, by substituting gold for the fraction of official reserves now held in non-gold form. So long as national currencies are linked by fixed rates pegged by central banks or other agencies that have discretion about how they react to inflows and outflows, these agencies will be in a position to exert great influence over the domestic policies of other countries, to offset inflows or outflows, and so to let maladjustments accumulate.

In such discussions, the issue is sometimes presented as if it were between "internationalists" and "nationalists," with any defender of the present system, or of any other system involving fixed exchange rates, regarded as an internationalist, and any proponent of flexible exchange rates, as a nationalist. I trust that my earlier comments have made it clear that this is not so. The issue is not between internationalism and nationalism but between freedom, economic and political, and bureaucratic interventionism, to use a milder term than dictatorship. Collectivism or interventionism is no less collectivism or interventionism by being on an international scale. The basic question is the relations among individuals, and their freedom to engage in economic and other transactions with one another, whatever nation they live in, not the relations among nations. To liberals, the nation is a convenient administrative unit, a means, not the ultimate end or object of policy.

It has always seemed to me extraordinarily curious that so many liberals have tended to favor independent central banks and, more recently, extensive international cooperation among central banks. Fearful as they are of arbitrary power in other areas, they have time and again come out in this area in favor of government by men instead of law, in favor of interventionism instead of the market. One reason, no doubt, is the confusion between a real gold standard and a pseudo gold standard. But I believe that there are two other reasons that may be more basic.

One, which has impressed me as a result of reading Frank Fetter's recent admirable survey of British monetary theory and policy,[7] is the accident that the Bank of England developed as it did in the high tide of British liberalism. As Fetter makes clear, this was an anomaly, and recognized as such at the time, not a consistent part of the liberal tide. The Bank Act of 1844 was a result largely of the recognition that an independent central bank with discretionary power over the quantity of money was inconsistent with a policy of laissez-faire and free trade. Either money should be issued by the government or its quantity should be determined by the market as under a pure specie standard. Peel's rule, requiring the bank to keep a 100 per cent marginal specie reserve in excess of a fixed fiduciary circulation, was intended to provide a mechanical formula that would remove any discretion on the part of the Bank. Unfortunately, the rule was applied only to notes, at a time when deposits were

[7] Frank Whitson Fetter, *Development of British Monetary Orthodoxy, 1797-1875* (Harvard University Press, 1965), especially chapter vi.

276

becoming increasingly important. Discretion over the issue of deposit money left the Bank with its freedom almost unimpaired. But whether, as I do, you think the result was unnecessary financial mischief, or, as so many defenders of the Bank have argued, a generally wise and benevolent policy despite some mistakes, the crucial point is that the development of an independent central bank in Britain was an aberration from general liberal policy, not a manifestation of it.

A second reason why so many liberals have favored independent central banks and international monetary arrangements resting on cooperation among them is that they have so often found themselves in agreement on substantive issues with central bankers. This certainly is often my own situation. I have great respect for the skill and competence of the central bankers and international money men, admiration for their devotion to their tasks and great confidence in the personal disinterestedness of the bulk of the present crop. And I agree to a much greater extent with them about desirable economic policies than with the men whom the American political system has currently put in charge of governmental economic policy. Yet delegating great economic power to the central bankers seems to me completely alien to our liberal principles.

Whether such a system be desirable or not, there remains the question whether it can long endure. On the domestic scene, history has given a fairly decisive answer: truly independent central banks are fair-weather institutions. When there is any serious conflict between the policies they favor and policies strongly favored by the central political authorities—generally as reflected through Treasury policy—the political authorities have inevitably had their way, though at times only after some delay. When, in the absence of such conflict, and during good times, there has developed considerable public support for the independent central bank, this has strengthened its hand in subsequent periods but has still not enabled it to prevail for long, though on some occasions long enough to do enormous harm—as in the United States from 1929-1933—or, if it has had strong and farsighted leadership, to do great good—as for a few years in France under Moreau.

277

On the international scene, the chances that such a system will be solely a fair-weather system seem to me enormously greater, at least in the world as it now is. Domestically, central banks have been established through avowedly political decisions, and are part of a broader political framework that confers legitimacy on their actions. In the international scene, present arrangements have mostly occurred by inadvertence. True, the I.M.F. was an explicitly created agency, but it was created for a purpose almost exactly the opposite to that which it has served —to foster exchange rate flexibility, not to impose rigidity. Central bank cooperation is certainly a happenstance. Of course, this is not a criticism nor by itself does it mean that the arrangements that developed were undesirable. As we all recognize, the most fundamental economic and political arrangements have developed in this way rather than through deliberate design. After all, that experience and possibility are a large part of the case for the free market.

More important for the present purpose, these arrangements stand by themselves and are not part of any broader political framework. When they come under stress, they will get no support from such a framework. Britain and the U.S. are now free to disregard the advice and the pressure of any international consortium of central banks. So long as the monetary arrangements are not part of a broader political structure, each case will be judged separately, and whenever the costs of compliance get very high, the system will collapse. It will smooth over minor difficulties, at the cost of a major crisis. What happened in 1931 to the system Norman so carefully constructed in the 1920's is a striking object lesson. And, I very much fear, we shall have another in the not too distant future.

Return to a real gold standard might well be desirable but is currently impossible. It would require abandonment by all countries of the use of monetary policy as an instrument to affect domestic employment or price levels. Substitution of a pseudo gold standard for the present pseudo gold-exchange standard would be a gain, but a minor one. Like the present standard it would involve political interventionism into international trade and payments, and occasional major crises, and would inhibit any real movement to freer trade. The desirable liberal alternative is currently a system of freely floating exchange rates with gold having no special official role. All present restrictions on the ownership, transfer, or price of gold should be removed, and gold should become a truly free market commodity. As I argued in my earlier paper, paradoxically, this is more likely to foster a real gold standard than is clinging to the form of a gold standard while giving up the substance. Liberals least of all need to be told that what appears the long way round is often the short way home.